THINKING PLACES

Where Great Ideas Were Born

Carolyn and Jack Fleming

Order this book online at www.trafford.com
or email orders@trafford.com

Most Trafford titles are also available at major online book retailers.

Print information available on the last page.

ISBN: 978-1-4251-2585-1 (sc)
ISBN: 978-1-4251-6754-7 (hc)

Trafford rev. 05/27/2015

www.trafford.com

North America & international
toll-free: 1 888 232 4444 (USA & Canada)
fax: 812 355 4082

Dedication

To our family, old friends and the countless new friends we have met along the way in our journeys to the thinking places of many interesting, creative people.

And

Remembering our friend, James Noble Harrell, poet, playwright, novelist, citizen of the world, whose boyhood thinking place was a tree house in a chinaberry tree in a small southern town.

A note from the authors:

This is a literary travel book. It is a tale of many journeys, with a collection of fresh insights into the lives of creative people. It also offers a philosophy and an attitude for travel – of openness to serendipity, to rare experiences, to new friends, resulting in unexpected lagniappe, or "a little something extra."

Study, Anticipate...
Be open to Serendipity and Lagniappe...
Follow your Quest with Passion...
CF/JF

Contents

Contents

Thinking Places of Creative Persons in America

Foreword

I feel most honored to have been invited by Carolyn and Jack Fleming to write a Foreword for their delightful book. If memory serves me, I recall writing quite a few Introductions and at least two Prefaces for various academic books during my thirty years as an English professor, but I do believe that this is my very first Foreword. I shall take seriously the fact that this particular type of essay is called a Foreword, not a Forewords. And therefore keep my comments short and to the point.

What an inspired idea the Flemings had in developing a book around the theme of the various "thinking places" or retreats which famous authors have chosen as they wrote their now immortal prose and poetry. I am especially impressed by the refreshing variety of writers the Flemings have decided to include. I would have expected such luminaries as Charles Dickens, William Wordsworth, Carl Sandburg and Bernard Shaw, but I was surprised and delighted to find Edvard Grieg, Glenn Curtiss, Booker T. Washington and Willie Morris among the chosen thirty-one. In addition, the Flemings include with each author both a Vignette which efficiently and effectively provides needed context for the author's life and writing career and, my favorite section, a lagniappe or "little something extra" which personalizes their essays by describing a unique and lasting inspiration acquired after visiting each site.

I was particularly charmed by one of the two lagniappes in the chapter of my favorite author Charles Dickens. It concerned a cookbook (that the Flemings discovered in the Reading Room of the British Museum), which was written by Catherine Hogarth Dickens, Charles Dickens' long-suffering wife. Poor Catherine must have sampled far too many of her own recipes since, during their marriage, she was transformed in the Flemings' apt description "from a slim pretty wife to a stout Victorian matron." Alas, Dickens left Catherine after nine children and twenty years of marriage for a second-rate actress who was half Catherine's age and dress size! By including this fascinating tidbit in their book, the Flemings provide us with far more than literary gossip; they actually give us a unique insight into why Dickens might have created such peculiarly conflicted female characters in the four novels he penned following his separation from his wife in 1857.

It is this joyous spirit of discovery and appreciation that makes *Thinking Places* such a rare gem in the crowded field of books about authors. I have spent my academic career reading and reviewing such books written by my fellow English professors. They, like the Flemings, attempt critical appreciations of the great British and American writers. But, unfortunately, many professors choose as their "thinking place" the Ivory Tower of Academe and thereby produce books that all too often end up illuminating the supposed genius of themselves, the critic, while ignoring or distorting the real genius of the famous authors.

Not so in this book. Fortunately, the Flemings do not belong to any of the trendy, off-putting schools of literary criticism: Freudian, Marxist, deconstructionist, post-structuralist. They play hookey from all of these somber, self-important, limiting schools of thought and, instead, give us a book that possesses the same spirit as recess–liberating, playful, enthusiastic and full of invigorating fresh air.

Well, enough of my own words. It is time for you to turn the page and enter the delightful world created by two lovers of literature whose joy for the written word is so contagious that you are bound to catch their own special thrill of the quill.

Elliot Engel,
English Professor,
North Carolina State University

Introduction

Many years ago when we visited the homes of Edvard Grieg of Bergen, Norway and George Bernard Shaw in Hertfordshire, England, we discovered that both Grieg and Shaw had a small, one-room garden house, a retreat, separate from the house. Here they produced some of the works that made them world famous. We decided to call these retreats "thinking places."

Later we came across a Victorian hut thinking place in Elmira, New York. We learned that Mark Twain had written here daily when he and his family had come to Elmira in the summers. In this thinking place, he wrote *The Adventures of Tom Sawyer, Huckleberry Finn, Roughing It*– in fact, most of the works for which he is justly renowned.

In nearby Hammondsport, New York, we saw what inventor/flyer Glenn Curtiss called a "thinkorium". It was built on top of his two-storey house. We concluded that there seemed to be a common element among many gifted people – the need for a special, cloistered place to nurture the creative process. That belief started our search for other thinking places.

As time went on, we discovered many, many thinking places. Creative people, whether writers, scientists, artists, musicians or inventors, frequently use a get-away place to think and be productive. Dylan Thomas wrote in a tiny, one-room, wooden structure perched on a cliff, overlooking the sea. Marjorie Kinnan Rawling's farmhouse-writing place was a table on a screen porch that overlooked the wild Cross Creek country in central Florida. Charles Dickens had a small Swiss chalet near his home in Rochester, Kent, England. Henry James' vividly described creative Garden Room at Lamb's House in Rye, Surrey, England was destroyed by World War II bombs, but nearby one may visit Virginia Woolf's home, Monk's House, and her garden writing hut. We were able to visit the home of Ernest Hemingway when he lived in Key West and wrote from early morning in a room level with the tree-tops, connected to the house only by a cat-walk; but Tennessee Williams' writing hut in

Key West is now part of a private residence, and could not be visited.

Not all thinking places, we came to realize, exist as an enclosed structure. Dickens, in his early years, walked the nighttime streets of London for instruction and inspiration. Charles Darwin had a "Thinking Path" at his country home near London; he walked this path consistently every day, regardless of the weather. William Wordsworth found inspiration in walking in the mountains of the Lake District.

A number of books and articles, mostly about living writers, show their houses or desks. Our collection of stories and descriptions of various thinking places is about creative people who lived in the past and their "thinking places" that can be visited today.

As we developed the idea for this book, our emphasis was on the place itself–the place where one may catch a glimpse today of where the creative process actually occurred: a location, a structure or a memorable site where a visitor may receive his own inspiration and, perhaps, as if in some mystical way, tap into the creative muse and be energized by its power.

Inquisitive travelers, we have always looked forward to "journeys with a mission," enlightening experiences with special destinations. As with any journey, the people we met and came to know a little better—both in the present and from the past—gave bountiful rewards and pleasure.

The subject matter of this book is not intended to be exhaustive; the vignettes and descriptions of the thinking places are summaries, which include some fascinating and less well-known aspects of the creative person's story. We hope that our distillations of these many wonderful stories will be as gratifying and helpful to the reader as they were to us, and lead the reader to seek more information.

It is very satisfying to travel and to reach a physical destination, but in this day of telecommunication and virtual reality there can still be satisfaction in armchair travel and the stretching of the mind and imagination by a "journey with a mission." Such a journey can give new visions and deeper insight. It is the authors' hope that readers may be stimulated to

---

think about and develop meaningful itineraries to "visit" in person or in thought, places that may give personal impetus for selecting and finding the reader's own "thinking place."

Serendipity and Lagniappe

Although our journeys to thinking places started, quite by chance, with visits to the homes of Grieg and Shaw, in later years, after study and planning itineraries in advance, we made journeys to multiple regions and specific sites. But, by serendipity, our unexpected experiences and visits often were as fulfilling as our target sites. We considered many of these as "Lagniappe" (a French-Cajun expression for "a little something extra," a supplementary gift).

One of our itineraries started at George Bernard Shaw's home north of London in Hertfordshire for a second visit. The next day we continued our journey to Thomas Hardy's home in Dorchester, southwest England, near the coast. On this trip we were to visit the homes of many well-known authors but, unexpectedly, one of the highlights of the trip was our staying at a bed and breakfast inn in a large cottage with a thatched roof! It had been built in the fifteenth century and it was added to a century later. The innkeepers and owners, Rosemary and Furse Swann, were delightful as host and hostess. In recent years, they had attached to the rear of the ancient structure a very attractive, glassed-in room—a thinking place—for their creativity in ceramic modeling. A door and hallway connect directly from the house to the modern room.

Rosemary Swann began working in terra cotta in the 1960's when she was living in Sweden. Her work often relates to traditional stories, such as the Garden of Eden and the story of Noah. Frequently, her work is humorous, with pigs as a favorite subject. Furse Swann taught English in schools and colleges until the mid 1980's when he gave up lecturing and began modeling. He said he is "mildly obsessive about sheep" and claimed to make goats, geese, deer, badgers, and Green Men as well. Their works are available in a number of galleries and at Yoah Cottage

Ceramics. Meeting these two creative people in such a unique setting was lagniappe, indeed!

This particular journey continued to one of Dylan Thomas' homes on the coast of Wales, where we had another serendipitous, lagniappe experience!

Yoah Cottage near Dorchester, England

Rosemary and Furse Swann

The Beginnings of

Thinking Places

Edvard Hagerup Grieg

1843 – 1907

The Griegs' Home; Composer's
Hut, near Bergen, Norway

Edvard Grieg

"Thou art my thoughts, my present and my future
Thou art my heart's supreme, its only joy;
I love thee more than any earthly creature,
I love thee dear, I love thee, dear,
I love thee now and for eternity,
I love thee now and for eternity!

One thought of thee all other thought drives from me,
Pledged to thy good alone this heart shall be;
For to whatever fate God's will may doom me,
I love thee, dear, I love thee, dear,
I love thee now and for eternity,
I love thee now and for eternity!"

"I Love Thee", music and words by Grieg

Journey   Bergen and the "Hill of Trolls"

Whenever you start a journey you cannot know its importance or how unexpected events may unfold and deeply influence your future.

Many years ago, we found ourselves on a local train en route from Oslo to Bergen, through the rugged, mountainous terrain of Norway. The passengers were mostly locals; also, there was an apparent scattering of other tourists with enough curiosity to take the long and winding journey. One of the tourists, in half German and half English, asked Carolyn, "Are you Sonja Henie?" (Norwegian Olympic gold medal figure skating champion and actress.) Carolyn, blushing, did look quite blond and Scandinavian to Jack, who said simply, "She surely does look a lot like her doesn't she?" Carolyn was embarrassed and protested. The wide-eyed tourist was very pleased with his fancied good luck on his meeting such a well-known celebrity in this remote place.

5

Anyway, about that time, the train slowed down and pulled into a village train station. We disembarked since we planned to stop overnight in the village of Geilo, "half way to Bergen", where there were a number of old inns. We had read about an ancient church in the village, and it seemed like a good opportunity to see Norway, "off the beaten path".

Actually, we were traveling to Bergen to catch a ship across the North Sea (a mal de mer, non lagniappe experience), to Britain and to see a smaller seaport and coastline so representative of Norway and its culture. We knew vaguely that Edvard Grieg, Norway's most celebrated composer, was, in some way, connected with Bergen and that Grieg's music was thought to represent well the land and spirit of Norway. We did not go to Bergen seeking Grieg, but by serendipity, we went to his home, Troldhaugen (hill of trolls), and *this proved to be one of the most significant journeys in our lives*—one that made an impact with far-reaching consequences: the origin of our long and varied quests for thinking places of creative people!

⌣⌣⌣

Vignette   Edvard Grieg   1843 - 1907

Seldom has a movie and Broadway musical been as aptly titled as *Song of Norway*, the life story of composer and concert pianist, Edvard Grieg. His music was imbued with his love of his native land. He had a genius for bringing folk music into his own distinctive compositions, which reflect the feeling and grandeur of the land and waters of Norway. When Grieg was born in Bergen in 1843, Norway was still a part of Sweden, and did not become independent until the bloodless revolution of 1905. Grieg declared, "I am not an exponent of Scandinavian Music but only of Norwegian. The national characteristics of the three peoples–the Norwegians, the Swedes and the Danes–are totally different, and their music differs as much."

Grieg became a part of the intellectual movement which fostered a re-birth of the spirit of Norway by recognizing the significance of its past. A fellow genius, dramatist Henrik Ibsen, was also a leader in this movement. He asked Grieg to compose the incidental music for *Peer Gynt*, his play about an imaginary Norwegian character. Grieg obliged, and his work has become one of the most beloved of the world's classics. The musical, *Song of Norway*, is indeed expressive of what Grieg wanted to give to his country.

It is a small irony that Grieg's great-grandfather on his paternal side was not Norwegian. He was a merchant from Aberdeen, Scotland who allied himself with the Pretender, Charles Edward Stuart in the eighteenth century. When the government troops overcame the Jacobites at the Battle of Culloden, Alexander Greige had to flee to Bergen where he found haven. He changed the spelling of his name to Grieg and a distinguished Norwegian dynasty was born.

Edvard Grieg's father, although a man of culture, was not musical, but his mother's musical talent presaged what her son would become. She was a soloist on the pianoforte and a composer of folk songs, some of which are still popular in Norway today. She was also a strict teacher of her son, who began his music lessons when he was six. From this point on, every influence and event in Grieg's life seemed to point to what he was to become. He heard music constantly in his home. When he was only twelve he began to compose. At fifteen, he met Ole Bull, a prodigiously talented musician who was impressed by the young Grieg's talent. Although Norwegian, Bull encouraged the Griegs to send their son to the Leipzig Conservatory in Germany. Grieg traveled with Bull in Norway and learned to appreciate the folk music of Norway.

Falling in love with a fine musician, a singer, was the next favorable progression in Grieg's own song of Norway. She was pretty Nina Hagerup, a cousin of Grieg's, and probably his childhood sweetheart. With her own tremendous talent, she lovingly assisted him. While they lived in Christiana, now a part of Oslo, Grieg became the conductor of the Philharmonic Society.

Two already famous musicians, Lizst and Tchaikovsky, became Grieg's friends and enthusiastic admirers. He concertized throughout Europe, frequently pushing himself for professional and financial reasons. He was an innovative harmonist, and his work became the model for many composers. His music was not universally well received at first. Some critics felt it unorthodox and dissonant when compared with Mozart and Beethoven. To others it was so melodious that it seemed only entertainment. Nevertheless, his works became increasingly popular, and Grieg was in constant demand in the major cities of Europe as a performer and conductor. His devoted listeners would have been amazed had they known that one of his hands had been crushed by a truck. It was said that he walked with a stoop because he had lost the use of one of his lungs when he was young. Although his concert tours frequently took him away from Norway, he and Nina always returned to their villa, Troldhaugen, for the summer. His thinking place there was in his little hut overlooking the fjord. Here he wrote some of his loveliest compositions.

He was a continual sufferer from asthma and, in his later years, endured excruciating arthritic pain. He died on September 3, 1907. The nation mourned his passing, and fifty-thousand people gathered, seeking to attend his funeral procession.

Time has proven that the music of Edvard Grieg, expressing the heart and soul of the land and people of Norway, also finds strong resonance in the hearts and emotions of listeners around the world. Grieg and his song of Norway are loved and remembered. "I Love Thee" is one of our favorite love poems.

Thinking Place   Troldhaugen and Composer's Hut"

Grieg's best-known works, *Piano Concerto in A Minor Op16* and *Peer Gynt Suite* (1875) were composed long before 1885 when he moved into his new summer retreat-home near Bergen. Troldhaugen was built on a hill overlooking Hardinger Fjord. According to local legend, the hill was a haunt for trolls, the fantasy little folk of the Norwegian forests. Grieg built the composer's hut in 1891. Although his productivity declined in his later years, nevertheless, he composed at least six major works while working in the hut from 1891 until his death in 1907. He had continued heavy schedules of touring Europe as a conductor and performer during these years.

The home at Troldhaugen is Victorian with folk art influence. It is highly decorated on the outside but baretimbered on the inside, in the tradition of a Norwegian farmhouse. It has been restored and refurbished, including the composer's own Steinway piano, a gift at the time for Nina's and Edvard's silver wedding anniversary.

The composer's hut is located down a path from the main house in a densely wooded area. The small brown hut is perched on the side of the hill, with its one window looking out over the trees and fjord. Inside, the gabled ceiling gives a sense of spaciousness to the little room. It is simply furnished: a desk and chair placed before the window, an upright piano with two candleholders mounted on the front panel, a footstool and a Victorian, tufted sofa.

One can feel Grieg's presence in this little room, as one visualizes: his sitting at the desk, and looking out the window over his beloved Norwegian forest, mountains and fjord; intermittently playing the piano and scoring on a sheet; then, resting on the sofa—thinking. And one identifies with his concern when he always left a note to possible intruders in the little hut when he was away from Troldhaugen, "Please don't disturb the papers—they are of no value to anyone but myself."

Today, there is much to see at Troldhaugen. In addition to the house and composer's hut, there is the Edvard Grieg Museum with permanent exhibitions and multimedia rooms, cafeteria and bookshop. Adjacent to the museum, Troldsalen, a sod-roofed concert hall with a seating capacity of 200 people is used frequently for chamber music and other concerts. The graves of Edvard and Nina Grieg are nearby, tucked away in the side of a cliff. Outside the entrance of the concert hall is the diminutive, life-sized statue of the five foot- one - inch tall composer— a veritable giant of Norwegian history and of the entire world of music.

Lagniappe

Our very special dividend, our lagniappe, from our visit to Norway was the gift that Edward Grieg's small composer's hut gave us. We were not looking for it. It found us! It was the beginning of our search for thinking places of creative people; a "gift that keeps on giving". An unexpected finding of a simple structure in a strange setting—this started an avalanche of awareness and pleasure to last us for a lifetime.

Another episode in our Norwegian journey was truly unique and a special bonus. When we got off the train in the old village of Geilo, we felt that we had stepped back into the world of Grimm, or Hobbit Land or, at least, into Disney's version of Olde Norway. The quaint, peaked houses with steep-slanting roofs, window boxes with flowers, wooden carvings and gingerbread trimming gave a fairy-tale air.

Near the center of the village, at that time, was a small, brown, wooden church building, said to be several hundred years old. It seemed deserted.

Fortunately, the door was open and we went in. We sat down on a bench in the dimly lighted, small sanctuary just to take it all in: the altar, the crucifix, the sturdy pews all lined up in the hazy light. Then, out of the small balcony area in back of and above us came a few soft musical notes, then the glorious sounds of organ music, from pianissimo to forte to double forte! It sounded familiar, reminiscent of "*A Mighty Fortress is Our God.*" The organist was there to practice for the next day's service!

Here in this remote, quaint village, deep in the forest, on the other side of the world from our home—through music in a holy place and with associated memories—we felt quite at home.

Photographic Credits:
All pictures in this chapter are courtesy of E.P. Nickinson, Jr.
Betty Nickinson is pictured in front of the Griegs' home.

Grieg's desk inside the hut

Grieg's Statue in garden

Piano inside the hut

George Bernard Shaw

1856 - 1950

George Bernard Shaw's home and writing hut, Shaw's Corner,
Ayot-St.Lawrence, Hertfordshire, England

George Bernard Shaw

"The worst sin toward our fellow creatures is not to hate them, but to be indifferent to them: that's the basis of inhumanity."

The Devil's Disciple

"An Englishman thinks he is moral when he is only uncomfortable."

Man and Superman

"Mark Twain and I are very much in the same position. We have to put things in such a way as to make people, who would otherwise hang us, believe that we are joking."

Table Talk

Journey   Shaw's Corner

When we returned to Shaw's Corner at St.Ayot-St. Lawrence, Hertfordshire, some twenty years or more after our first visit there, we began our first planned, organized itinerary in search of thinking places. We arrived at Shaw's Corner late in the afternoon during the off-season for tourists. We had written in advance for an appointment. Fortunately, the gentleman in charge of Shaw's home, which is under the National Trust, was most cordial and helpful, in spite of the late hour. We were able to tour the house with him leisurely. Many of the items on the shelves, such as Shaw's Oscar statuette, were shielded with paper covers, but we were allowed to see them–and even hold the Oscar. Viewing Shaw's office, one of his thinking places, with his desk and old typewriter gave us a feeling of admiration and awe. We saw his piano, his rows of books on shelves, as well as his collections of hats and walking sticks–many recognizable from snapshots we had seen in the past.

We planned to return the next day to see GBS' gardens, the writing hut and the little statue of St. Joan.

We were referred to a most interesting country inn nearby for a memorable evening and lodging.

After our visit to the gardens the next day, we continued our journey to thinking places beyond.

Vignette   George Bernard Shaw   1856 – 1950

Born in Ireland, self-educated in the Reading Room of the British Museum in London, Shaw compressed the work of at least three lives into his ninety-four years. His fifty stage plays, many of which are frequently revived today, gained for him a distinction among many critics, as the greatest playwright in the English language of the twentieth century. Some would add, "since Shakespeare." His wit, his use of irony and paradox, his social criticism stamp his body of work with originality and a one-of-a-kind quality that is recognized as "Shavian," with more than just a touch of the Irish. Born in Dublin of Irish gentry, he described his background as "revolving impecuniously in sort of vague second cousin-ship around a baronetcy." He was not as successful as a novelist, but he excelled as a critic, in not just one but three different fields – art, music and theatre. But fame did not come quickly. After he moved to London to join his mother and sisters, he worked for more than nine years, never earning more than the equivalent of thirty dollars by his pen.

He was a prolific letter-writer, and his correspondence has been published in volumes, notably to actresses Ellen Terry and Mrs. Patrick Campbell, also Granville Barker. Shaw was a social-ist and a member of the Fabian Society. In the service of his political beliefs, he was a pamphleteer and an excellent public speaker. He was an avid photographer, a pianist who played for his own pleasure and a man who walked daily for his health. He was a vegetarian. He loved hats! Shaw is to date the only Nobel

Prize laureate (for Literature) who also received an Oscar (for *Pygmalion,* the basis for the musical, *My Fair Lady.)*

He was married to the understanding, and probably amiable, Charlotte Payne-Townshend. Theirs was a good marriage, presumably marked more by understanding than passion, and it lasted for fifty-five years. He outlived his wife by seven years, and after his death, his ashes were mingled with hers and scattered in the garden.

George Bernard Shaw had little reason ever to be bored or lonely. He entertained himself in solitude when he played the piano or wrote countless letters to his friends, famous personalities in their own right. His letter-writing consumed a great deal of time. His correspondence with just one person, famed actress, Mrs. Patrick Campbell, filled an entire volume. Much of it passed between them before they had even met. Best of all, he had the companionship of one of the sharpest minds in England — his own.

If this seems to be a full lifetime of activity, it doesn't account for his major claim to fame and his durability as a writer. He was foremost a playwright who made his own rules. He wrote some fifty plays, some history-based and some comedies, which became a forum for his ideas, both original and provocative. His prefaces for the plays, prose essays, are equally famous as the exposition of his ideas. Dramatic action was less important to him than brilliant dialogue, characterization or the presentation of his own take on religion, politics or how the human race could improve itself. Some of his famous works include: *Saint Joan, Man and Superman, Heartbreak House, Pygmalion, Caesar and Cleopatra, Candide* and *The Chocolate Soldier.* Notice how many have been made into movies.

Unlike many of his fellow writers, from the Victorian to the early twentieth century, Shaw is still read today, and his plays are as popular as ever and are performed in countless venues. The annual, delightful Shaw Festival at Niagara-on-the-Lake, Canada always features George Bernard Shaw's plays.

What are the qualities that make Shaw seem timeless? The answers will vary with his admirers. Perhaps his originality of viewpoint and expression, enlivened by his wit and keen intelligence, may be one of many judgments. Shaw, both as man and artist, was one-of-a-kind.

Thinking Places

Knowing his propensities and his personality, one would expect his thinking place to be out-of-the-ordinary, and it was! Picture a quite small, wooden hut, furnished simply with a table for writing, a chair and a cot. But there was a telephone for emergencies.(See picture below.) It was placed in the bottom of the garden, quite apart from the house and any domestic distractions.

What made Shaw's thinking place truly Shavian? It was the mechanism he had placed under it, a turn-table. In changing seasons or times of the day, he was able to turn his thinking place to catch the sun through the small windows of his made-to-order private room. We smile when we view this practical example of Shaw's creativity, and most likely he anticipated our reaction.

Lagniappe   Ayot- St. Lawrence

The Brockett Arms is a short walking distance from Shaw's Corner. We agreed with their brochure that this delightful fourteenth century inn retains all the traditional features that one would find in a country inn. The brochure reads, "Surrounded by the beautiful, rolling Hertfordshire countryside, Ayot St. Lawrence is one of the loveliest villages in the county with a wealth of history and intrigue that few can match. The Brockett Arms itself was originally 'the Monastic Quarters for the Norman Church until the Reformation when the Catholics were outlawed.' The Inn offers lunch, candlelit evening meals and, on occasion, Cream Teas." It was a delight to find this warm and cozy place on a very dark and windy night, thanks to the advice of our new friend at Shaw's Corner.

The next day, when we re-visited the Garden hut we were struck with the utter simplicity of Shaw's thinking place, where he created timeless, celebrated plays. In the garden nearby, we viewed the small statue representing one of his plays, *Saint Joan*.

Another point of interest in the area includes one of Shaw's favorite buildings (although he was not a churchgoer), the Greek-inspired eighteenth century church of New St. Lawrence. It is a near perfect reproduction of the Temple of Apollo at Delos. Nearby in the county is Hatfield House, a magnificent stately home and an outstanding example of Jacobean architecture. Hatfield Forest covers one-thousand acres. Old Hatfield village is also nearby. For many, the powerful personality of Shaw, his thinking place, and his creativity dominate the entire area.

Niagara - on-the- Lake, Canada

Occasionally, lagniappe begets lagniappe. Such was our experience with George Bernard Shaw. Our growing interest in him led us to attend the Shaw Festival in Niagara-on-the-Lake in Ontario, Canada. The Festival, in our opinion, lived up to its reputation as one of the finest theatre experiences on the North American continent. The small town itself wins our vote as one of the prettiest, most charming places we have ever visited– anywhere!

On our second visit, among the plays we saw, was a production of *Man and Superman* combined with *Don Juan in Hell*, a six hour happening! But they did give us a brief lunch break. Later that same evening we saw the original version of *Pygmalion* (three hours) which has a "surprising" ending for those more familiar with the musical adaptation, *My Fair Lady*. Shaw made certain that there was never a dull moment that entire day!

On that second visit we also discovered *The George Bernard Shaw Vegetarian Cookbook,* 1987, by Dorothy Bates, who revised the original by Laden and Minney. Thanks to Anna Pope of Book Publishing Company we are permitted to share part of our lagniappe with you.

Vegetable Charlotte

3 carrots
2 white turnips
1/2 pound Brussels sprouts (We would substitute chopped broccoli.)
1/4 cup butter (Southerners, like the author, may use a bit more.)
5 slices whole wheat bread
Butter a round one-quart dish. Cook each vegetable until tender in lightly salted water, drain and puree in blender or processor. Cut bread in half on the diagonal, butter on both sides. Using all but one slice, line baking dish with bread. Spoon in the pureed vegetables, swirl spoon through to mix vegetables but retain separate colors. Use remaining two triangles of bread for top of dish. Bake at 375 degrees about 20 minutes. (Note: You may want to jazz this up with garlic, seasoning salt or your own concoction.)

The highest form of lagniappe is a return visit to a favorite place that you thought you never would see again. In 2007 here we were in Niagara-on-the-Lake again, seeing a Shaw play. It was *Saint Joan,* his strongest play, we thought. Remembering the little statue in Shaw's garden, we wondered if *Saint Joan* was his favorite play too.

Photographic credits: Pictures in this chapter and those in the following chapters were taken by co-author Jack Fleming, unless designated otherwise.

Interior of the hut

Some of the many hats worn by George Bernard Shaw

St. Joan's statue in the garden

Mark Twain

1835 - 1910

Mark Twain's summer home with relatives at Quarry
Farm and writing hut near Elmira, New York, USA

Mark Twain

"To promise not to do a thing is the surest way in the world to make a body want to go and do that very thing."
The Adventures of Tom Sawyer

"Nothing so needs reforming as other people's habits."
Pudd'nhead Wilson

"Man is the only animal that blushes. Or needs to."
Life on the Mississippi

Journey   Elmira

Many years ago, we traveled to Elmira, New York, quite by chance. We had been to Baddeck, Nova Scotia to visit Alexander Graham Bell's summer home, researching the historical Bell and Glenn Curtiss relationship for our musical play about early flight. We motored through the colorful fall foliage of the Adirondack Mountains and beyond, en route to Curtiss' hometown in Hammondsport, New York, in the Finger Lakes region.

Passing through Elmira, we remembered that Mark Twain (Samuel Langhorne Clemens) spent many summers in Elmira and was buried there. We read in our travel guide more about Twain's years in Elmira and that his Victorian writing hut was now located on the Elmira College campus.

We found the Woodlawn Cemetery in a beautiful setting with rolling hills, huge, ancient trees, and many impressive Victorian monuments. Twain's grave is in the Langdon-Clemens plot along with twenty other gravesites of the two families. The plot had been established in 1870 on the death of the father of Twain's wife Olivia, "Livvy" Langdon Clemens. Interestingly, there are two impressive shaft-monuments in the lot: One is a substantial column of classical design inscribed with "Langdon"; the second one is a more modernistic-looking rectangular shaft of similar height with two large, bronze medallions with the names of "Mark Twain" on the top and "Gabrilowitsch" below. The latter monument is twelve feet or two fathoms high (corresponding to the old river parlance, "mark twain", for two fathoms deep, called out by the leadsman on Mississippi river boats to reassure the pilot of the depth.) Why was "Gabrilowitsch" on Mark Twain's monument? We learned later that, actually, "Mark Twain" was added to his son-in-law's monument, rather than the other way around, some twenty-five years after Twain's death.

The Clemens' daughter, Clara, in 1919 had married Ossip Gabrilowitsch some ten years after they had met in Europe, where Clara was studying piano. She later switched to voice training and was talented enough to go on the concert stage. Ossip Gabrilowitsch, born in St. Petersburg, Russia had been a child prodigy, playing the piano at age five. He went on to become internationally famous as a concert pianist and conductor of the Detroit Symphony Orchestra. Ossip and Twain were great friends and spent many hours talking about "everything, but music." Ossip, for years had stated that on his death, he wanted to be buried at the foot of Twain.

When Ossip died, Clara discussed a memorial to Ossip with the celebrated sculptor, Erfrid Andersen, who suggested a monument to honor her father as well as her husband.

We went on to see the attractive campus of Elmira College where Twain's octagonal, Victorian style writing hut is located. It is now called the "Mark Twain Study." This hut was like a magnet, and it drew us back to Elmira. On a return trip, we visited the Elmira College Office of Admissions and obtained information about Twain's summer home, Quarry Farm, where the hut was originally located. Now owned by the College, Quarry Farm is about two miles from town. The Center for Mark Twain Scholars is located there. We walked up the old stone steps near the house where the hut had been. This was a very special place. Irreverent Twain would have scoffed if we had used the word "hallowed," but it was close to it.

Mark Twain was a traveling man all of his life. No doubt, he was fascinated by the comings and goings of the riverboats on the Mississippi during his childhood in Hannibal, Missouri. As a child, he must have longed for journeys down the Mississippi and adventures somewhere out there in the world. His dreams of travel and exciting experiences came true as his life unfolded. His later dreams of an idyllic life with a loving wife and family came true in Elmira and in Hartford, Connecticut. Our journeys to Elmira and Quarry Farm transported us back in time where we could stand on the ground and touch some of the objects which meant so much to Mark Twain during a happy, productive and meaningful phase of his life.

Vignette   Mark Twain   1835-1910
(Samuel Langhorne Clemens)

It is tempting to say that Mark Twain, an American original, was both a Victorian and a contemporary writer. In fact, his ever popular, *The Adventures of Tom Sawyer*, was the first book ever typed on a typewriter. However, it is difficult to limit him to a single category. His writings, in both subject matter and reader appeal, span time and space. His work is universal and as fresh today as when it was first published. Ernest Hemingway paid him a Hemingway-sized compliment, "All modern American literature comes from one book by Mark Twain called *Huckleberry Finn*." Some consider Twain as America's greatest writer.

Most people know what he looked like, either through photographs or the numerous one-man shows that attempt to re-create him today. He popularized the white linen suit and Panama hat, wearing them everywhere, long years before Tom Wolfe wore his white suit in Manhattan.

Rudyard Kipling so admired Twain that in 1889 he traveled

from India, unexpected and unannounced, to see him. Kipling described the man and his Elmira, New York setting in the following passage: "A big, darkened drawing room; a huge chair; a man with piercing eyes, a mane of grizzled hair, a brown mustache (Twain described his own mustache as red), covering a mouth as delicate as a woman's, a strong square hand shaking mine, and the slowest, calmest, levellest voice in all the world saying, 'Well, you think you owe me something, and you've come to tell me so. That's what I call squaring the debt handsomely.' " Still quoting Kipling, "The thing that struck me first was that he was an elderly man; yet after a minute's thought, I perceived that it was otherwise, and in five minutes, the eyes looking at me, I saw that the gray hair was an accident of the most trivial. He was quite young. I was shaking his hand. I was smoking his cigar, and I was hearing him talk—this man I had learned to love and admire fourteen thousand miles away."

Kipling perceived the aromas coming from the dining room and assumed that lunch would be soon. Twain himself never ate lunch and considered that his guest wasn't hungry either, so Kipling later went away hungry. And what was Twain's reaction to his soon-to-become famous visitor? The two men were kindred spirits and subsequently respected each other for a lifetime. With Twain's characteristic humor, he answered his wife's inquiry about the visit, "He is a stranger to me, but he is a most remarkable man — and I am the other one. Between us, we cover all knowledge; he knows all that can be known, and I know the rest."

What were Twain's literary qualities that make him the object of admiration over half a century later? First, his humor, both gentle, irreverent and even biting when used in satire; his characters so memorable and knowable; his natural-sounding dialogue—he was the first author to use American-regional dialect in literature; his concern for man's foibles and hypocrisy and the ever-present evil of society itself.

Before he became famous, Mark Twain, with only a public school education, worked at a variety of occupations: typesetter, printer, volunteer soldier in the Confederate cavalry, silver miner, and most significant, a steamboat pilot on the Mississippi River, an experience which gave him his pseudonym, "Mark Twain." As a young man learning the lore of the Mississippi River, did Twain ever dream of foreign lands? He did become quite a traveler, journeying to other parts of the United States, the Holy Land, Europe and eventually, around the world. (He discovered that he was talented as a platform lecturer and, like Charles Dickens, he used his lecture fees to overcome his financial problems. Actually, his lectures provided a major part of his income.) He was a passenger on the first steamship to cross the Atlantic– another Mark Twain first.

On one of his voyages, he saw the photograph of Olivia Langdon, the sister of a fellow passenger– and fell in love. It was a love match. They were married and had four children. He and "Livvy" built a large home in Hartford, Connecticut. The family entertained themselves with readings and amateur theatricals and was happy until the sadness of later life. Although they lived in Hartford nine months a year, they spent the summer months in Elmira, New York at Quarry Farm, the home of Livvy's sister who built the unique octagon-shaped hut or thinking place for Twain on a hill nearby. Its many windows revealed a beautiful view of the area. Twain himself said that he did most of his writing at Quarry Farm for two decades. He collected notes and outlines in a small wooden chest all during the year, and then did his concentrated writing in the hut at Quarry Farm, working for five to seven hours straight without interruption.

Travel may have been a spur to Twain's writing. He wrote one or more books after visiting the following places: Hawaii; San Francisco to New York via Panama; Nevada and the West; Europe and the Middle East; and traveling on the Mississippi (three books). In this period he wrote *Huckleberry Finn,* generally considered his greatest book.

A Connecticut Yankee in King Arthur's Court belongs to the period when Twain had financial difficulties, which resulted in bankruptcy. He worked hard to pay off all his debts–and he was successful!

Grief over the death of his wife and two of his three daughters, a son dying as an infant, resulted later in a pessimistic, even bitter, outlook in Mark Twain. His comic bent was replaced by a cynical attitude.

A high moment of recognition did come to him in 1907. He was awarded an honorary degree of Litt.D. from Oxford University. A fellow recipient was Rudyard Kipling. In their ceremonial gowns, did the famous writers recall their long-ago first meeting at Quarry Farm when they had talked for two hours, smoked two cigars – but had no lunch? Perhaps Kipling chuckled and reminded Twain of the clever letter he had received from him twelve years earlier.

Dear Kipling,
August, 1895

It is reported that you are about to visit India. This has moved me to journey to that far country in order that I may unload from my conscience a debt long due to you. Years ago you came from India to Elmira to visit me, as you said at the time. It has always been my purpose to return that visit and that great compliment some day. I shall arrive next January and you must be ready. I shall come riding my ayah with his tusks adorned with silver bells and ribbons and escorted by a troop of native howdahs richly clad and mounted upon a herd of wild bungalows; and you must be on hand with a few bottles of ghee, for I shall be thirsty.

Affectionally,   S.L. Clemens

There are few people in history who have commanded such a universal audience and warm respect as Mark Twain. Like the river boatman assisting the pilot to navigate safely calling, "mark twain, " Twain's writings and persona give guidance and reassurance to those who come to count on him for insight into the human condition.

Thinking Place   Summer Thinking Place

Samuel Clemens loved to tease Susan Langdon Crane, his wife's older sister, a bright, happy and unflappable person. They enjoyed each other's company, disagreeing about their divergent religious and philosophical views. Everyone loved "Aunt Sue."

Sam (Mark Twain) called her, "Saint Sue" — and for good reasons. Susan and her husband, Theodore Crane, built in the spring of 1874, as a surprise, the unique octagonal study or writing hut at their Quarry Farm. When Samuel Clemens arrived for the summer, he was surprised, indeed, stunned with pleasure and duly impressed. According to Twain's niece, Ida Langdon, "the site...was the top of the knoll not far away from the farmhouse. It was approached by a path...through an orchard – a path bordered by daisies ... (and other flowers.) At the end of the path, wide stone steps curved up the knoll to the Study."

Elmira and Quarry Farm, and now, this unique, secluded writing/thinking place gave Mark Twain "a foretaste of Heaven." Each summer he and Livvy escaped the frenetic life at Hartford where there was a constant deluge of drop-in neighbors, "callers from the ends of the earth," visits from distinguished writers, churchmen, journalists and actors and Twain's "comings and goings" to his own lectures and conferences.

Twain described it to a friend in Edinburgh that same year: "My Study is a snug little octagonal den, with a coal-grate, 6 big windows, one little one and a wide doorway (the latter opening upon the distant town.) On hot days I spread the study wide open, anchor my papers down with brickbats and write in the midst of the hurricanes..." He had a beautiful view from his thinking place far above the valley below. He described a sunset in September, 1876 in a letter to friends: "The farm is perfectly delightful this season. It is as quiet and peaceful as a South Sea Island. Some of the sunsets which we have witnessed from this commanding eminence were marvelous...I don't know whether this weird and astounding spectacle most suggested heaven, or hell. The wonder, with its constant, stately and always surprising changes, lasted upwards of two hours, and we all stood on top of the hill by my study till the final miracle was complete and the greatest day ended that we ever saw."

Twain went to his Study on most mornings about ten o'clock. According to Ida Langdon, "He often gave a little caper of delight as he left the house, and laughed one of his affecttionate laughs. One knew that was good-bye for the day." He did not eat lunch and worked until five p.m. All the children understood that they were not to go into the "quiet zone" near the hut. However, when Twain was working on *The Prince and the Pauper*, he wanted the childen's input. He frequently would call out or blow a horn, and the children would come trooping into the "quiet zone" and sit on the stone steps while he read the latest chapter of this story they loved very much. The children poured out their reactions and suggestions. "He listened with intense interest" and with "considerable amusement" for this was, in Twain's words, "a yarn for youth." What a whimsical image to remember...little children in a forbidden, magical place; sitting on the stairway ascending to the secret room; hearing an exciting story as it was being born; and competing to give advice to a kindly wizard and story-teller... who seemed to be listening to them.

Lagniappe   Elmira

When we returned to Elmira and journeyed with expectancy to Quarry Farm, we saw the stone watering troughs along the side of the steep road going up the hill to the house. Each of them had the name of one of the four Clemens' children. These troughs, now filled with dirt and flowers, were for watering the horses as they made it up the steep hill back to home. It was a reminder of their consideration for the horses, and that in Twain's time, it was not an easy journey into town.

The highlight of our visit to Quarry Farm, of course, was seeing the site of the steps to the writing hut, but our dividend – our lagniappe—was in town, on the campus of the college.

We visited the Elmira College library where Mark Twain books and memorabilia are located. The curator showed us a prize of their collection—a moderate sized, wooden box, faintly inscribed "Samuel Clemens." Some had been using it for throwing in umbrellas and miscellaneous items for years, until it was recognized as the box Twain had used to accumulate notes during the winter in Hartford, and then brought to Quarry Farm each summer for use in his writing. Since Mark Twain did write in the Study, parts or all of his many books, including *Huckleberry Finn, Tom Sawyer, Roughing It, Life on the Mississippi,* and *The Prince and the Pauper,* we felt we were looking into a box that once held the beginnings of so many stories we knew, and familiar characters released from this genie's box by the vivid imagination of the master magician and spinner of yarns—Mark Twain!

Photographic credits: Picture of Mark Twain courtesy of Twain House, Hartford, Connecticut.

Mark Twain

Interior of Twain's writing hut

Glenn Curtiss

1878 - 1930

Glenn Curtiss' Thinkorium on top of his home; currently
in the Glenn Curtiss Museum, Hammondsport, New York

Glenn Curtiss

"What is the need of racing unless you think you are
going to win; and if you are beaten before you
start, why take a chance?"
(His rule for motorcycle racing.)

Curtiss, Glenn H., The Curtiss Aviation Book

"...sensations of an aviator—feeling a peculiar
realization of the immediate presence of the Supreme
Being, overwhelmed with the magnitude of the
universe, with a sense of being a part of it,
Untrammeled, unaffected by ordinary things ...
now, minutely weighing his life in his hands as if it
were something far removed from himself; breathing
an air full of vigor and inspiration, with a sense of
exaltation pervading every cell of his body."

Curtiss, Glenn H., The Curtiss Aviation Book

Journey

In the late 1980's we collaborated with composer, Allen Pote,
to write a musical. Aviation pioneer, Glenn Curtiss, was one of
the heroes.

In the musical, *Seaplane*, the lyrics of the opening song tell
about Hammondsport, New York at the time Glenn Curtiss was
starting his flying career:

"Gotta' lotta' things happenin' in Hammondsport!
Gotta' lotta' action in Hammondsport!
There's no denying in Hammondsport
That the world is centered in Hammondsport!

Balloons are flying in Hammondsport!
Dirigibles are sailing in Hammondsport!
There's no denying in Hammondsport,
That the world is centered in Hammondsport!"

There's no denying that Hammondsport was an exciting place to be in 1908 when Captain Baldwin's dirigible factory and Curtiss' development of airplanes were going full force. We were also excited about our first journey to do research for a musical about early flight and to see all the places we had read about in the stories of Glenn Curtiss and the Village of Hammondsport! In addition, it was fall and the foliage was at the height of color. At our bed and breakfast, they served grape pie for breakfast. This was, indeed, a very special place!

The village square with probably few real changes since Curtiss' day, is still a picture-book image of Americana. The Victorian bandstand has a border of wooden, musical notes. Smellies Drugstore building is across from the square. Up the street, still intact, is Lulu Mott's boarding house, where many young student flyers stayed.

We walked to the lakeside, visualizing the beehive of activity that was going on along the beach in Curtiss' day when they were developing the amphibious hydro-aeroplane. We saw the quaint, gabled train station close to Keuka Lake. Talking with someone on the square, we were told, "They called him GH, for 'Glenn Hammond'. GH drew the plans on the wall; they built the plane and then GH tried it out. Friends of GH were usually friends for life."

We visited the Curtiss museum, at that time still on the second floor of the old school building. (Later the Curtiss Museum was to be moved to its new building adjacent to Pleasant Valley.) What a thrill to see the reconstructed, early Curtiss plane at this developing museum. At the time, Tony Doherty, curator of the museum, took us on a tour. His father, Gink Doherty, was close to Curtiss and, in fact, piloted the reconstructed machine that Dr. Langley tried to fly, just months before the Wrights flew in 1903. But that's another story. We were touching hands with those close to important history. Outside the old school was the small, one-room structure, the "Thinkorium." It had been on top of GH's two-storey house. (Today, it is inside the new museum.) This became one of the first four locations that inspired us to find other thinking places.

We had hopes of pulling it all off–writing the book and lyrics for a musical about early flight. The story would start in Hammondsport with Glenn Curtiss and his good friend, Dr. Alexander Graham Bell, then move to Pensacola where Curtiss' airplanes were used in the Navy's first "aeronautical station". The climax would be the first crossing of the Atlantic Ocean by an airplane, the Navy-Curtiss, NC 4. (The huge, original sea-plane is now displayed in Pensacola's National Museum of Naval Aviation.) It was a tall order, but the material was won-derful—and true! Our friend and collaborator, well-known composer, Allen Pote, was to come up with some of his greatest music for *Seaplane*. Eventually, there would be three different runs in as many years in Pensacola, each production attracting marvelous talent. Hammondsport's Keuka Lake Players would take to *Seaplane* like a duck– or a Curtiss hydro-aeroplane– to water; they too, brought together wonderful talent for their many productions.

Seaplane flew–in Hammondsport, Pensacola and the Ken-nedy Center in Washington, D.C. By this time we considered ourselves just two of the many, many people who made it happen. The lyrics for the finale came to speak for all of the *Seaplane* team:

To build a dream…takes more than one of us…
    and even then
We may never know…just when or where the
    dream will end…
We may never know just how far a dream will go
    …we can only help to make it grow.
We stand on the shoulders of dreamers before us
    …hearing the echoes… joining the chorus
    …together we can build a dream!

Vignette   Glenn Curtiss   1878 - 1930

Glenn Hammond Curtiss was a true boy scout before the Boy Scouts of America existed. He was "the fastest man on earth" before he ever piloted a plane. He was a friend and colleague of Alexander Graham Bell before he owned a telephone. He was a champion bicycle racer before he was the owner of a small bicycle shop. He was the engineer and developer of the motor on the first airship (dirigible) in the U.S. military before he knew how to fly.

Eventually, Glenn Curtiss became an inventor-designer of aeroplanes, (as they were spelled then), including the first airplane (Navy-Curtiss 4, a seaplane) to cross the Atlantic; an award-winning airplane pilot; the largest manufacturer of airplanes in the U.S.; a real estate developer and founder of two cities in Florida; an inventor of the first recreational vehicle – a trailer equipped with beds for sportsmen.

He did this with an eighth grade education and with no family backing except for the love of his mother and grand-mother, both widows with low income.

Curtiss grew up with the ideals taught to many young Americans in the nineteenth century. Like Thomas Edison and other inventors of the day, he showed early in life the ingenuity that accompanied the burgeoning of American enterprise. He could fix anything, take anything apart and put it back together. If his limited schooling did not provide an answer, he, like Edison and other like-minded inventors, would simply figure it out for himself.

He was interested in speed, first on bicycles and then on motorcycles. In 1907, he rode a motorcycle of his own design and manufacture at Ormond Beach, Florida. It had the first V-8 engine on a motorcycle and he tore up the one-mile track record, "faster than a racehorse, faster than a train locomotive." He raced at 136 miles per hour on a Florida beach to become, in the newspaper headlines, "The fastest man on earth." It was both his riding skill plus his phenomenal machine that won the day. (The motorcycle has been displayed at the Smithsonian and at the

Glenn Curtiss Museum in Curtiss' hometown, Hammondsport, New York.) Little did Curtiss dream that, eventually, his machines would be going even faster–in the air!

Glenn's father, a harness dealer, died when Glenn was four years old, and he grew up without a father figure. His grandfather, a minister, left in his small estate a plot of ground that was planted in grapes, but family resources were meager. Glenn learned to make do, working at odd jobs and puttering at home. He read about gasoline motors, figured out and fashioned a carburetor out of a tomato can and rigged up a small motor. Later, when he mounted a motor on a bicycle, his vehicle and career took off!

When his sister, Rutha, became deaf at age six, Glenn moved with his mother and sister to Rochester, New York where Rutha could receive better training. In Rochester, Glenn began work at Eastman Kodak, where he invented a device that made his work go faster, and he also delivered telegrams for Western Union. On most weekends he demonstrated the qualities of a good scout when he rode the seventy rough miles to Hammondsport on his bicycle to see his grandmother and to care for her.

When his mother remarried, Curtiss moved to Hammondsport. Local druggist, Jim Smellie, sponsored Smellie's Pep Cycle Boys, and Glenn was the star racer. "Tank" Waters became a racing partner and a lifetime friend. Mr. Smellie later transferred the bicycle business to Glenn, and someone let him use a building on the square. Best of all, Lena Pearl Neff married him when she was seventeen and Glenn was twenty. They moved in with his grandmother. Lena also liked cycling. She learned to ride a motorcycle, and in 1910, she was one of the first women in the area to drive the new-fangled automobile.

GHC, as he styled himself on his papers, was soon successful making bicycles, which he shipped all over the country. His logo was fashioned after the distinctive Ford logo. (Henry Ford and Curtiss became good friends in later years.) In 1903, he won the American Amateur Championship for motorcycle riding, and he broke many records. His motorcycle feat at Ormond Beach in 1907 topped them all. Not only did he have a superb machine, but he also had a natural ability for racing, as he would have later for flying. He popularized the racing crouch.

Soon his engines caught the attention of Thomas Baldwin, who specialized in balloons and dirigibles, and they worked together successfully. Captain Baldwin moved his airship factory to Hammondsport.

A scientist and international celebrity also wanted to know more about the Curtiss engines. Alexander Graham Bell, from his summer home in Canada, contacted Curtiss whose life thereafter would be changed forever. The Wright brothers had flown first in 1903, but through a strange set of circumstances, partly due to the Wright's secrecy and their concern that someone might steal their invention, there was widespread question about their flight. Bell, Curtiss and three others formed the Aerial Experiment Association. Their aim was simple, as Bell put it, "To get into the air." In fact, Bell had had a long-term interest in flight—equal to his interest in the telephone. Bell had tried to stabilize the flight of manned kites with huge sets of silk-covered tetrahedrons bound together. Mrs. Bell put up her own money for the trial and error process.

The experiments of the AEA began, at first, at Bell's summer home in Baddeck, Nova Scotia, then on Keuka Lake in Hammondsport. The group met in Curtiss' room—the Thinkorium— atop his two-storey house. They experimented with motors and with gliders, finally stabilizing flight with small wings between the two main wings. The A.E.A. planes were the first in America to use these ailerons for stabilizing flight instead of the wing warping of the Wrights. Finally, they had a spectacular climax to all their experiments. It was July 4, 1908. A crowd gathered in Pleasant Valley and waited all day for good weather so Glenn could take off in the little yellow plane, the *June Bug*. Representatives of the Aero Club and the *Scientific American* were official observers. It was the first pre-announced, public flight by an aeroplane in America. A movie camera filmed it for another first in the history of flight.

Many achievements followed– the first plane to land on a ship; the first plane to take off from a ship; the first practical, amphibious airplane (which flew to a Navy ship, was hoisted on and off the ship, then flew back to land); the first flying boat; and, in 1919, the creation of the three Navy-Curtiss (N-C) sea-planes which attempted the first transatlantic flight. The NC-4 made it all the way, and all the crews were safe. All of these pioneering accomplishments earned Glenn Curtiss the title of "Father of Aquatic Aviation." Curtiss personally won many fly-ing records, some with great daring, such as flying under a bridge in New York's Hudson River. The French proclaimed him the "Champion Aviator of the World" after Curtiss won the Air Show race in Rheims in 1909.

All was not guts and glory. The Wright Brothers were unhappy. The main dispute was not their claim to being the first to fly. The problems grew out of continued experiment and development by the AEA and Curtiss himself, who made dis-tinctive improvements and advances. The Wrights felt that their patents entitled them to assess anyone who flew an airplane or who tried to develop an airplane in the U.S. Wilbur and Orville Wright spent much time in court suing Curtis and many others for patent infringement. Curtiss countered with his own claims. Wilbur died in 1910, but the suits went on. Not until the advent of World War I was the fight resolved. The U.S. Government stepped in, bought the patent rights from Wright and Curtiss business interests and made possible the continued progress of aviation in America. A new company was formed for manu-facturing planes for the armed services—the Curtiss-Wright Company!

Glenn and Lena kept their home in Hammondsport but lived in Long Island, New York. Then they moved to the Miami area, built a home and two planned cities, named Opa Locka and Hialeah, one Indian pueblo in design and the other of Moorish-inspired architecture. Glenn Curtiss became as successful in real estate and development as he had been in aviation. It was said that he made more in his Florida ventures than he had with airplanes. He and a partner sold a million dollars worth of building lots in ten days. For each city he built an airport. He gave a golf course and additional property to the city of Miami. That property became the Miami International Airport.

G.H., the bicycle racer from Hammondsport with an eighth grade education, founded eighteen corporations in Florida, served on civic commissions, donated extensive tracts of land and water rights to local government and strongly promoted the growth of the Miami region. He received an Honorary Doctor of Science degree from the University of Miami.

In May 1930, Curtiss celebrated the twentieth anniversary of his award-winning flight from Albany down the Hudson River to New York City. He flew the same route in an eighteen-passenger Curtiss Condor airliner with a professional pilot handling the take-off and landing. Two months later, G.H. had appendicitis, and following surgery, he died with lung embolism at age fifty-two. He was buried in the tree-shaded cemetery at Hammondsport, in Pleasant Valley, where he had taken off nearby in the *June Bug* in 1908. Townsfolk and well-known people from around the world gathered to remember and honor this talented man who gave so much to his hometown, to his nation and to the world. Airplanes flew over the crowd and dropped flowers.

It has been said that the Wrights were the obstetricians of aviation; their contributions, though magnificent indeed, were limited to the very early years. Curtiss nurtured flight's early growth and development; he was the long-term pediatrician of aviation. Glenn Curtiss was truly the embodiment of the American success story: self-starting, hard working, indefatigable and visionary. He was a good scout, a good friend, and a good citizen–truly, an All-American winner!

Thinking places   Glenn Curtiss's Thinkorium

Glenn Curtiss was a man of action. No doubt, his mind was usually turned on high speed, or like his motors, occasionally idling until the next burst of energizing, new ideas. G.H.'s thinking places were wherever he was. He was a master of improvisation, figuring out problems on the spot by trial and error. He had no training in mechanics or engineering, but he became one of the leading experts on motors, first by building a motor for his own bicycle, then developing it further. He became one of the major motorcycle manufacturers in the United States. In fact, his motors drew the attention of Alexander Graham Bell and thus started their relationship in The Aerial Experiment Association.

Usually, Curtiss was not a methodical experimenter like the Wright Brothers, who planned and demonstrated each detail. Curtiss would often draw any changes in the design of an aircraft on the wall of his shop, and then, always good with his hands, and in working with his crew, would just produce it.

Curtiss did need a place to get away from the busy shop to sit down and think. He needed to talk things over with his associates, especially when Bell and the other members of the A.E.A. came from Baddeck, Nova Scotia to Hammondsport. His two-storey home was in the midst of his developing shops and surrounding vineyards on Castle Hill, over-looking Hammondsport. Curtiss built a one-room addition–on top of his house! The view of the lake and the bustling town below must have been a sight to see and revved up the thinking of all who went there. G.H. called it his "thinkorium." It was almost like being, as Dr. Bell would say, "into the air." It contained a table, some chairs and a globe–perhaps working plans and models. Mostly, it was a place to plan and formulate–to think!

In later years, when the Curtiss' house was razed, the Thinkorium was saved and refurbished. When we first saw it, the Thinkorium was outdoors on the grounds of the original Curtiss Museum at the site of the old school building. Now it is safely ensconced in the new museum, alongside the many other treasured items: motorcycles, earlier Curtiss planes, and other memorabilia that inspire thoughts of a very practical thinker and his thinking places.

Lagniappe   Hammondsport

Charles Champlin, retired television, drama and movie critic of *The Los Angeles Times,* said of *Seaplane:* (Hammondsport's, Pensacola's and early aviation's own musical), "It's *Music Man* with wings!" He also said that the production and effort was a phenomenon in Hammondsport akin to the annual firemen's parade when all of the people of Hammondsport and the vicinity were brought together every year on a joyous occasion.

Charles Champlain's roots go deep in Hammondsport. His grandparents, the Champlins and the Massons, had owned and directed the Pleasant Valley Wine Company since the 1860's. Charles's mother was a sixteen year-old schoolgirl in 1914 when she recited a poem at the dedication of Curtiss's *America,* the first plane built to make a trans-Atlantic flight.

The people of Hammondsport gave us and composer, Allen Pote, not only Honorary Citizenship of Hammondsport, but also more than three summers of fine theatrical performances, unforgettable experiences and relationships. After some performances, cast and crew would meet in The Village Tavern, a pub that featured *Seaplane* banners and posters alongside the old pictures of early Curtiss airplanes. They made us feel like home folks.

Our special lagniappe from Hammondsport and *Seaplane* was being part of a small, All-American town for several years. That included sharing the camaraderie and warmth of many new friends. We touched hands with the past, embraced the present and celebrated a take-off of aspirations for the future of all of us who participated.

Lagniappe was indeed bountiful from the beginning and throughout our entire Curtiss and *Seaplane* experience. In our journeys from Pensacola, to Baddeck, Nova Scotia, to Hammondsport, to the Azores, to Washington, D.C., and back home, so many people–many new friends–helped us to gather and confirm the pieces of the story, and others contributed to putting the subsequent production together.

Our first consultant for the information about the life and times of early Naval Aviation in Pensacola, circa 1914, was Anna Lamar Switzer, wife of an early naval pilot who later became an admiral. Anna, a beautiful lady in her late 70's, had been a little girl when she witnessed the first boatload of aviators and (Curtiss) aeroplanes arrive in Pensacola harbor in 1914. Later, from a balcony she watched a long line of young naval aviators waiting to dance with a pretty, flirtatious belle from Baltimore, Wallis Warfield (later to be the Duchess of Windsor). And that became part of our story, as well as Anna's admonition to "make it very romantic, just like it was!"

Charles Towers, the only son of *Seaplane* hero, Admiral Jack Towers, helped us greatly, as did Mrs. Pierre Towers, widow of Admiral Towers. We received invaluable assistance also from U.S. Navy Admirals, Maurice Weisner, Lloyd Mustin and Magruder Tuttle and from the author of the definitive biography of Admiral Towers, Dr. Clark Reynolds.

One of our greatest honors came when Charlie Towers and his wife, Lois, asked us and Allen Pote to represent them at Yokosuka Naval Base, Japan for the decommissioning ceremonies of the destroyer, the U.S.S. John Towers, DDG 9. The Fifth Fleet Band played excerpts of music from *Seaplane*! As sailors lined up at multiple levels around the railings of the retiring vessel, then, to the strains of *Seaplane's* "I Want to Make a Mark," "Man Must Fly" and "To Build a Dream," the crew sadly filed off the ship for the last time.

The harbor at Yokosuka, Japan was a long way from Hammondsport where Glenn Curtiss and Jack Towers, Naval Aviator # 3, flew over Keuka Lake with primitive aircraft of canvas and bamboo. It was a long way from Trepassey Bay, Long Island when, in 1919, the N.C. (Navy Curtiss) Expedition, led by Commander Towers, flew in huge seaplanes of canvas and wood across the Atlantic and into the modern age.

Learning their story was lagniappe indeed.

Photographic credits: Pictures of Curtiss' Thinkorium and the *June Bug* flight, the latter from a mural at the museum, are courtesy of Glenn Curtiss Museum, Hammondsport, NY. Picture of members of Aerial Experiment Association below are from the Gilbert H. Grosvenor Collection of Photographs of the Alexander Graham Bell Family (Library of Congress).

Members of the AEA; Glenn Curtiss on the left;
Alexander Graham Bell in the middle

June Bug in flight

NC4 (Navy Curtiss) seaplane
pictured on a poster for the musical, *Seaplane*

Thinking Places

of

Creative Persons

in the

British Isles

William Wordsworth

1770 – 1850

The Wordsworth Homes: Dove Cottage in Grasmere and Rydal
Mount, with a Thinking Path near Ambleside, Cumbria, England,

William Wordsworth

> "That best portion of a good man's life,
>   His little, nameless, unremembered acts
>   Of kindness and of love."

"Lines Composed a Few Miles above Tintern Abbey"

> "The music in my heart I bore
>   Long after it was heard no more."

"The Solitary Reaper"

> "I wandered lonely as a cloud
>   That floats on high o'er vales and hills,
>   When all at once I saw a crowd
>   A host, of golden daffodils."

"I Wandered Lonely as a Cloud"

Journey   Grasmere

Our journey ahead was to one of the most beautiful parts of England – the Lake District. Our mission was to learn more about William Wordsworth, the man. Many surprises would gradually unfold. For instance, we learned that Wordsworth fell deeply in love with his wife–ten years after they had married.

Wordsworth was born and lived most of his life in the Lake District near Grasmere, in Cambria, England. His burial site at St. Oswald's Church, Grasmere, is one of the most visited literary shrines in the world. Our journey to Grasmere began in the late afternoon near sunset when we dined in an outdoor setting on the edge of a small stream. We saw the ancient church in the distance, St. Oswald's, and looked forward to our visit the next day to the churchyard where legions of visitors had preceded us.

Picturesque Grasmere nestles by the lake, surrounded by

low mountains. Although the town is now filled with many hotels, inns, bed and breakfast places and the usual assortment of tourist shops, it retains its quaintness and charm. The center of interest, of course, is St. Oswald's churchyard, but Dove Cottage, Wordsworth's home for nine years and the adjacent Wordsworth Museum, are also major sites of interest. We later visited nearby Rydal Mount in a rural area on the road to Ambleside. Rydal Mount was Wordworth's home for thirty-seven years. Here he died when he was eighty. St. Oswald's Church was built in the thirteenth century. The nave includes a number of memorials, including one to Wordsworth and several to the early Le Fleming family of Rydal Hall. St. Oswald's Church, named after a seventh century Northumberland Christian king who once preached at this site, is the parish church for the village of Grasmere, Rydal and Langdale. Each of these townships has its own gate to the churchyard.

Most travel accounts of suggested journeys to Grasmere include strong recommendations to visit the famous Grasmere Gingerbread Shop, situated at the lynch gate of the church. According to Manchester 2004, Encyclopedia of Greater Manchester, the shop building was originally the village schoolhouse from 1660 to 1854. For more than 130 years, there has been a celebrated bakery "where Sarah Nelson's original secret recipe has been scrupulously followed." Gingerbread is dispatched from here to all parts of the British Isles. In fact, the distribution is worldwide. We liked it too!

Grasmere is much more than a churchyard, inns and gingerbread. It is a place of tranquil beauty, a refuge from the big city; an historic place with many reminders of a less complex society and way of life; a place where we pause and salute the more gentle art of the poet–with reverence for the written word; a place where we connect with the grandeur of the land and the lakes–and feel a sense of place.

Vignette   William Wordsworth 1770 - 1850

The life and work of William Wordsworth progressed from springtime to an early winter. Whatever the circumstance, he earned and holds the title of the great Nature Poet. In nature he saw more than just beauty. He saw the expression of divinity and moral teachings. Some say, incorrectly, that he was born an old man. The view of him as an austere, somber man is misleading. Who was the real Wordsworth?

William Wordsworth, as a young man, was a rebel, a liberal at the very least, in his poetry, his politics (early on) and in his love life. He wrote sublime poetry. Most of it. In ballad, sonnet and blank verse, he gloried in his own belief that all living nature feels the joy of being alive. As he grew older, he became more conservative. If you want to know what Wordsworth thought about Wordsworth, read his long biographical poem, *The Prelude; Or Growth of A Poet's Mind.* Even longer proportionally than the title was the period of time that he kept it on the shelf—forty-five years. He wrote it in his youth, considered it his magnum opus, revised it, had it copied by his dutiful wife and sister (no typewriter) and then stipulated that it could only be published after his death. Much mystery still exists about this man.

His story begins, as many sadly did in his day, "and then he was left an orphan." His mother and then his father died when he was quite young. Of his five siblings, he was closest to his sister, Dorothy. After he went away to grammar school and to live the rest of the year with a married couple, he and Dorothy did not meet again for nine years. When they did finally get together, they never parted again for very long. Literature has other examples of brother-sister associations—the Lambs, the Rossetti's, the Gordons (Lord Byron), but the Wordsworths appear to be the most loving of the kindred souls.

Before William and Dorothy were reunited, and between terms at St. John's College, Cambridge, William met Annette Vallon in France. Both were smitten with each other, but there were problems. She was Catholic. He was Protestant, hoping at the time to become a curate. He was twenty-one and she was twenty-five, and her parents disapproved of the match. The result of their ardent affair was a child whom they named Caroline. He admitted his paternity when the child was christened. He went away to think it over, but he kept up with Annette. Dorothy corresponded with her.

Then William decided to marry Mary Hutchinson whom he had first known as a child. His love letters to her won his suit. Before they were married, he made another trip to a neutral place in France, to Calais, "where it has been said that no one goes in the summer time if he doesn't live there." With Dorothy in tow, they visited with Caroline, now nine and Annette, who styled herself "the widow Williams," a name that may have been a trifle unsettling for William. What must have been their conversations in the visit that lasted for a month? They must have come to an understanding because William and Dorothy returned to England with marriage ahead for William and Mary. Dorothy continued her correspondence with Annette. The mystery widens.

And now we come again to Dorothy, of whom Coleridge said, "She is a woman indeed!—in mind, I mean, and heart—for her person is such, that if you expected to see a pretty woman, you would think her ordinary—if you expected to find an ordinary woman, you would think her pretty!" There was no equivocation about her personality. She was bright, vivacious, and attractive to men and had a talent for friendship. Did she also have a talent for writing? Most likely she did, although she had little time left in the day after serving as both William's amanuensis and housekeeper.

Certainly, she would not have considered competing with her beloved brother with whom she had shared a home for years before his marriage, and afterwards would continue to live with his family in their very small house. For a contemporary judgment of Dorothy's talent, read Thomas Carlyle in a letter he wrote to an associate about Dorothy's writing: "Finished Miss Wordsworth's Journal. I do not know when I have felt more than in reading it. She saw so much more than I did, though we were side by side a great part of the time." Frequently, Dorothy's journal was a prose rendering of what Wordsworth would express poetically.

There is no doubt that William and Dorothy were mutually dependent on each other and delighted in each other's companionship on their long walks, their travels and in those moments when they would lie in the grass together and simply look up at the sky. If William's wife, Mary, wondered if she could ever come up to Dorothy in William's eyes, it did not prevent her from becoming an intimate friend to her sister-in-law.

William had many literary friends in the day when a visit might turn into a month's stay. His best-known association was with Samuel Taylor Coleridge. The two men are famous for their collaboration on the literary manifesto, *Lyrical Ballads*, which argued against pseudo-classicism. Wordsworth championed the feelings of the common man as proper subjects of poetry; Coleridge in his "rudderless poetry" wanted to free the imagination. The "Preface" to the first and second editions (Wordsworth authored the second on his own) was the rallying cry of the Romantic Movement, one of the greatest eras in English literature. In his own poetry, Wordsworth was both the philosopher and a lyricist. Hazlitt said of his friend, "He may be said to take a personal interest in the Universe."

In politics, Wordsworth was a liberal in his youth. He was in sympathy with the French Revolution until the Reign of Terror betrayed its principles. Later the liberal he had been became the defender of the status quo. He allowed himself to be named Poet Laureate, an honor in itself but one his still liberal colleagues might have considered a "sell-out" politically.

In Wordsworth's springtime, the first half of his life, he accomplished his greatest work. Most students probably memorized in school some of the joyful lyrics that comprise Wordsworth's gift of springtime. Consider: "I Wandered Lonely as a Cloud", "My Heart Leaps up When I Behold", "To the Skylark", "She Was a Phantom of Delight" (written to his wife, Mary),"On the Sea-shore near Calais" (to his daughter, Caroline.) Finally, from the *Prelude*, "Bliss Was It That Dawn to Be Alive, But to Be Young Was Very Heaven!"

It is understandable why "winter" has been associated with the latter part of Wordsworth's life. He and Mary lost three of their five children, two when aged four and six, and Dora, named for her Aunt Dorothy, died just before her forty-fourth birthday. For a time, his friendship with Coleridge was ruptured. His brother, John, "the silent poet," was lost at sea. Dorothy "lost her mind" in 1835, although she did not die until 1855, five years after William's death. His friends, Scott, Lamb and Coleridge died before he did.

Even in winter there are bright, sunny days. The poetic principles that Wordsworth and Coleridge had advocated were understood and accepted. Wordsworth, the man and the poet, was validated.

Thinking Places

Much has been written about William Wordsworth's love for long-distance walking in the lake country, often alone, and frequently with his sister, Dorothy, or his friend Samuel Taylor Coleridge. Did his walking exercise give him more than panoramic views and a feeling of being one with Nature? Was it more than that? Did this give him a physical as well as a psychological stimulant to his bursts of creativity? (See descriptions in sections on Dickens, Darwin and Kipling who also had lifetime habits of taking long walks.)

When we visited Dove Cottage at Grasmere, where Wordsworth lived from 1799-1808, we saw the small rooms of the cottage and realized how crowded it must have been. In 1802 when William's wife, Mary, moved in, Dorothy stayed on in the house. Over the next few years three children were born. Frequently, there were overnight guests. One can appreciate his need for a getaway place.

We saw the log-supported shelter or "Indian shed" that has been reconstructed in the steep gardens back of the house.

Somewhat secluded and surrounded with vegetation, it was originally built in 1802. (Higher up the hill a "moss-lined summer house" had been built in 1804-1805). It did allow Wordsworth a semi-remote place nearby to think and, pacing up and down, to compose and memorize his poems, always speaking aloud to himself. After returning home he would write them down in his room or dictate them to Dorothy or Mary. Also, Wordsworth wrote poems while in the sitting room of Dove Cottage. At that time, the window overlooked the meadows and the lake.

In 1813, with increased income, the Wordsworths moved to a very substantial two-storey house, Rydal Mount, near Ambleside, with an inspiring view of the low mountains of the area. Nearby, a most picturesque path wound its way along the side of a steep incline. The path led to a stone lean-to shelter, larger than the one near Dove Cottage. Just beyond, and visible from the shelter, was a striking, panoramic view of the mountains, forest and lake (see attached picture).

One might assume that the process for creating serene poetry would be associated with a peaceful setting and a calm, quiet demeanor of the poet. This was not always true with Wordsworth. According to Johnston, "Sometimes they (Wordsworth and his friend, John Fleming) used to walk the five miles around the lake in the early morning, talking and memorizing school verses. Sometimes they worked up verse compositions of their own, quietly murmuring and musing together as they strolled along, a very intimate kind of communication. Wordsworth later made this strolling, outdoor communication his own, 'booing and hawing' as he walked back and forth in his garden like a metrical shuttle, creating and memorizing his own verses for later dictation to his amanuenses at home. No one other than Coleridge or Dorothy—and Fleming—ever accompanied him in these exercises."

Hunter Davies quotes a letter of Dorothy's. It is an apt description of Wordsworth's thinking place and its effect on him. "In wet weather he takes out an umbrella; chuses the most sheltered spot, and there walks backwards and forwards and though the length of his walk be sometimes a quarter or half a mile, he is as fast bound within the chosen limits as is by prison walls. He generally composes his verses out of doors and while he is so engaged he seldom knows how the time slips away or hardly whether it is rain or fair."

Visiting the Lake Country and feeling the inspiration of the setting, one can readily understand why Wordsworth found so much to draw him to the paths through this land of beautiful mountains, forests and lakes.

Lagniappe

Our special gifts from our visit to Grasmere, as we looked back on it several years later, was our eventually getting to know Wordsworth even better through the writings of Hunter Davies. He is the author of the principal, full length, popular biography of Wordsworth. Hunter Davies's *William Wordsworth*, addressed to the general reader, draws from the published letters of Wordsworth, his sister, Dorothy, and Coleridge and Southey.

Davies, in his delightful style, discusses in detail the interpersonal relationship of all of the above-mentioned players on the stage at Dove Cottage and Rydal Mount, and much, much more.

Hunter Davies lives in the Lake District near Cockermouth and writes with authority on subjects related to the area, including Beatrix Potter. We first met Hunter and his attractive wife, Margaret Forster, in Samoa, in 1992. (She is also a well-known writer. A movie was made of her novel, *Georgy Girl*.) All of us were attending the occasion that marked the beginning of the restoration of Vailima, home of Robert Louis Stevenson and his wife, Fanny. Hunter was in Samoa to do research for his book on Stevenson, *Teller of Tales, In Search of Robert Louis Stevenson*. At that time we had a similar purpose in finishing our musical play, *Imagination, RLS in the South Pacific*.

How satisfying it must be for Hunter to write about fellow but former residents of the Lake District–Wordsworth and

Beatrix Potter–while looking through his study window at scenes that they had also admired – the mountains and forests of Cumbria, the beautiful Lake District of England.

Wordsworth 's hut at Grasmere

The Lake Country — view from Wordsworth's hut

Hunter Davies and Margaret Forster at a book signing

Jane Austen

1775 - 1817

Jane Austen's Home at Chawton, Hampshire, England
and her thinking-writing place in the dining room

Jane Austen

"A lady's imagination is very rapid; it jumps from admiration to love, from love to matrimony in a moment."

Pride and Prejudice

"One half of the world cannot understand the pleasures of the other."

Emma

"It is a truth universally acknowledged, that a single man in possession of a good fortune, must be in want of a wife."

Pride and Prejudice

Journey   Chawton

The themes of Jane Austen's books are as current today as they were during her lifetime. This is attested to by the current popularity of her books and movies about them, and by the thousands of visitors to the Austen house in Chawton, Hampshire. We saw scores of school children and others of all ages when we visited the house one summer afternoon.

Jane Austen started writing at Steventon at an early age, but publication of her works did not begin until she was thirty-five and had moved to Chawton, to her brother's large and comfortable house in the country. She had lived in Bath for a time but did little writing there in its big city atmosphere.

The Austen home is now a museum with displays on upper floors of period clothes and other items. Our greatest interest centered in the living room, furnished with eighteenth century furniture and the site of Jane Austen's thinking and writing place in this house.

Vignette   Jane Austen   1775 - 1817

Professor Elliot Engel has stated that Jane Austen was, "the first great female author in our language" and "the foremost comic ironist in the English language." She would doubtless have received the Nobel Prize if she had lived two centuries later, but if she had, the world would have lost her irreplaceable depiction of life among the gentry in the eighteenth century

She wrote anonymously, sometime signing a book "by a lady," and she did not want anyone outside her family to know of her writing. Nevertheless, some discovered her secret, and she won many plaudits from her literary contemporaries. Sir Walter Scott, Samuel Coleridge, and Robert Southey were admirers of her talent and Alfred, Lord Tennyson said she was "next to Shakespeare." Jane would have laughed at this overstatement. All she wanted to do was to write about what she knew, and the people of her own social class.

She is as popular today as contemporary writers of best sellers. Jane Austen Societies exist all over the world; many promote conferences and tours. People find that her work is easy to read, full of humor and irony, with characters as truly memorable as a favorite aunt. Movies and television specials have been made of three of her six books.

Her growth in popularity was slow at first with an important exception. The librarian to the Prince Regent told Jane that His Royal Highness might like a dedication of one of her books. She duly dedicated *Emma*, but she wasn't happy about it. In this example, the quite modern-thinking Jane revealed herself as a feminist. She wrote in a letter that she hated the Prince "because of his treatment of the Princess, whom I shall support as long as I can because she is a Woman."

Jane was one of eight children—five boys and three girls of a rural vicar and his wife. Jane was closest to her sister, Cassandra, and, when separated, they wrote charming letters to each other.

It was evidently a happy family. Her mother taught the children at first, and then her father taught them along with boys outside the family for extra income. Jane was one of his apt students; she knew French, some Italian, English history and piano. Cassandra said that the music Jane copied in a manuscript was neatness itself. How fortunate for the printers when they received her novels. Jane also was blessed with a pretty singing voice.

Her genius, and most authorites agree on that assessment, was nurtured in the home. The family entertained each other with amateur theatricals in the barn fitted out for that purpose or in the drawing room when the weather was cold. As a young girl she wrote the script for these entertainments. She also began writing short stories. Life was pleasant. The family went to dinner parties and dances, which included country-dances and eventually, the waltz. They had servants, but the women did some cooking in that period. Reverend Austen farmed, and Mrs. Austen raised her own potatoes. The Austens were far from wealthy, but they did have a carriage and horses. Even so, Jane and Cassandra enjoyed lengthy walks. (Is there some connection between walking and literary productivity? See the vignettes of Dickens, Darwin, Wordsworth, Yeats and Sandburg.) In these early, impressionable years, Jane was observing and absorbing details of the life around her, the only life she wanted to record. She did what her heroines did in her books – needlework and card playing, which included whist and backgammon – and gossiping.

According to her nephew, Jane was "not so regularly handsome as Cassandra but rather tall, slender, animated and very attractive." Her hair was probably auburn. The portrait of her painted by Cassandra was considered unflattering. She never married, but did she have romance in her life? Yes! She accepted one marriage proposal, but reneged on it the next day. During a summer vacation at the beach, she met a young minister, and they seemed to be smitten with each other. Alas, they never saw each other again since he died soon afterwards. She later said that she considered that her books were her children.

From an early age Jane Austen applied herself to her writing, as if she sensed that she had very little time to live. It is amazing how well she used what time she had. She wrote her first novel,

Love and Friendship, and *A History of England* when she was only fourteen. Four of her books came out within a period of five years, and two were published posthumously. She was thirty-five when the first book, *Sense and Sensibility,* was released. Then *Pride and Prejudice, Mansfield Park,* and *Emma* appeared between 1811 and 1815. *Northanger Abbey* and *Persuasion* were published after her death. She wrote the first three at their home in Steventon when she was twenty-three years old. Actually, *Pride and Prejudice* was written before her early releases, but it required fifteen years to achieve publication.

Then followed a fallow time for Jane when the family moved to Bath. She much preferred the country. After her father died, Mrs. Austen and her two daughters moved to Southampton where Jane did not write at all. In 1809 the women moved to a permanent home on Jane's brother's large estate in Chawton, Hampshire. Jane began to write again. She had only seven and a half years to live and to write at Chawton.

Two of Jane's brothers, both admirals in the Royal Navy, died at advanced age, one at ninety-two and one of cholera when he was seventy-two. When Jane died in 1817 of what may have been Addison's Disease, she was only forty-two. Cassandra was with her. The two sisters had moved to Winchester to be near Jane's doctor. She is buried in Winchester Cathedral, but she left behind a host of people who live in her immortal books.

Thinking Places

Our searches for thinking places were often related to remote getaway places, such as garden houses or lonely paths in the woods.

Jane Austen's thinking place at Chawton was the exception. She did her thinking and writing in the midst of family activity in the dining room by a window. It was not considered lady-like to be writing stories. This was a man's prerogative in her century.

Jane wrote carefully on a small table with a straight chair, and she used small pieces of paper. On hearing the sound of someone coming into the room, she quickly tucked her pages into her lap or covered them with blotting paper.

Across the room was a doorway leading to a staircase and to the outside. This door made a creaking sound when anyone was coming in, thus serving as an alarm system for her. The day we visited Jane's dining room and thinking place, the door was still creaking.

◦◦◦

Lagniappe   Chawton

In a world that is constantly changing, it is reassuring to find something or someone who remains the same. We found that quality in Jane Austen and her world. We were not alone in this discovery. In the nearly three centuries since her death, Jane Austen is as popular as ever for creating characters that live beyond the page in situations, actions and conversations that make us smile as we read.

Her home at Chawton was furnished so typically for her time, it was as if Jane had just stepped out of the room. It was a revelation to see the circumstances of her writing some of the world's greatest literature, often secretly, sitting in the center of family home activity. She was a self starter with grit and gumption! How feeble are our own excuses for needing a perfect place and quiet to write or concentrate.

Having a better understanding of the "Austen Attitude" of meeting life with equanimity, originality, wit and grace was our lagniappe for our visit to Jane Austen's world. In Jane's case, we should say, "Lagniappe extraordinaire!"

Period dresses displayed in upstairs rooms

The Austen dining room

Jane's creaking door alarm

Jane's writing and thinking place in the dining room

Thomas Carlyle
1795 – 1881

Jane Carlyle
1801 - 1866

Carlyle Home at 24 Cheney
Row, Chelsea, London, England
and attic Thinking Place

Thomas and Jane Carlyle

"The greatest faults, I should say, is to be conscious of
none."

Heroes and Hero Worship: The Hero as Prophet TC

"Blessed is he who has found his work; let him ask no
other blessedness. "

Past and Present TC

"Oh Lord! If you but knew what a brimstone creature I
am behind all this beautiful amiability."

Letter to Eliza Stoddert JC

"The surest way to get a thing in life is to be prepared for
doing without it, to the exclusion even of hope."

from her Journal JC

Journey

From the 1840's onward, Thomas Carlyle, famous
worldwide as a writer and lecturer, and his wife, Jane Welsh
Carlyle, widely known in London for her quick-witted charm
and skillful homemaking, were famous hosts of their age. Their
guest lists were long, including some of the most famous literary
and intellectual personages of the day.

When the Carlyles moved from Scotland to London in 1834,
they found a "small" three-storey townhouse in Chelsea near the
river embankment at 5 Cheyne Row. (Years later the number
was changed to 25 Cheyne Row when houses were built on the
other side of the street.) They rented the house for thirty-five
pounds sterling; a year later they were given a thirty- year lease.
At the time, it was considered an "unfashionable" area in
London. Today, it is quite the opposite.   They resided in this
sturdy and comfortable town house for the rest of their lives.

Chelsea, bounded on one end by the Cheyne Road area and, at the other end, by Sloane Square with the huge Peter Jones' Department Store, is connected by King's Road Shopping district with its designer shops, the Royal Hospital for Pensioners, and several museums.

Our journey to the Carlyles' home started in Knightsbridge near Chelsea at Lennox Gardens, our flat for six months in London years ago, in less frenetic times. Then our recurrent problem of communicating with the ticket seller for the "tube" (subway) was solved by faking a British accent to get a ticket to "Sloe-own Skwah" (Sloane Square). Cheyne Walk and Cheyne Row now have many small round, blue plaques on the townhouses, honoring illustrious people who once lived there, such as Gabriel Rosetti, George Meredith, and Algenon Charles Swinburne. Henry James lived nearby for years in Carlyle Mansions, when he was not in his country home in Rye. J.M.W. Turner, James McNeil Whistler, Leigh Hunt and Augustus John also were connected with the area. Others who lived in the neighborhood included George Eliot, Oscar Wilde and Mark Twain, the latter for a year.

Outside, in the back of the house, is the garden with its high walls giving a sense of privacy, but not free from neighborhood noise. It was   probably too noisy for Thomas Carlyle's main writing and thinking place since he required complete quiet. According to Professor Brent Kinser, Thomas and Jane did spend much time in the back garden, often writing letters. Thomas did most of the garden work and Jane, an animal lover, kept a hedgehog in the garden area.

Of special interest in the house is the Library or Drawing Room on the lower floor and the Attic Study (See Thinking Place) on the top floor. The Library, a previously small room, was transformed to its present state in 1843, and redecorated in 1852. The shelves are full of books, part of Carlyle's collection. The screen, with portraits and engravings assembled by Jane in 1849, was one of Carlyle's favorite items. Carlyle's green, leather-upholstered reading chair, was given to him on his eightieth birthday by John Forster, Dickens' biographer. What a sense of awe one may have when realizing what happened in this room: conversations of Dickens, Darwin, Browning and many more; the rewriting of *The French Revolution* over many years, Carlyle having been told his large manuscript had been burned by accident; and many other significant events and ghosts of the past.

c⌣⌣o⌣⌣⌣⌣

Vignette

Thomas Carlyle   1795-1881

Jane Welsh Carlyle   1801-1866

Perhaps Carlyle suffered from a "genius complex," which he may have had from youthful age. His father was a stone mason with a modest income and thus was unable to give him much support. Carlyle charted his own future. At fourteen he enrolled in the University of Edinburgh. He had no transportation, so he walked the one hundred miles to Edinburgh, taking days to make the trip. He was imbued with the conviction that he was set apart from ordinary men to accomplish great things. Many years later he had done just that and had become one of the most famous men in London, not only as a writer but as a political critic and social philosopher.   There was, however, a price to pay!

Carlyle's family had little income, but he considered them the best of the best. In contrast, Jane Welsh was from a well-to-do family, and daughter of a prosperous doctor. She loved her mother, but they did not tolerate each other well. Jane was very bright and charming but sometimes, it was said, Jane's wit could be biting.   At age eighteen she was attending an exclusive school, Miss Hall's, in Edinburgh, when her beloved father died. Jane dropped out of school, returned to her hometown, Haddington, and taught school to pay her way.

Before Carlyle came along for Jane, there was Edward Irving, her handsome tutor. They fell passionately in love, but Irving was already engaged, and he felt an obligation, strongly reinforced by his future father-in-law, to go through with the marriage and sadly rejected Jane. But, later, it was Irving who introduced Thomas to Jane, and he became a close friend of

Carlyle's as well as Jane's. The new Mrs. Irving never became a friend of Jane's.

Jane had hoped to marry a genius, and in due time, genius met near-genius. After five years of courting, and over her mother's resistance, Jane and Thomas finally became engaged. Their letters to each other reflected a strong intellectual compatibility and mutual, deep respect, as well as affection. At one point, the wedding had been set into the future, and Carlyle wanted to call it off, but Jane talked him out of his hesitation. Before their marriage Carlyle insisted that he did not want to accept any part of Jane's inheritance. When they married Jane made over her legacy to her mother.

The couple lived in Edinburgh, and then on property at Craigenputtock for six years. This remote place seemed to bring out all of sociable Jane's aches and pains, made worse by the isolation. It brought inspiration to Carlyle. Next they tried London, then back to Scotland, then finally and permanently, to London. After their marriage, Jane discovered that Carlyle liked to do almost everything alone. Yet, they were tender and affectionate, especially in their letters to each other. He called her pet names, like "Screamikin." She called him either Carlyle or "Mr. C." She never addressed him as Thomas. (In the Victorian era, it was common for a wife to forego the use of the first name.)

Thomas was a constant and prolific writer and became a popular lecturer. He had an informed opinion on everything as he became famous in London and abroad. Other famous people, Dickens, Darwin, Browning, Ruskin and Thackeray among them, attended the Carlyles' evenings at home; Tennyson and Mazzini, the Italian revolutionary, were regular visitors. Chopin played their piano; the piano is on view today in the Carlyle home. At these soirees, Thomas, with a talent for discourse, would hold forth in monologues, perhaps unaware that Jane's ready and sometimes ascerbic wit also captivated other guests and assured the attendance of some. Jane often was the center of attraction of her group. People enjoyed repeating her remarks and witticisms. Friends flocked to their evenings at home. These social occasions, with an attentive audience, (often with two audiences, we assume), must have been the Carlyles' happiest.

Both Jane and Thomas wanted their home to be appropriately furnished. Jane saw her role as provider of a suitable environment to nurture his genius, busying herself making improvements in their home in London, changing the household furnishings twice in a space of ten years. She truly enjoyed making life easier for Thomas because she loved him, and indeed, Thomas was devoted to her but, at times, when they both proved difficult to live with, they may have wondered why each had wanted to marry a genius in the first place. Various biographers have taken sides about both Thomas' and Jane's virtues and human imperfections. We agree with all those who considered Thomas and Jane as two of the most brilliant authors and personalities of their times. We also agree with Professor Brent Kinser that they "were one of the remarkable couples in the history of belles-lettres."

The Carlyles discovered, with a few exceptions, that they could not take vacations together. Ironically, Thomas had written before they were married, "Oh Jeannie! Oh my wife! We will never part, never through eternity itself; but I will love thee and keep thee in my heart of hearts!" Jane replied, "Yes, surely, we will live together and die together and be together through all eternity."

But after they were married, both spent a great deal of time away from home, separately, on visits to other people, but their letters in the interim showed their great regard for each other. Sometimes, one would be leaving, as the other would be returning home. Still in their own way, they loved each other.

Thomas could be intent, overbearing and unpleasant at times, but he made and kept friends. He was so busy writing, as if he had a sense of being pre-ordained to produce masterpieces, that often he had little time for Jane. When a work was finally completed, he needed to go away alone, usually to Scotland.

Jane was often alone during gloomy London days with her canary, Chico, and her dog, Nero, to keep her company. She regretted that she had no children. She always had a maid to help with housekeeping, but a steady succession of maids through the years presented various problems. Time hung heavy for Jane. She spent her spare time writing letters, little dreaming and never knowing, that some day her letters would make her nearly as famous as her husband.

One problem Jane couldn't seem to alleviate for Thomas was noise! Carlyle had a pathological hatred of noise. He could neither work nor sleep if there was noise. The Carlyles attempted to build a soundproof room under Jane's supervision.

A calamity awaited Carlyle. He had asked John Stuart Mill to read his only copy of *The French Revolution*, hand-written, of course. Imagine his despair when Mill had to tell him that his maid, thinking the papers were trash, had burned the entire first volume. To his great credit, he showed forbearance and understanding. He rewrote that lost volume, adding six more. His work also included: *Sartor Resartus; On Heroes, Hero-Worship and the Heroic in History, Past and Present; The Life of Schiller; The History of Frederick II of Prussia; The Early Kings of Norway,* and *The Life of John Stirling*. Carlyle, the scholar, wrote about the letters of Boswell, Byron, Walter Scott, Walpole, Voltaire and Dickens. He had published the letters of Oliver Cromwell and others. He himself was an ardent letter writer, and during their courtship he had been a mentor to Jane in her letter writing.

In 1866 Carlyle's lifetime dream came true, recognition in his native Scotland. This had eluded him earlier. He was appointed Rector of the University of Edinburgh, the most prestigious academic position in Scotland! This was an honorary position, not requiring residence in Edinburgh. Jane shared Thomas' joy; they were ecstatic! The appointment called for an address by the recipient and Thomas set about the task of preparation with fervor, making sure that everyone around him suffered along with him. When Thomas traveled to Edinburgh, Jane declined to make the trip because of her frail health. Carlyle prepared well, memorizing his speech, including long passages from the classics. He did not write it down, choosing "to speak from the heart"; nor did he use notes when he gave the oration. The speech lasted an hour and a half. Members of the audience, including many luminaries such as Dickens and Huxley, were spellbound. At the conclusion there was a prolonged, standing ovation.

Before Thomas had time to return from Edinburgh, Jane Welsh Carlyle, while riding in her coach, died quietly and unexpectedly, presumably from a heart attack. She was sixty-five, beloved by many who knew her. Thomas returned home in a state of shock and disbelief. He was inconsolable with guilt and depression. He knew he had always loved her; he hadn't fully realized just how much until her passing. He discovered her letters, and recognizing her great talent, decided to edit them for publication. They filled more than three volumes. Through the letters, he understood all she had done for him and how lonely she must have been. His footnotes that are personal in nature are expressions of his deep regret. He did not delete any passage, even those that put himself in a poor light. Carlyle, on reviewing Jane's letters remarked about her "talent" and "genius," "...my little woman...Not all the Sands and Eliotts and babbling cohue of 'celebrated scribbling women' that have strutted over the world, in my time, it seems to me, if all boiled down and distilled to essence, make one such woman."

The last eighteen months of Jane's life may have been her happiest. She had had an especially serious episode of illness (recurrent "pain") and went away for a cure. When she returned her health seemed to be restored, and they had a touching and joyful homecoming. Carlyle appropriately was more attentive. Thereafter, Jane wrote to her sister, "I cannot tell you how gentle and good Mr. Carlyle is! He is busy as ever, but he studies my comfort and peace as he has never done before." He bought her a carriage, something he had put off in the past. This had greatly pleased Jane.

Carlyle never remarried. He lived at Cheyne Row for fifteen more years, continuing his literary output. For the last few years he was unable to write because of a disabled hand, but he often used an amanuensis for dictation.

Carlyle had started writing *Frederick the Great* in 1852 and completed it thirteen years later with great acclaim. His reputation suffered a temporary setback in the 1850's when he published a series of *Latter-Day Pamphlets* offering controversial views on former slaves, the Irish and corporal punishment, unpopular in many quarters. It was a failure, even losing him some of his friends and admirers like John Stuart Mill and John Ruskin. But with time, in his older age, he regained the high respect of his peers and friends who gathered around him, and he became fully restored as "The Sage of Chelsea."

At the library of the University of West Florida, volumes of books on and by Thomas Carlyle fill shelf after shelf. They furnish further validation that Carlyle had attained the goal that he had set for himself when he was only fourteen. Carlyle was also a master letter writer. Over ten thousand of his letters have been saved, many of the originals in a dozen different libraries.

Thinking Places

From an early age, Thomas Carlyle had a thinking place. At age fourteen when he returned from The University of Edinburgh, he found his parents' home too small for serious study, especially with six bothers and sisters, adding to the confusion. He was resourceful though and found just what he needed. It was a ditch near the house—a dry ditch—that provided a secluded spot for quiet concentration.

After he married Jane Welsh, he no doubt had a study or thinking place in the different places they lived before they settled permanently in Chelsea. At the house on Cheyne Walk, Thomas tried writing in every room, seeking to get away from the noise of the street and from next door. As mentioned above, he wrote *The French Revolution* in the library or drawing room. Thomas didn't just like quiet; he simply could not abide noise. In order to write and to think, he required solitude, unbroken by noise of any kind. Neighbors moved next door with a flock of chickens, and a rooster. Another neighbor had a cow. The crowing of the rooster drove Thomas wild. Letters were exchanged. Then he trembled with exasperation when they played the piano next door. Letters were exchanged. Carlyle would become furious and beside himself at times. He would finally storm out of the house for a walk!

The Carlyles were determined to build a soundproof room and they set about remodeling the attic. A new staircase and windows for ventilation were built. They attempted to insulate the walls and ceiling. Unfortunately, the sounds of the Thames River were accentuated, and the plan was unsuccessful. Carlyle persisted in his "insulated" attic study for twelve years, and then returned to the ground floor for his solitary writing.

In the attic study, one may see Carlyle's desk, made by an amateur carpenter friend of Jane's father, and bookcases with some of Carlyle's works. In a display case are his walking stick, manuscripts and other memorabilia.

As for Jane, her thinking place at Cheney Row was probably in her bedroom and on any surface where she could write her many entertaining letters, her chief occupation. Perhaps she did some of her writing while sitting on a bench in the walled-in gardens in the backyard.

<hr />

Lagniappe

Our first trip many years ago to Cheyne Walk to visit the Carlyle house was enlightening but depressing. It was difficult to be unaware of opportunities lost for both Thomas and Jane when reading of their sometimes stormy marriage. A feeling of lagniappe received just wouldn't come. At the time we had a limited, prevailing version of the story of the Carlyles: that childless Jane was a victim of a Victorian, unhappy, sexless marriage to an irascible, stern Thomas Carlyle. Our lagniappe arrived belatedly when communicating with Carlyle scholar Brent Kinser and reviewing recent publications by Dr. Roger L. Tarr; Ashton; and Fielding and Sorenson, giving the other side of the story. According to Professor Tarr, "the alleged tragedy of Jane Welsh Carlyle's life is one built upon ignorance and founded upon falsehood"...."she has become the symbol of presumed oppression in Victorian marriage." ..."in fact, the seeming pathological violations of Jane Carlyle's life have been going on—largely unchecked until the recent and welcome appearance of Rosemary Ashton's *Thomas and Jane Carlyle: Portrait of a Marriage* (2002), and Kenneth Fielding and David Sorensen's *Jane Carlyle: Newly Selected Letter)*--since her death in

1866(2004)." Tarr gave the following summary: "Their marriage was not perfect. Carlyle was demanding, punctual and certainly stern. Jane was ascerbic, witty and equally stern. They clashed frequently. There was thunder, but always it was followed by redemptive rain."

Due to our limited vision, we had wondered if the Carlyle chapter would be of interest to our readers. Should it be included? It is now one of our favorites after learning more of their story. It is special lagniappe to learn that currently there is vigorous discussion by Carlyle scholars, bringing up new and refreshing ideas!

Additional lagniappe came to us while doing further research at The University of West Florida library on this remarkable couple. Not only were there shelves devoted to Thomas, but there before our eyes was an entire shelf devoted to Jane, containing volumes of her letters and several full-length biographies. It was confirmation of her acceptance as a premier letter-writer in literature.

Thomas deserves a salute and full credit for his devotion to Jane and his years of toil in recording her letters and preserving them. To realize more fully that Jane received appropriate credit for her own formidable talent and that Thomas dedicated himself completely to assure Jane's place in literary history—this was truly lagniappe for us.

This short letter below, written by Jane before she married, one of the three thousand saved, gives a flavor of her writing and personality. Most of her letters were not short, and often she did not bother with separating into paragraphs.

Friday, December (1812)

Sir,

I am quite ashamed of having kept the books so long – A series of engagements which have cruelly massacred my time since my return home is the only apology I have to offer for myself —

You would receive from Mr. Irving the second volume of Alfieri which, by mistake, I read first –

Your attention in supplying me with so much amusement and edification deserves from me the strongest expressions of gratitude–but as I have not come into the world with the gift of making speeches, I must leave it to your imagination to supply all that I ought to say.

Yours,

Jane Welsh

In spite of challenging and sometimes stormy times together, Thomas and Jane Carlyle gave much pleasure, support and intellectual stimulation to each other, and to their peers and people of their times– as well as for posterity.

©NTPL

Portrait of Jane Carlyle by Samuel Laurence, Carlyle's House, Chelsea (The National Trust)

©NTPL

Portrait of Thomas Carlyle by Robert Tait, Carlyle's House, Chelsea (The National Trust)

The Carlyle's walled –in garden

Charles Darwin

1809 - 1882

The Darwin Home, Down House, Downe, London Borough of
Bromley, England; and Sandwalk, Darwin's Thinking Path

Charles Darwin

"Man with all his noble qualities with his godlike
intellect which has penetrated into the movements and
constitution of the solar system still bears in his bodily
frame the indelible stamp of his lowly origin."

The Descent of Man

Journey   Downe and Darwin's World

The village of Downe, a tiny speck on the map south of London, and nearby Down House, make up only a small package of
land and houses; yet, like a small package of dynamite, Down
House gave birth to explosive ideas in 1859 with publication of a
book by Charles Darwin.

One way to drive to rural Downe is to combine the journey
with a trip to Churchill's impressive Chartwell (Weald of Kent),
Lord Sackwell's elaborate and historic Knole Castle (near Seven
Oaks), and Anne Boelyn's beautifully restored Hever Castle (a
short trip south of Chartwell.)

A highlight of our trip in this area was an overnight stay in a
five- hundred-year-old inn, just north of Westerham. In the inn's
cheerful, beamed and low-ceilinged tavern, the dinner turned
out to be British food at its best! Later, the small bedroom was
quite comfortable and two weary travelers welcomed the
modern bed. We wondered who were some of the many other
weary travelers who had stayed in this room through the centuries? What were their stories and where were they going?

And, speaking of weary, how exhausted Charles Darwin
must have been from time to time on his five-year voyage on the
HMS Beagle around the world. As we drifted off to sleep, these
thoughts gradually faded from our consciousness, just as the
years and stories of the previous occupants of this room had
faded away with time.

They knocked on our door at an early hour. We enjoyed an English breakfast –"white coffee"(with milk) or tea, cold toast in a metal toast rack, orange marmalade, butter, broiled tomatoes, fried eggs and English-style undercooked bacon. Fortified, we were on our way to Biggin Hill, Downe and Down House.

The village of Downe had added the "e" to its name shortly before Charles and Emma Darwin moved into Down House in 1842, and the Darwins did not want to change the spelling of the name of the old house. By that time, Charles had spent five years on the voyage, become famous as a naturalist, married and spent five years with a busy professional and social life in London. Charles was a lover of nature at heart and longed for the country life.

Moving to Down House allowed him to pursue his experiments and writing while completely immersing himself in his family, home, gardens and nature walks. Darwin stated, "I never saw so many footpaths in any other country. The country is extraordinarily rural and quiet with narrow lanes and high hedges and hardly any ruts. It is really surprising to think London is only sixteen miles off."

At the time of our journey to Downe and Down House, the entire area still seemed "extraordinarily rural and quiet", as described by Charles Darwin. Today's cared-for condition of Down House and its properties, and educational facilities, are continuing tributes to the Darwin family–and to the genius and humanity of a man whose life's journey was dedicated to seeking to understand the mysteries of life on our planet.

Vignette   Charles Darwin 1809-1882

What books would be on your list of the ten most significant books of the last two hundred years? Even if we define "significant" in different ways, *On Origin of Species* would most likely appear on your list. It is an understatement to say that Charles Darwin's massive work subtitled *By Means of Natural*

Selection on the Preservation of Favoured Races in the Struggle for Life was controversial in its day. Columns in newspapers and periodicals, caricatures, sermons, private and public conversations took up the debate. Although written as a scientific work, Darwin's readable style made it accessible for the lay person to read; it must have been the topic of the day. First published in 1859, after thirteen months of writing and years of collecting specimens, Darwin revised it for the many editions to follow. He always considered it a work in progress.

To say that *Origin* is still controversial today is also an understatement. Those who oppose its premise do so for religious reasons and for their own interpretation of data. They frequently serve on school textbook committees, thus keeping the issue current.

There are several ironies in the Darwin story. Charles studied medicine for one year at Edinburgh University but dropped out, one reason being that his tender nature rebelled at witnessing surgery performed without anesthesia. He then went to Cambridge University, planning to become ordained in the Church of England. An inspired teacher, the Reverend Professor Henslow, helped Darwin realize that his true interest and ability was in natural history. After his graduation, Professor Henslow secured him an invitation for a long voyage that would change his life and his mission.

Sometime after the voyage in 1839, he married. His beloved wife, Emma, faithful to the Church, became deeply concerned that his belief in the theory of evolution might prevent their future reunion in Heaven.

Most ironical of all, another naturalist, Alfred Russell Wallace, propounded a theory similar to Darwin's and sent Darwin his findings. Darwin commented, "I never saw a more striking coincidence!" A conference was held, and both men gave credit to the other, but Wallace generously stated that Darwin's work pre-dated his own.

Charles Darwin seemed destined to become a naturalist. As a very young boy in a portrait with his sister, he is shown holding a pot of flowers. From childhood through university, he assembled botanical and zoological collections. At Cambridge he requested a cram course in geology. After his graduation, he received a life-changing invitation to become a naturalist on the HMS Beagle for two-and-a-half years to circumnavigate the globe, starting in South America. Darwin recognized some reasons not to do it. He knew it would be dangerous; he suspected that he had heart trouble because of palpitations. His revered father was at first opposed to his going, but Darwin realized that it was a unique opportunity, and he went anyway. He probably didn't consider how long he would be seasick, existing for days at a time on only sea biscuits and raisins. He did have two land excursions, lasting four months each, and he collected in all thousands of specimens, which he sent back to England.

The voyage stretched to nearly five years. During that time, he witnessed a volcanic eruption, experienced an earthquake and storms at sea and became seriously ill with a fever. The latter may account for his ill health, endured for the rest of his life. (This could have been due to a chronic infectious disease transmitted by the bite of an insect.) In spite of all of these exigencies, he demonstrated his genius in the field of natural history—and came home with remarkable specimens in botany, zoology and geology—the beginning of a theory and the foundation for his life's work.

What was he like, this man who was called an ape and a worm by some of his contemporaries? In his most familiar portrait, we see a long-bearded Darwin, his eyes peering solemnly from the jutting plateau of his forehead, a formidable-looking man. His children saw him as the patient and tender-hearted father who played with them, frequently on his hands and knees, allowing them to interrupt him in his study. His daughter stated that her father was one who considered them, "creatures whose opinions were valuable. The best of us came out in his presence."

Now let Emma, his wife of forty-three years, speak. "He is the most open, transparent man I ever saw and every word expresses his real thoughts. He is particularly affectionate and very nice to his father and sisters, and perfectly sweet tempered." They had ten children, but three died at an early age.

Like her husband, Emma's buoyant personality added to the happiness of the household. She played the piano every night and also read to Darwin. Well-educated, she was a good match for Darwin. She ran the Sunday School, taught village children how to read, and ministered to the poor. Although she had servants, Emma was not obsessive about keeping a constantly neat house. She valued peace and contentment. She was a realist who said "yes" to life.

By all accounts, Darwin was an enthusiastic man, friendly, modest, fair in his judgments, generous in sharing credit, and thrifty. He was frequently worried about money although he didn't need to be. He liked to play billiards and to walk. Though frequently ill with disagreeable and painful symptoms, he continued to work and was a prolific writer. He wrote twenty-four books and many articles.

A week before their wedding Charles wrote to Emma, "I do hope that you may be as happy as I know I shall be. I think you will humanize me, and soon teach me that there is greater happiness than building theories and accumulating facts in silence and in solitude."

Toward the end of his life, Darwin commented to a friend, "My theology is in a muddle." Many of his critics would agree with this statement. Some others might ask simply,"Is it possible that as Darwin loved the natural world he must have revered the creative force that some would call "God"?

As Randal Keynes, great-great-grandson of Charles Darwin, related in his book, *Annie's Box*, subtitled, *Darwin, His Daughter and Human Evolution*, Darwin was overwhelmed with grief on the death of his young daughter. He could not justify the concept of a loving God who would strike down such an innocent, lovely child. He quoted Darwin who expressed the opinion that pain and suffering is "the inevitable result of the natural sequence of events, i.e., general laws rather than intervention of God".

Darwin did not relate to the term "atheism" but considered himself an "agnostic," intermittently unsure of his beliefs and at odds sometimes with the organized church.

. According to Keynes, when asked about his views on the grounds for belief in God, Darwin stated, "the impossibility of conceiving that this grand and wondrous universe, with our conscious selves, arose through chance, seems to me to be the chief argument for the existence of God."..."the mind still craves to know whence it came and how it arose."..."nor can I overlook the difficulty from the immense amount of suffering in the world."..."The safest conclusion seems to me that the whole subject is beyond the scope of man's intellect; but man can do his duty."

Today, when one sees myriad advances in science since Darwin's time and contemplates our tiny planet in the immense universe of billons of stars (suns) in billions of galaxies, it is comforting to realize that we are in good company with those who feel that so much is beyond our comprehension; but we "do our duty" and develop our own belief systems from the information that we garner through study, life experiences and, for some, through faith.

Darwin always expected to be buried in the country churchyard near Down House, but England gave him her highest honor, a place in Westminster Abbey.

Thinking Places

At Down House, Darwin had a work place, which he called "a capital study". (See picture below.) Everything he needed was conveniently arranged around a Pembroke table in the center of the room. Papers, letters, a book or two, were placed here. Other items, such as specimen bottles and the material that he was currently working on were laid on a revolving drum table between windows. He could use his microscope on a shelf by sitting on a low stool by a window; files, shelves and cupboards were located around the room. Everything was in reach of the most important piece of furniture in the room—a blue armchair placed on top of an iron frame with wheels. A foot cushion for his feet and a lapboard that stretched across the arms of the chair completed his writing and reading needs. In this armchair he wrote *On Origin of Species.* His study and other rooms may be seen in the beautifully restored house, opened to the public in 1929 and maintained by English Heritage.

Darwin was a creature of habit and discipline, observing specific hours for accomplishing everything he did. Daily he arose before sunlight, took a short walk outside, had a small breakfast by himself, and then did his best research from 8:00 to 9:00 AM. He had specific times for reading letters, for listening to Emma's reading of novels, for meals, for family activities; and, in the afternoon, for more research and scientific reading, resting, then a short stroll. But at noon, for one hour, he reserved time for walking on his path he called Sandwalk, no matter what the weather might be. He had leased 300 yards of extra land, a quarter of a mile from Down House, to make a footpath around its perimeter. He had a fence installed and planted trees and shrubs with a wood on one side; it was truly one of his thinking places—his "Thinking Path." To keep count of each round that he made without conscious thought, he put rocks at the beginning of the path and kicked one aside, one by one, as he made each turn. On occasion Emma went with him, but his walking was primarily a solitary routine when he did his best thinking. His dog Polly, a white terrier, often accompanied him.

Today one can be trained to increase levels of Alpha brain wave activity, which possibly may be associated with creative thinking. Perhaps Darwin discovered one-hundred-fifty years ago that his walks helped induce a state of mind with alert relaxation open to bursts of inspiration; this was, no doubt, invaluable in his creative work. (See the section on William Wordsworth for apparently a similar experience.)

Lagniappe

We did not know about Darwin's Sandwalk before we visited Down House. Sandwalk, another prime example of a secluded thinking place was, indeed, an unexpected bonus of our visit. We had not expected such lagniappe since we had already been repaid for our efforts by seeing Down House and Darwin's study. In its comfortable rooms it was easy to imagine the daily life of this loving and lovable Darwin family, who had joys and sorrows, hopes and worries just like all of us, no matter how we have evolved into the human creatures that we are.

Beyond the Darwin's large back yard, we saw Sandwalk stretching ahead of us, a well-worn path, shaded by trees, beckoning invitingly. We did not place stones at the beginning to measure our circuits, as Darwin used to do. We knew we wouldn't walk very far, but still we started with some hesitation. After all, this was Darwin's own Thinking Place. We felt as if we were intruding, particularly since we had brought a camera to record the view.

As we proceeded, we felt as if we were back in pastoral Kent in another century, in Darwin's time. As the British would say it was a fine day. We even heard bird song and wondered if Darwin ever imported to Down House the kind of finches that he observed and included in his notebook.

The walk was half over when we suddenly became silent, each of us conscious that we should be trying to think creatively, considering where we were. We had walked back to where we had started, when we admitted to each other that we had had no illuminating thoughts. Our only reward, more than sufficient, was the beauty of the path through the woods and our sense of being in a very special place where much high-powered thinking had occurred.

On the way back to the house we stopped by Darwin's greenhouse as Darwin had done countless times. We looked in - and there was our additional lagniappe! On a shelf, among other growing specimens was a pitcher plant! The sight of it was what Darwin would have called, "a striking coincidence." The pitcher plant grows wild in a limited number of places in Escambia County, Florida, our home. Something like a Venus flycatcher, it has been placed on the endangered species list since it plays an important role in the ecology of swamplands. The State of Florida has been buying up the Pitcher Plant Prairies, the swampy lowlands where it grows. We realized that Darwin had a special interest in carnivorous plants and, probably, in pitcher plants. We visualized that he would have applauded the spirit of Florida's action in behalf of the environment. We learned later that Darwin published extensively about his work with carnivorous plants. We cherished the connection, no matter how slight, of how this special little part of nature tied together such different people, countries and historical moments.

Darwin's greenhouse
and carnivorous plants

Charles Darwin,1840, by George Richmond
Courtesy of the Darwin Heirlooms Trust
© English Heritage Photo Library

© English Heritage Photo Library
Darwin's study and indoor thinking place at Down House

Charles Dickens

1812 – 1870

Charles Dickens' last home, Gad's Hill Place, near Rochester,
Kent, England and his Swiss Chalet Thinking Place

Charles Dickens

"Any man may be in good spirits and good temper when he's well dressed. There ain't much credit in that."

Martin Chuzzlewit

"There is a wisdom of the head, and a wisdom of the heart."

Hard Times

"It was the best of times, it was the worst of times."

A Tale of Two Cities

"Oh, but he was a tightfisted hand at the grindstone. Scrooge! A squeezing, wrenching, grasping, scraping, clutching, covetous old sinner! Hard and sharp as flint, from which no steel had ever struck out generous fire; secret and self-contained, and solitary as an oyster."

A Christmas Carol

Journey   Rochester

We were on the road to Rochester, Kent and the ancient Royal Victoria and Bull Hotel, reflecting on how many Dickensian images we have tucked away in our minds: the Christmas cards showing snowy scenes with stage coach and four, heralded by long horns; Victorian scenes of warm fires, holly wreaths and Christmas merriment; groups of carolers in winter garb and tall hats singing near an eighteenth century lamp, and on and on. Our thoughts also were filled with memories of past Dickensian experiences: attending the annual December play, "A Christmas Carol" held in a local church parish hall during our childhood; traveling to the Broadstairs Dickens Festival in England with our small children years ago to see "A Christmas Carol," odd to us that it was put on during the summer months; trudging along the streets of old London on a

103

bitter, cold and foggy night, on a walking tour of streets and inns described in Dickens stories, such as the George, and the George and Vulture.

One of our richest experiences ever was getting to know Mr. John Greaves, The Honorable Secretary of the Dickens Fellowship. We met him at the Dickens House Museum in London and later had him as our guest for dinner, where he entertained all of us for hours. He and Dickens would have been fast friends. In fact, when he recited from Dickens, playing in turn the varied and colorful characters, he became, in face and gesture, a character out of Dickens. His repertory included seventeen hours (!) of memorized pages from Dickens, including different brogues, accents and inflections. He started performing during World War II, entertaining the British troops. Servicemen and women must have felt as we did that "An Evening with John Greaves" was an evening of a lifetime, filled with information, hilarious stories and great fellowship. We later learned from Professor Elliot Engel, another esteemed Dickens scholar and lecturer, that the Honorable Mr. Greaves was revered by Dickensian experts everywhere. Mr. Greaves gave us Dickens' own recipe for Christmas Punch. We lift our cups to the memory of The Honorable Secretary!

Professor Engel, an internationally acclaimed writer and lecturer on four continents, is a modern-day "John Greaves." He has been a master teacher for us with his lectures, personal conversations on several occasions, and his tapes discussing Dickens (and multiple other authors.) He brought the great-great grandson of Charles Dickens to Raleigh, North Carolina, Dr. Engel's home base, for The Dickens Festival we attended. For more about books and audio, video and DVD recordings of many leading authors look up Dr. Elliot Engel's information-filled *Authors Ink* newsletter and _www.AuthorsInk.com_.

Traveling itself can be closely associated with Charles Dickens. In his early serial stories, *The Pickwick Papers*, the traveling characters visited over a hundred inns. In fact, a book was written about the inns mentioned in *Pickwick Papers* alone. Dickens' life, also, was filled with travel, much for personal pleasure and much for lecturing, including two tours of the United States.

Rochester and environs represent Dickens' early childhood happiness and aspirations, as well as his later life when he had reached the pinnacle of success and had satisfied his dream of acquiring as his home, Gad's Hill Place, at Higham, near Rochester, Kent.

Our goal was to see Dickens' small writing hut, which originally was on his wooded property adjacent to Gad's Hill. The hut, a miniature Swiss chalet had been shipped in 58 packing crates to Dickens by a friend. The assembled Swiss Chalet Hut was used frequently by Dickens. Today the hut stands outdoors on the grounds of the Charles Dickens Centre in Rochester. The Centre, with exhibits, murals and audiovisuals about many of Dickens' works is delightful and a Lagniappe experience in itself.

The Royal Victoria and Bull Hotel looked exactly like a Victorian inn depicted on the Christmas cards of our memory. According to the Inn's brochure, "The present inn is some four hundred years old. Previously another inn stood on the same site. 'The Bull' was a Coaching Inn on the London to Dover road. Mail coaches stopped off here daily to change horses, and to allow passengers to obtain refreshment."

The brochure went on to state, "One of the hotel's most famous visitors was Princess Victoria, later to become Queen, who stayed on the night of 29th November 1836. Dickens stayed here on many occasions and featured the hotel in two of his most famous works. In *The Pickwick Papers*, the hotel was featured as 'The Bull at Rochester' and it was where the Pickwick Club stayed on their first journey. In *Great Expectations*, the hotel was referred to as the 'Blue Boar' and the main character, Pip, took his indenture as apprentice Blacksmith at the Guildhall opposite. Pip in later life stayed at the hotel."

Like Pickwick and his club members, after a long day's journey, we felt warmly disposed and comfortable in the old "Bull at Rochester" and looked forward to the next day's adventure.

Vignette   Charles Dickens 1812-1870

Who has not heard the name, Charles Dickens, one of England's most famous authors? Young people have read *David Copperfield* and *Oliver Twist*. Adults have their choice of a formidable list of novels, including *A Tale of Two Cities*, *The Pickwick Papers*, *Nicholas Nickleby*, *Bleak House*, *Barnaby Rudge*, *Our Mutual Friend*, and an unfinished work that has been made into a play, *The Mystery of Edwin Drood*. He popularized the serial and kept his public waiting in suspense for the next issue. When *The Old Curiosity Shop* was running, a crowd of people in New York met the ship bearing the latest installment. The waiting fans wanted to assure themselves that Little Nell had not died. (She had. Dickens always chose an emotional and sentimental effect.)

As Professor Engel has pointed out, Dickens was also the first to popularize the paperback. Dickens was adept at merchandising and would have approved of the plays, musicals and movies that have been based on his works. Annually he produced Christmas stories, five in all. The most famous is *A Christmas Carol*, featured in countless places every year.

He had a great talent for dialogue and imaginative plots, and many of his characters–and their names–are unforgettable. He was a keen observer and reporter of social conditions in England–the plight of abandoned children and their exploitation by society, the evils of the penal system, the pitiful condition of the innocent who were victims of society–and is credited with helping bring reform.

Dickens' own life reads like a novel. From the age of five to ten, when his family lived in Chatham, Kent, Dickens was very happy, particularly in the company of his father, an optimistic but improvident man. Hardship and poverty followed for young Charles when his father was imprisoned in debtors' prison, taking his family to live there with him. Only Charles, at twelve, stayed out of prison to work in a blacking factory, sharing his meager salary with his family. He remembered his later childhood as lonely and harsh. When his father received a small legacy and was released from prison, he insisted that Charles should attend private school. Dickens's education was minimal, but his genius and his personal initiative prepared him for his illustrious career.

To augment his income and further promote his books, Dickens made two trips to America where his dramatic readings were immensely popular. If Dickens had had no talent as a writer, he probably would have become famous on the stage. He was a mesmerizing reader of his own work. Sometimes he would became so involved emotionally after a dramatic passage that he would take to his bed, almost unable to speak. This self-imposed strain probably led to his early death at fifty-eight, but he lives on today, not only as the most important writer of Victorian England but also as an author who speaks to all ages.

Thinking Places

The tremendous literary output of Charles Dickens required more than one thinking place. One of the most significant was the London streets at night. He thought nothing of taking a ten or twenty mile hike, frequently from dusk to dawn. Not only was he doing his solitary thinking, he was also observing the varied life of London, which found its way into his books, twenty-one in number, including the unfinished, *The Mystery of Edwin Drood*.

In Broadstairs, Kent, in his home, Bleak House (also the title of one of his novels), a visitor may see his study with his desk by a window, facing the North Sea. On the desk he placed a china monkey, without which he supposedly was unable to write. Dickens wrote to the Duke of Devonshire, " The freshness of the sea and the association of the place (I finished *Copperfield* in this same airy nest) have set me to work with great vigor."

At Gad's Hill was his most unusual thinking place, his Swiss chalet, one used in spring and summer. He had it placed on a secluded part of his wooded property across the Rochester High Road It had two stories, a ground floor and a "first floor," (second floor to Americans) the latter containing six windows. The study was designed to be full of light with mirrors attached to the walls. According to his son, the very theatrical Dickens used mirrors intermittently during his writing sessions, acting out his characters with exaggerated facial expressions and body movements.

From his desk on the second storey, he could see cornfields and in the distance, the Thames River. A telescope was positioned on his desk. The chalet's charm was enhanced by the Swiss decorative trim. Dickens never tired of the chalet, and later had an underground tunnel constructed under the road so that he could visit the chalet unobserved. Dickens usually wrote most of the morning and walked in the afternoon.

In his last days his health had been failing noticeably to those around him. Perhaps with a sense of urgency, trying to finish the story of Edwin Drood, he returned to the chalet to work all afternoon on June 8, 1870. That evening he was seized with a stroke, which proved to be fatal.

Today the chalet has been moved to the grounds of the Charles Dickens Center in Rochester, Kent.

Dickensian Lagniappe

Our Dickens adventures resulted in two giant instances of lagniappe on two different trips. The first came years ago on a visit to Broadstairs for the Dickens Festival in June. We arrived just in time for a production of *A Christmas Carol* with no time to search for lodging. Afterwards we asked someone for hotel suggestions. "Everything is sold out," he replied. When we mentioned having seen the excellent performance, he said, "Oh, you're Dickensians, are you?" – and he spent the next hour until he found the owners of a private home who would give us lodging. Thus, another blow was struck for Anglo-American friendship!

The other instance of lagniappe came from a British friend who facilitated our receiving a ticket to the Reading Room of the British Museum. There we found a cookbook written by Mrs. Charles Dickens, nee Catherine Hogarth, but under a pen name, "Lady Maria Clutterbuck." The title of the book was *What Shall We Have For Dinner?* Charles Dickens, Jr. vouched for the authorship and said his mother used as her nom-de-plume the name of a character she had played in one of his father's amateur theatricals. The book is a curious relic of the Victorian era. Mrs. Dickens states her reason for the book: "to rescue many fair friends from such domestic suffering (their husbands not coming home to dinner) that I have consented to give to the world bills of fare." Seasons (both for food availability and weather temperature) and the number of people dining divide these. Bills of fare for two or three persons have fewer dishes than eight or ten or fourteen, eighteen or twenty. One menu for eight or ten persons for a winter time meal suggested:

"Curry Lobster. Haunch of Mutton. Broccoli. Browned Potatoes. Pigeon Pie. Oyster Patties. Maintenon Cutlet. Potatoes. Boiled Turkeys. Oyster Sauce. Two Woodcocks. Hare. Four Snipes. Cabinet Pudding. Apple Tart. Charlotte Russe. Jelly."

While Catherine was giving unadorned recipes for Bubble and Squeak, Lamb's Head and Mince, Scotch Minced Collop, Kalecannon, Prince Albert's Pudding, and Rice Blancmange, Charles was writing in Barnaby Rudge: "It was a substantial meal; far over and above the ordinary tea equipage, the board creaked beneath the weight of a jolly round of beef, a ham of the first magnitude, and sundry towers of buttered Yorkshire cake piled slice upon slice in most alluring order."

And while dapper dresser, Charles, was recording in *The Pickwick Papers*, twenty-five breakfasts, thirty-two dinners, ten lunches, ten teas, ten suppers and sixty-five light refreshments, poor cookbook author, Catherine, was changing from a slim, pretty wife to a stout Victorian matron. It's sad to report that

Dickens asked for a divorce, forcing Catherine to leave her home and her children. There was another woman, a long kept secret.

And what about Charles who stayed relatively thin? This passage from Martin Chuzzlewit probably speaks for the fashion-savvy novelist:

"... had his little table drawn out close before the fire, and fell to work upon a well-cooked steak and smoking hot potatoes, with a strong appreciation of their excellence, and a very keen sense of enjoyment. Beside him, too, there stood a jug of most stupendous Wiltshire beer; and the effect of the whole was so transcendent that he was obliged every now and then to lay down his knife and fork, rub his hands and think about it."

If Catherine had only written as well as her husband, her cookbook might not have been shelved and forgotten in The British Museum!

Here is the recipe for "Dickens Christmas punch" relayed to us by The Charles Dickens Museum, thanks to Sophie Slade.

<u>Smoking Bishop</u>

6 Seville Oranges
4oz sugar (1/2 cup)
Cloves
1 Quart of strong red wine
1 Bottle of ruby port

Bake the oranges in a moderate oven for approximately 20 minutes until golden brown, and then place in a warmed glass or pottery bowl with 6 cloves pricked into each fruit. Add the sugar and pour in the wine, but not the port. Cover and leave in a warm place for a day. Then, squeeze the oranges into the wine and pour through a sieve. To keep for future use, bottle in sterilized bottles and seal at this stage, omitting the port. To serve immediately, add the port to the liquid and heat in a pan, but do not boil. Serve in warmed goblets and drink hot. Or, pour into bottles and stand in a pan of simmering water; this keeps it hot and makes pouring easier. If Seville oranges are out of season, use 5 sweet oranges and one yellow grapefruit instead.

Charles Dickens

Catherine Dickens

Robert Louis Stevenson

1850 – 1894

Vailima, the home of Robert Louis Stevenson
near Apia, Samoa; medallion showing RLS's
usual writing place--propped up in bed

Robert Louis Stevenson

"For my part, I travel not to go anywhere, but to go. I travel for travel's sake. The great affair is to move."

Travels with a Donkey

"There is no duty we so much underrate as the duty of being happy."

An Apology for Idlers

"Give us grace and strength to forbear and to persevere.
Give us courage and gaiety, and the quiet mind, spare us to our friends, soften to us our enemies."

Prayer (inscribed on his memorial in St Giles)

Journey   Around the World to Samoa

We began following the long trail of Robert Louis Stevenson's journeys, not in Edinburgh, his birthplace, but in Samoa, a small island in the South Pacific. Like many people, we had encountered RLS in childhood, reading *A Child's Garden of Verses* and *Treasure Island* and, much later, *Dr. Jekyll and Mr. Hyde*. RLS had written, "The whole tale of my life is more interesting than any poem." We had much to learn about his life and wide travels.

We identified with Stevenson's love of journeys and new experiences. We were looking for material for a new musical. We learned all we could about RLS' adventurous life, his sailing to many islands in the South Pacific and living the last four years of his short life in Samoa. It sounded like a good prospect for a play, but Samoa was a long way from home to research one chapter of RLS' life. (We did it anyway.)

115

At that time, two people influenced our going to Samoa. Our friend, Admiral Maurice Weisner said, by all means, we should go. He had been to Western Samoa on an official visit, as Commander in Chief Pacific U.S. (CINCPAC). In fact, the Samoan leaders, the Paramount Chiefs, honored him as a "High Chief." We learned more later about the Samoans' continued traditions of a tribal society with the highly respected High Chiefs as the controllers and arbiters, much as it was in RLS' day. Interestingly, the spokesman for the High Chief is called the Talking Chief.

The other person who influenced us was James Michener, whose book was made into that wonderful musical, *South Pacific*. In a long telephone conversation with Michener we suggested that he consider the fascinating story of early flight and the history of aviation in a future book. We had read in *The World is My Home* about his interest in flying and his three airplane crashes in the Pacific area. He wrote that when flying, in case of a forced landing in the sea, one should always take with him a wide-brimmed hat and a mirror—the latter to signal to ships that may come into range. (Later, we thought about this when we were flying over the South Pacific from American Samoa to Apia, Samoa in a small, frail airplane.) He invited us to his classes and a visit with him in south Florida, but, sadly, we put it off until too late.

During World War II, Michener, who had been a college history professor, was assigned to the South Pacific as a journalist. Since his orders were, at first, loosely applied as "tours of inspection," he "caught a ride" flying to many (forty-nine) of the Pacific islands, observing some of the societal conditions, as well as the drama and everyday life of the sailors and GI's. Later, he was sent on missions by the "brass" to investigate courts martial and irregularities.

We valued his opinion when he wrote that one of the most memorable experiences he had in the Pacific was coming in on the road from the airport in Samoa to Apia, the principal town; "the next hour was one of the most wonderful in my life."

We discovered that Michener, like Stevenson, had great admiration for the Samoan people. We learned more about Samoa through Michener's wrtings. Early in his World War II visits to Samoa he had met Aggie Grey, "a magnificent woman in her late forties who would become known as the queen of the South Seas, honored by writers of several nations and by her own government who used her portrait on the most popular postage stamp." Michener and Aggie remained lifetime friends.

One of the delights of Samoa today is staying at Aggie Grey's Hotel. Michener wrote the foreword to *Aggie Grey, A Samoan Saga* by Faye Alailima, an American, married to a Samoan chief. Michener stated that Aggies' story "runs on like a novel," that began "a hundred years ago when Willie Swann, roving son of a British colonialist fell in love with Pele, daughter of a battling Samoan chieftain." They married and Aggie was their daughter. Aggie grew up to become an effective entrepreneur, operating a boarding house even before World War II. It became the famous Aggie Grey's Hotel. During the war, she sold food and native goods to the members of the military. Michener denied strongly the rumor that Aggie, the determined lady, was the model for Bloody Mary in South Pacific. He encountered the real, Tonkinese Bloody Mary on Espiritu Santos near Guadalcanal; the Frenchman's plantation was also there.

With hard work and business acumen Aggie ended up with the premiere hotel in the South Pacific. Michener wrote that during WW II when he was stationed in American Samoa, he and everyone else did all they could to get leaves to go to Apia "to get a taste of the excellent island food at her palm-thatched hotel, and to join her and the beautiful girls who appeared at night to dance the famous siva-siva." RLS had written about these spirited Samoan dances. Later, we too enjoyed the excellent food and evening shows at Aggie's attractive dining area. The shows were performed by Aggie's daughter-in-law and granddaughter—and by staff members who were porters and waiters by day and dancers by night!

One afternoon we learned even more about traditional Samoan life when we interviewed Faye Alailima while sipping a cool, tropical drink in Aggie's courtyard. Faye's adventures of adjusting to a communal, extended-family culture in Samoa are related in her enlightening book, *My Samoan Chief*.

In due time, we learned more about RLS and climbed to the top of Mount Vaea (walking for an hour or so nearly straight up, well, almost), to visit his gravesite. Engraved on his tomb is RLS' famous Requiem, "Under the wide and starry sky, Dig the grave and let me lie. Glad did I live and gladly die And I laid me down with a will. This be the verse you grave for me: Here he lies where he longs to be; Home is the sailor, home from the sea*, And the hunter home from the hill." . (* should be "home from sea".) After completing the arduous and heated journey down the mountain, we dived into RLS' pond, fed by a cool mountain stream

RLS' home, Vailima, is at the base of Mount Vaea. His family reported that in his last days, RLS gazed frequently at the mountaintop and seemed to anticipate his burial there. When we visited the old, deteriorated house, we saw a sign indicating that a group in Provo, Utah planned to restore the house. We later contacted them and learned that they had served as Mormon missionaries in Samoa in their youth and, recently, had banded together to help save a Samoan rainforest. Now they were going to restore Vailima as a gift to the Samoan people. Our subsequent communications began long-time friendships with them and many other Stevensonians.

A year later, we returned to Samoa for the ceremonies beginning restoration. The groundbreaking ceremonies were impressive with talks by local officials and visitors, choruses singing RLS' "Requiem" put to music – and, later, food provided by Aggie's Hotel staff. We came to know better as our very good friends: Rex Maughan, the principal benefactor, and Jim Winegar and Dan Wakefield, leaders from Utah. We touched hands again with Ellen Schaffer, aged eighty-nine at the time, and the retired curator of Silverado Museum in St. Helena, California where many RLS relics are located. We had visited with her during the prior year when she rode with us to Mount St. Helena, California, now Robert Louis Stevenson State Park. This was where Fanny and RLS spent their honeymoon in an old, abandoned miner's cabin. How kind it was for our Utah friends to sponsor the trip to Samoa for Miss Ellen to fulfill her lifetime dream.

As mentioned in the Wordsworth chapter, at this time we first met prolific writer, Hunter Davies, and his wife, Margaret Forster, both popular and well-recognized British authors. Hunter Davies has written books about two of our other interests, William Wordsworth and Beatrix Potter. Hunter was on the trail of RLS and his later book, *Teller of Tales, in Search of Robert Louis Stevenson*, proved to be outstanding.

Hunter was especially interested in the opinion of a physician who was also interested in RLS, since RLS' chronic health problem has long been a source of speculation by many writers. It had been assumed generally that RLS had tuberculosis, but Jack, a cardiologist, but not a pulmonary specialist, gave several reasons why he deduced that RLS did not have tuberculosis: a definitive diagnosis was not made (X-Ray diagnosis had not been discovered); no one close to him contracted the disease in spite of RLS' many episodes of active, acute illness. Jack proposed that RLS's lung hemorrhages were possibly due to other causes, such as residuals of lung infection from childhood and perhaps constitutional, heritable disorders. Later, in his book, Hunter quoted Jack's hypotheses.

The following year we came back a third time for the exciting, big event, the 100th anniversary of RLS' death! Stevensonians from "all over the world"–Scotland, New Zealand, Japan, England and the U.S.A., to name a few, assembled for the dedication of the beautifully restored and refurbished grand old home at Vailima! (See section below, Lagniappe in Paradise). By that time, we had written the book and lyrics for *Imagination! A Children's Musical/Whimsical* about RLS in the South Pacific. Allen Pote, an internationally known and respected composer, wrote the music. In two separate events, it was heartwarming, on this far-off island, to hear children from the RLS Elementary School and students from Samoa College perform some of the songs from *Imagination!*

RLS loved "travel for travel's sake" and, in spite of a lifetime of poor health, he covered a good portion of the globe in his short life of forty-four years. After our journeys to Samoa, eventually, not necessarily in this order, we followed RLS' footsteps: in Edinburgh, Scotland and environs; in Grez, France on the river Loing near Fontainebleau where RLS met Fanny, his wife-to-be; in the Cevennes Mountains in France where he hiked for ten days with Modestine, a cantankerous donkey; in California–Monterrey and St. Helena, Napa Valley, where he courted, then married Fanny; later, Hyeres near the southern coast of France, RLS' happiest time, perhaps because *Treasure Island*, as well as *Silverado Squatters* were accepted for publication; in Saranac Lake, New York where he visited Dr. Trudeau for advice about RLS' lung condition; in Hawaii, where he stayed awhile visiting his step-daughter and the King of Hawaii; in his series of voyages to many Pacific islands; in Samoa where RLS lived his last four years, some of his healthiest and most fulfilling ones, before he died and was buried on Mount Vaea. We were able to follow most of RLS' journeys except for Davos, Switzerland and isolated islands in the Pacific.

Our ultimate RLS experience came when we were motoring from the Eistedfodd celebration in Llangollen, northern Wales toward a target in lower Scotland. We made better time than expected and found ourselves on the outskirts of Edinburgh at twilight. No rooms were available on this short notice. The annual, popular Edinburgh Festival was going on! In our desperation, we called our Stevensonian good friend, Alistair Ferguson, the Honorary Secretary of the Robert Louis Stevenson Club of Edinburgh. To our delight he was able to get us a room at a house that recently had started a limited bed and breakfast operation. It was–of all places–17 Heriot Row, RLS' family home from 1857 onwards! Since RLS' boyhood room, over-looking the old lamplights on the street below, had only one bed in it, we took turns sleeping in that room! We alternated with a bed down the hall in the room that Cummy, RLS' nurse and teller of many scary tales, had used for years. Wow!

Early on, just before leaving on a trip to Samoa, we met a Stevensonian, an attractive lady in California. We agreed to take a medal commemorating a loved one and place it near RLS' grave, an action she said would be meaningful to her. She said something that we would come to appreciate in the expressions of many others, later, "Once Stevenson gets hold of you, he'll never let you go!" We found this to be true as we met more and more Stevensonians through the years and attended many events honoring this fascinating man, forever young and vibrant!

Vignette   Robert Louis Stevenson 1850 - 1894

"Those whom the gods love die..." not just "young" in years, but young in heart–no matter their age. This is the spin that Robert Louis Stevenson put on the familiar words in his essay, *Aes Triplex*. It is also the philosophy by which the beloved novelist, poet, essayist, short story and letter-writer chose to live and die. Always aware that he would probably die early in life of lung disease, Stevenson decided that he would not just timidly taste of life but that he would explore life in as many dimensions as he could.

That he succeeded is the testimony of many people who either knew him personally or have studied his life. All say that Stevenson's life was even more exciting, more filled with adventure than even the most soul-stirring of his books. One does wonder how many more tales of adventure, of poems that are easy to remember and to recite were stillborn when he died —too young—at age forty-four. No one would have thought that a frail, sickly child, probably spoiled and over-protected by his mother and his nurse, Cummy, would grow up, still frail and sickly, to live through the following adventures:

- Carousing in his youth in a dangerous section of Edinburgh;
- Traveling alone except for a donkey in the mountains of France;
- Sailing the Atlantic in pursuit of a woman with whom he had fallen in love at first sight; enduring the cold and privations of an emigrant railroad car, as he crossed the American continent in further pursuit of the same, aforementioned love; living in San Francisco and Monterey, California in

hunger and poverty, with only twenty-five cents daily for food, while his love, named Fanny, made up her mind;

- Honeymooning in an abandoned miner's shack inhabited by rattlesnakes;
- Living and writing in the highlands of Scotland; then the mountains of Switzerland; discovering the charm of southern France, in spite of illness; then settling in Bournemouth, England, re-establishing old friendships;
- Journeying to the Adirondacks mountains, New York in the coldest of winters to visit a famous doctor in search of health;
- Chartering a sailing ship, the *Casco*, to explore the Pacific, the Marquesas and Tahiti. (On board was his wife, Fanny, terrified by the sea, her teen-aged son, RLS' mother, always prim and correct in her Victorian lace cap—and a coffin, intended for RLS, should the need arise. Try to imagine their conversations, month after month at sea.)
- Sailing to Hawaii where Hawaiian royalty became friends;
- Visiting many Pacific Islands on the *Equator* where some of the inhabitants were hospitable, and some, including cannibals, were not;
- Discovering a remote island where the royal princess would save his life with her concoction of raw fish and other undisclosed ingredients;
- Landing in Samoa where he would make the Samoan life and Samoan causes his own, and be called "Tusitala", teller of tales
- Traveling to Australia several times, braving ocean storms;
- Sailing back to Hawaii; enduring typhoons and tropical heat;
- Settling in Samoa as the Laird of Vailima, with servants in Scotch plaid lava-lavas (Samoan one-piece garment).

You may have decided, as we did, that RLS's life contained more adventure, met by pluck and courage, than any of the characters of his many books.

Perhaps when he played imaginary games on his counterpane at 17 Heriot Row in Edinburgh, Stevenson was building his future store of imagination, of a bravery that sometimes seemed to deflect danger; of good spirits that made hardship bearable and a philosophy that he expressed in "An Apology for Idlers": "There is no duty we so much underrate as the duty to be happy." The quotation continues, "By being happy, we sow anonymous benefits upon the world, which remain unknown even to ourselves, or when they are disclosed, surprise nobody so much as the benefactor." Surely Stevenson, as he looks for undiscovered islands in another life, must be greatly surprised at the millions of people he has made happy.

Undoubtedly, RLS would agree that no discussion of his life would be complete without the inclusion of his wife, Fanny. She was not conventionally beautiful, but both Sam Osbourne, her first husband, and Stevenson fell in love with her on first meeting. Not many women would have followed RLS to almost the ends of the earth, as she did– willingly and with good grace. Out of necessity, she learned to garden and worked hard as a laborer in an environment strange to her. She papered certain walls of their home at Vailima with Samoan tapa cloth and chose colors that would make it attractive. She was a born homemaker, a superb and inventive cook but first, she was as much an adventurer as RLS was. When her first husband went away to California and Nevada, mining for gold, she followed him, two children in tow–from Ohio to New York, then by ship to Central America, then across the Isthmus of Panama, actually walking part of the way. For other escapades, Fanny's life in a mining camp, for instance, read *This Life I've Loved* by Fanny's daughter, Isobel (Belle) Field. (In 1936, when *Gone with the Wind* was the #1 best-seller for fiction, *This Life I've Loved* was the #1 best-seller for non-fiction.)

Another of Fanny's early adventures illustrates that she was a feminist before her time. When she was betrayed by her husband, Sam Osbourne, it seemed that she had no other place to turn. She took her three children to Belgium where she could study painting, possibly as a way to earn a living in the future. Rejected by the officials in the art school, who were scandalized that a woman would even consider taking art lessons (and from live models?), she traveled with her children to Paris, then to Grez, near Fontainebleau. It was in the Barbizon artist colony at

Grez that RLS looked through a window and lost his heart. Fanny was bohemian, talented, strong-willed, and irresistible to a number of men in her life, in a word, fascinating!

We highly recommend biographies of both Stevenson and his one-of-a-kind wife, Fanny. RLS wrote about Fanny, "Teacher, tender, comrade wife, A fellow-farer true through life. Heart whole and soul-free, The august father gave to me."

For further inducement to read about Fanny, consider this odd turn-of-events. After Stevenson died, Fanny employed as her secretary and companion, Edward Salisbury Field, "Ned." For the next eleven years they were never apart. He had said of her, "She is the only woman I would die for." Fanny was nearing sixty; he was twenty-three. At the time, Fanny was dedicated to one great desire—to see another edition of Stevenson's works published and to assure his literary immortality. Perhaps she thought that Ned would be helpful in her great goal. Ned was a playwright. Coincidentally, Fanny's grandson, Belle's son, was also a playwright. In due time, both Ned and Austin had plays running on Broadway simultaneously. After Fanny's death, her daughter, Belle, married Ned. She was fifty-six; he was thirty-four.

Stevenson was not completely successful in his portrayal of women. Perhaps he should have sharpened his pen by writing about two distinctive women very close to him, Fanny and Belle. Stevenson wrote in almost every literary form. He demonstrated his versatility in poetry, essays, short stories, travel books, a Samoan history and, of course, novels. His two plays, with W.E. Henley as co-playwright, were not successful. The volumes of his letters reveal his kind and generous personality in depth; he is considered one of the most prolific letter-writers of all time.

After more than a century, the experts are still writing about his life and his work. Some of his books have never been out of print. *Treasure Island, Kidnapped, Master of Ballantrae,* and *Travels with a Donkey* satisfy the need for adventure in all of us. Also, *The Strange Case of Dr. Jekyll and Mr. Hyde* is a strange case in itself. One day, after a dream and much labor, RLS showed Fanny the short story he had just written about Dr. Jekyll. Fanny read it and told RLS that he had missed the point of his own story. "It was an allegory," she said. Much to her surprise and horror– perhaps appreciation that he so valued her critical eye, he threw it into the fire. Stevenson rewrote the entire story – with sincere thanks today from millions of readers, from playwrights and from moviemakers. Today the very title has become an idiom in the English language.

What of the man himself? From all accounts, he loved people, was generous and tender-hearted. He was good company, made friends easily and kept them. He enjoyed writing and receiving letters, and seeing as much of the world as he could. He was grateful for his life in Samoa, which he loved, even though it was not a paradise in every respect. The Samoan people loved RLS in his day, related to him and called him, affectionately, "Tusitala," teller of tales; they still refer to him by this name. In short, he was a man who lived abundantly, then died suddenly with a stroke, with little warning, not only young but also young in heart.

Thinking Places

Like the title of Michener's book, *The World is My Home,* Stevenson, more than most of us, could call the world his home. Thus, he had many far-flung thinking places. Perhaps the place he spent more time writing was in his bed or on a couch, propped up in a characteristic position. This image was immortalized by sculptor Augustus Saint-Gaudens in a medallion in 1887-88, created while RLS was living. In the large, original version RLS was holding a cigarette. RLS' memorial with a smaller version of the medallion is now in St. Giles Cathedral in Edinburgh. In this sculpture RLS is holding a pen, changed from RLS' usual cigarette, in deference probably to its location in the cathedral.

Another image of RLS familiar to Stevensonians is his standing, dictating to his step-daughter, Belle, his amanuensis at Vailima. RLS arose early, wrote propped up in bed or walked on the porch, composed his thoughts, and then later dictated to

Belle. RLS was a constant letter-writer. It was said that he would answer anyone's letters. No doubt, he thought a lot and formulated many of his ideas while writing letters in a variety of places. In regards to RLS' creativity, he gave most of the credit to his "Brownies", whom he described as, the "... little people who manage man's internal theatre...substantive inventors and performers...who do half my work while I am asleep and...do the rest for me as well while I am awake"...and who are "sometimes capricious and play a role in bad dreams."

RLS' strong imagination as a child was nourished by the many gripping and lurid stories of his long-term nurse, Cummy, to whom he dedicated *A Child's Garden of Verses*; and by his experiences as a youth with his lighthouse-building father on the coasts of Scotland. As an adult, RLS' many thinking places were, indeed, all over the world. In turn, he nourished the imagination of generations world-wide.

Lagniappe

In many respects, Samoa is an idyllic South Sea island paradise. Certainly, the realities of civilization have made their inroads in Samoa, but the island and its warm, friendly people retain much of their traditional charm and beauty. Fa'a Samoa, The Samoan Way, familiar to RLS more than a hundred years ago, persists today.

Each of our four journeys to Samoa had special features and unexpected pleasures. On the first visit we were introduced to a most interesting landscape and culture. On our second trip we made many new friends and saw the beginning restoration of RLS' home. Our third visit was a gathering of Stevensonians from around the world, as they observed the one-hundredth anniversary of the death of RLS and celebrated the restoration of Vailima. On the fourth visit in 2005, we saw further refinments in the restoration of Vailima.

As a backdrop in the small town of Apia, on our third visit, festivities honored both RLS and the Samoan Games. Rowing teams from all over Samoa were preparing for the South Pacific Games. The old outrigger canoes, familiar to visitors to Hawaii, had been replaced with modern, sleek crew shells with teams of both young women and young men. One could see the crews practicing into the late afternoon, silhouetted in the subdued light of a colorful sunset.

It was touching to see the parade and the small floats honoring RLS –and "Vailima" beer! One of the floats had a sign: on it, "Tusitala."

One morning before daylight many visitors and towns-people, including a robed choir of youngsters, assembled at the base of Mount Vaea, near Vailima. Lighted candles, each pierc-ing large leaves to catch the dripping wax, were given to everyone. It was impressive to see the flickering candles carried by so many individuals as they climbed up the mountain, all dedicated to honoring one man, frail in body but giant in spirit. On the night following his death, the Samoans had built a road winding through wilderness forest to the top of the mountain. When RLS was living they had built "The Road of The Loving Heart," near Vailima, honoring him.

After a hard climb up the mountain, everyone assembled at the top around RLS and Fanny's graves designed like Samoan Chiefs' graves, made of mortar and painted white. Inscribed on RLS' grave are his poem, "Requiem", a Scottish thistle, and the blossom of a hibiscus; on hers, appropriately, the flower is a tiger lily. Below the mountaintop graves, the Pacific stretched beyond view, and ocean breezes flowed over the tropical trees and vegetation. Skilled actors with strong Scottish accents gave readings. The townspeople and a youth choir sang songs. A kilted Scotsman played on the bagpipes and a Samoan played on a native instrument near the graves, for a memorable image and a photographer's dream-shot. An exhilarating ex-perience! They would have liked it—RLS and Fanny.

After descending the rugged mountain, in the increasing heat of midmorning, and at the end of the trail many of us dived into RLS' cool mountain pool, as we had done on our second visit. The following day everyone assembled at Vailima for the dedication ceremonies. The magnificently restored house, with galleries and verandahs and some of the walls decorated once more with tapa cloth, was now much like it was in RLS' and Fanny's days. In true RLS fashion, the event blended well the Samoan and Scottish cultures. The speeches with warm comments about Tusitala, singing and dancing by Samoans in native dress and the fellowship of admirers, was unlike any other occasion we had ever attended.

As always, the most important part of the experience was meeting or resuming "auld acquaintances" with so many interesting Stevensonians, automatically, our friends. All bonded easily. Just to mention a few (all are experts on RLS, in one way or another): our good friends and restorers of Vailima, Rex Maughan, the principal benefactor, and Jim Winegar; Gavin Bell, Scottish writer whose *Search for Tusitala* took him to many Pacific islands; John Cairney, Scottish actor and writer, later professor in New Zealand; Karen Steele, British actress and writer, who wore a striking necklace once owned by Fanny Stevenson; Bob Watt, writer and wonderful representative of Scotland with his kilts swirling on the dance floor; John Sheddon, also, of Edinburgh, excellent portrayer of RLS in many theatrical events and readings; Elizabeth Stuart Warfel, writer and Stevensonian, extraordinaire; Fay Alailima, already described above; Peter Hunt, writer, of Australia; Kumiko Koiwa, of Yokohoma, petite, devoted Stevensonian and artist who honored us by including our sketch in her interesting book, with its text mostly in Japanese; Elayne Waring Fitzpatrick, writer and college professor, along with a host of her attractive, fellow Stevensonians in the large contingent from the Monterey, California area; and many more.

All this truly warmed the heart and filled the memory bank. They would have liked it—RLS and Fanny.

If you wish to be a part of a most interesting, world-wide Stevensonian fellowship, consider joining the Robert Louis Stevenson Club in Edinburgh, Scotland or the chapter in Monterey, California. (Check the internet for extensive information about their activities and many other RLS museums and library collections, including the beautifully restored RLS House Museum in Samoa). In 2003, Vailima was listed by Patricia Schultz in her book, *1000 Places To See Before You Die*. We agree! Tour the grand, old home; climb Mount Vaea to the top and visit RLS' and Fanny's tombs; jump in the mountain pool at the end of the trail – and then relax at Aggie's!

Photographic credits: Pictures of RLS , family and staff at Vailima; and RLS in Samoa **are** courtesy of The Writers' Museum, Edinburgh.

RLS , family and staff at Vailima

RLS

Carolyn with students at
RLS Elementary School, Apia, Samoa

Rudyard Kipling

1865 – 1936

Bateman's, the Kipling home near
Burwash, Sussex, with Kipling's desk and chair

Rudyard Kipling

"We're poor little lambs who've lost our way, Baa! Baa! Baa!
We're little black sheep who've gone astray, Baa-aa-aa!
Gentlemen rankers out on a spree, Damned from here
    to Eternity,
God ha' mercy on such as we, Baa! Yah! Baa!"

"Gentlemen Rankers"

"Though I've belted an'flayed you
By the living Gawd that made you
You're a better man than I am, Gunga Din!"

"Gunga Din"

"Bite the bullet, old man, and don't let them think you're
afraid."

"The Light That Failed"

Journey   Sussex

We have sung one of Kipling's poems set to music. Maybe
you have sung it, too:

> "On the road to Mandalay
> Where the flyin' fishes play
> And the dawn comes up like thunder
> Out of China cross the bay!"

These words encapsulate the talent, travel background and
power of one of the most famous writers in the English language
in 1903. And so, remembering Kipling, we were on the road to
Bateman's, his country home in Sussex.

Rudyard Kipling was a prolific English writer of novels,
poems and short stories, many of them about his early days in
India and Burma (now Myanmar.) He lived a few years in

133

America, and then moved back to England. By then he had become so famous that his home in Rottingdean, East Sussex, had become a tourist attraction from nearby Brighton. The Kiplings moved to Bateman's, a more secluded home in the country, near Burwash, Sussex. The seventeenth century house, a sanctuary in the wooded landscape, was Kipling's ideal home, and he lived there until his death, over thirty years later.

Kipling had purchased the large stone house and thirty-three acres, with surrounding buildings, for 9,300 pounds sterling. The old mill had been constructed in 1750. Today on the grounds are the gardens, a carriage house where Kipling's Rolls Royce can be seen, the mill pond and mill, an unusual pear tree arch, and a quiet area overlooking the Dudwell River. One can imagine Kipling's pleasure in taking long walks through the grounds and the surrounding countryside or paddling about on the mill pond with his children.

We first visited Bateman's on a crisp winter day, off-season, just as we had in our separate visits to Shaw and Woolf's homes. The caretaker kindly gave us free access to the house. Years later, on our return visit on a sunny day, we were able to explore the grounds as well as the house more thoroughly.

The timbered ceilings, oak paneled walls, the large fireplace and the massive furniture emphasized Bateman's seventeenth century origin. As we had seen at Shaw's Corner, all of the objects on the desks and mantlepieces were carefully covered with little paper "tents" or dust jackets. Veddy British and indeed very practical. Of course, the highlight of the visit was seeing Kipling's study.

Although young Rudyard Kipling was a victim of the British Empire system at the time, he was also the beneficiary of the system with his own experience in India. Kipling became one of the greatest advocates of the Empire and the perceived destiny of the British people to spread their culture to the world.

Most readers of Rudyard Kipling would visualize him physically as a large, vigorous man, a caricature of "John Bull," one of Britain's symbols. Kipling's strong writings, his lifestyle and his unshakeable advocacy of an invincible British Empire, gave the impression that he was a sturdy, hardy man of strength. Actually, Kipling was in frail health most of his life. He was of short statue and weighed about 120 pounds.

Bateman's, a very substantial, fortress-like house, perhaps suggesting an island in itself, is an appropriate metaphor for the man who loved England and became the "Poet of the Empire."

Vignette   Rudyard Kipling 1865-1936

What do you know of Rudyard Kipling? Surprisingly, more than you think. Starting with childhood, you probably read *The Jungle Book* or *Just So Stories*. When you were in your teens, your blood may have thrilled to the rhythm of "Gunga Din" from *Barrack Room Ballads*. You may have heard someone sing, "Mandalay" or "The Recessional". Sometime in college days, you sang with your crowd, Yale's "Whiffenpoof Song." Maybe you didn't know that this was a parody on a Kipling poem. If by this time, as a young adult, you have been impressed by his mastery of vocabulary, including Cockney dialect and use of Indian words, his vision and descriptive talents, his compassion and use of irony, his belief in action, you may have read Kipling's masterpiece, *Kim*. If you have read a biography of Theodore Roosevelt at the same time, you may have concluded that the two men had similar personalities and beliefs.

What you may not know is that much of Kipling's life is reflected in his writings. One of the saddest stories you can read is "Baa, Baa, Black Sheep" when you discover that it mirrors five –and-one-half years of Kipling's childhood. It is a pitiful story of child abuse and an indictment of the casual, mindless treatment of their children by some foreign-service parents of the nineteenth century. In "Baa, Baa, Black Sheep," the eight-year-old boy and his six-year-old sister were deposited with a cruel, narrow-minded woman who kept children for their parents, who were part of the British Raj serving in India. His parents (Mr. and Mrs. Kipling) had not investigated the woman, only that she wrote an acceptable letter. Nevertheless, they left the children in England with no explanation to them and no good-bye. The parents returned to India, and although they corresponded, they did not see their children again for five years. A lonely Ruddy was beaten, shamed and had no one to turn to for comfort. The despotic Aunty Rosa liked his sister, Trix, but was cruel to Ruddy.

Does this sound like a page from a Charles Dickens' novel? It could have been. There were other parallels between Dickens and Kipling. When Kipling arrived in London as a young man, his rise to fame and popularity was immediate, "as meteoric as Dickens' had been," it was said. The two novelists had something else in common. They liked to walk at night, finding it, presumably, an aid to creativity. Kipling wrote, "I did not know then that such night-walkings would be laid upon me through my life, or that my fortunate hour would be on the turn of sunrise, with a sou' breeze afoot."

Kipling's life illustrates how circumstance manipulates the flowering of creativity. In "Baa, Baa Black Sheep" Kipling transmuted his early life, miserable as it was, into an unforgettable story. Another example from his family shows how Kipling's bad luck became his good luck in the field of literature. His first cousin was Stanley Baldwin. (He later became Prime Minister when Edward VIII abdicated to marry Wally Simpson.) Baldwin's parents were better off financially than the Kiplings, and were able to send their son to Harrow and to University. Kipling lamented that he could not follow Stanley. Instead, he had to leave the United War College at seventeen for financial reasons and go to India. His parents secured his appointment as Assistant to the Editor of *The Civil and Military Gazette* in Lahore. Kipling felt that by leaving England he was giving up his last chance to get ahead. Little did he dream that his literary career would take off in India. The color, the exotic scenes, the languages and the people of colonial India furnished the background for his stories and ballads. His genius made the most of his material.

When he did return to England, he would already be famous. (Incidentally, he did not hold it against his parents for the five years of separation. He said of his mother that she was "the wittiest woman in India," and he remained very close to his father in later years.)

While in India, Kipling worked hard at his craft, in spite of dysentery and malaria. When he returned to England, he married Caroline, an American and the sister of a friend and collaborator who had died. Caroline was beautiful, almost three years older than he was, and in some ways, almost a mother figure to him. They were happy together. They lived a few years in Carrie's home in Brattleboro, Vermont. A family quarrel, precipitated by a brother-in-law, caused them to leave Brattleboro, where they were living, and resulted in their leaving America. They returned to England and lived in Rottingdean in East Sussex. Later, they settled in the house in rural Sussex called "Bateman's," but continued their world travels, especially to South Africa to escape cold winters.

The Kiplings' life was full of tragedy: a daughter died of flu, which almost took Kipling himself; their son, only eighteen, was killed in the Boer War. Kipling became disillusioned by the war.

Kipling's literary offerings brought great commendation before World War I, but afterwards were condemned by some as imperialistic. Above all, he believed in activism, and acting from his British Methodism, stressed moral obligation and responsibility. His view that England should be a responsible colonial power may have been idealistic, even sentimental, but it was sincerely felt. He believed that England should spread civilization and that the "White Man's Burden" was the acceptance of responsibility by, in his opinion, the more powerful race. He was a great believer in discipline and in craftsmanship. He believed that the individual should make sacrifices for the good of the whole of society. He was a complex man, intuitive and capable of seeing beneath the surface of affairs. T.S. Eliot championed him in 1919 and again in 1959 by proposing the toast to "The Unfading Genius of Rudyard Kipling." Kipling refused all honors offered by the British government. He did accept the Nobel Prize in Literature in 1907, the first Englishman so honored.

Thinking Place

The large study, with beamed ceilings and book cases lining two walls, appeared very substantial and, according to reports, was much more orderly and neat than it would have been in Rudyard Kipling's time. One could visualize a roaring fire in the fireplace, and Kipling standing there, throwing unwanted pages of manuscript into the fire. He had told an onlooker once, "after looking at old papers, I got to thinking—no one's going to make a monkey out of me after I die."

In the center of the room is Kipling's ten-foot long, early seventeenth century, French walnut, draw-leaf table, still with smudges of ink stain on it. A pair of world globes rest on the floor, one on each side of the table, and nearby a large, Algerian waste-paper basket, much used by Kipling. As he wrote, "Mercifully, the mere act of writing was, and always has been, a physical act, no problem to me. This made it easier to throw away anything that did not turn out well, and to practice, as it were, scales." He often went through four or five drafts of his writings.

In front of the desk was a huge, early eighteenth century, English walnut armchair. Small blocks attached to each leg of the chair made it just the right height for the table. A Good Companion Imperial typewriter waits for use on the table, but Kipling, a poor typist, used it only occasionally. "The beastly thing simply won't spell." His secretary typed his manuscripts after Kipling wrote them out with pen and ink. That Kipling was "extraordinarily messy" is an understatement, we were told. He had on his desk "an outsize, office pewter inkpot on which I would gauge the names of the books and talks I wrote out of it." Stabbing the inkpot with his pen, he splashed ink on the desk and on his clothes. As a young man in India, he had received frequent rebukes because of ink stains on his clothes, so that he looked "like a Dalmatian dog." This ink spillage was partly compounded by Kipling's using small camel hairbrushes to ink out sentences and passages of his manuscripts on his many revisions.

Kipling's daughter described her father's work habits, "R.K. usually worked in the mornings if he had anything in hand, either doing the actual writing, or pacing up and down in his study, humming to himself. Much of his best-known verse was written to a tune. He was utterly absorbed in it and quite oblivious to anything else." Like the children around Mark Twain, Kipling's children, "learned very early to keep any requests or plans until he was safely finished, until he 'came back' as they called it and was ready to enter their daily life."

In the afternoons, Kipling joined in games in the parlor or explored the grounds and mill pond with the children and the dogs. Often after tea, he would read one of his stories to the children. "When he came to a pathetic passage, he would 'choke up', and when there was a funny part, how he would laugh!"

Kipling's desk in his study, his main thinking place was always "badly congested" with piles of papers and "certain gadgets," including a "long, lacquered, canoe-shaped pen tray, full of brushes and dead fountains" and other clips, bands, pens, etc. A tiny, weighted fur seal sat on some of the papers." A leather crocodile described in the past was no longer there.

In the study, Kipling wrote *Puck of Puck's Hill* and *Rewards and Fairies*. The latter included the famous poem, "If." He wrote many other stories here, expressing his "deep sense of the ancient continuity of the place and people in the English countryside."

How lucky the Kiplings were to find refuge and contentment in this sturdy, stone house, full of antiquity, fireplaces with roaring fires, as well as the warmth of family life and friends. How lucky we were to visit this special thinking place of a great writer—a discerning contributor to his readers' insight and understanding.

Lagniappe

Walkers, like Kipling, Wordsworth, Dickens, Darwin, Yeats and Sandburg, loved to explore the countryside, often finding new trails, leading to smaller, intriguing paths. This happened to us as we followed the trails of Rudyard Kipling's life. We found some unexpected associations and relationships.

What did Rudyard Kipling, a thoroughly English, Englishman, have to do with an American University's popular song? For about four years, Kipling did live in Brattleboro, Vermont where he wrote *Captains Courageous* and *The Jungle Book*. These portions of his life works helped him win the Nobel Prize. While nearby in Vermont, he did not drop over to Yale University to write the well-known "Whiffenpoof Song." However, a parody of his poem, "Gentlemen Rankers," did result in the famous Yale song. Many of the words are the same – "We are poor little lambs who have lost our way, Baa, Baa, Baa." In their time, Rudy Vallee, Bing Crosby and Perry Como made the lyrics well known as a singing commercial.

Did Kipling connect with the Boy Scouts? Although we think of scouting as very American, it was, of course, founded by an Englishman, Sir Robert Baden-Powell. Kipling was a friend of Sir Baden-Powell and later became a Commissioner in the British Scouting Program. Kipling's son was a Boy Scout, and Kipling was the author of "The Scout's Patrol Song," which became the official Scout song. In his 1908 booklet, *Scouting for Boys*, Baden-Powell described and recommended "Kim's Game," which was based on Kipling's story, *Kim*, published in 1901. The game consists of collecting thirty or so small articles on a tray, uncovering them briefly, then recounting the items to a third party; a game promoting attentive observation and memory, like the title character in the book, *Kim*.

So, for those with curiosity, sometimes one trail leads to another, and then to smaller intriguing pathways often leading – to a little something extra.

©NTPL

Rudyard Kipling

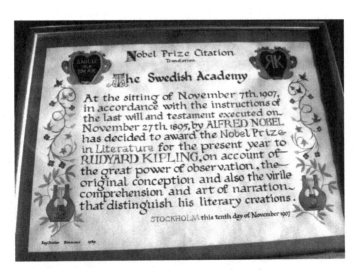

Kipling's Nobel Prize in Literature

William Butler Yeats

1865 – 1939

Thoor Ballylee near Gort,
County Sligo, Ireland

William Butler Yeats

"A pity beyond all telling
Is hid in the heart of love."

"The Pity of Love"

"But I being poor have only my dreams;
I have spread my dreams under your feet
Tread softly because you tread on my dreams."

"He Wishes for the Cloths of Heaven"

Journey   Counties Sligo and Galway

Yeats had strong ties to the West of Ireland and deep feelings about one of the loveliest parts of the Emerald Isle. Even though he was schooled in London and Dublin, some of his mother's family lived in County Sligo. He visited them frequently during the summers and spent his time learning about folklore and Celtic mythology. Yeats later said, "The place that has really influenced my life most is Sligo." He is buried in Dumcliffe Village churchyard, near Sligo City. We went to his gravesite, joining the many thousands who visit there each year.

In Sligo City, at Victoria Hall, the Yeats Society has offices, and the W.B. Yeats Exhibition is open to the public. A map of the area with sites where Yeats was inspired to write specific poems is available on their web site. We went to one of the places nearby—Lake Innisfree. How familiar the lines:

I will arise and go now, and go to Innisfree
And a small cabin to build there of clay and wattles made:
Nine bean-rows will I have there, a hive for the honey-bee,
And live alone in the bee-loud glade.

The lake, from our viewpoint was still quite remote, quiet, and non-commercialized. There were no bees. Understandably, this was the peaceful place where the poet yearned to escape the gray city.

During a significant period in Yeats' life, 1917-1928, he lived in Thoor Ballylee, a restored, ancient Norman tower. Thoor, means castle in Irish; Ballylee is south of Sligo and close to Gort, the market town of the area. Yeats had many reasons for his attraction to this area, especially because two good friends lived near by, Edward Martyn at Tulua Castle and Lady Gregory of Coole Park, two estates passed down from old families in this section. Yeats had visited with them frequently for many years. The three of them formed the Irish National Theatre, which became the well-known Abbey Theatre in Dublin.

At Coole Park, we saw the spacious fields which once were the grounds of a large country house and estates often visited by Yeats. We saw the famous beech tree (See section on Irish Lagniappe.) Our journey to the west of Ireland brought many memorable happenings and shamrocks along the way.

Vignette   William Butler Yeats 1865 - 1939

In his early creative years, they called William Butler Yeats "The greatest of modern Irish poets." In his full poetic flowering, they called him "The greatest modern poet in any language." He was awarded the Nobel Prize in 1923.

"Willie,"(a rather inappropriate nickname for a poet who could be austere and formal, even snobbish), also had a talented brother, Jack, who was considered the most famous Irish painter of his generation. Their two sisters were also gifted.

His father gave up the law to become a fine painter, and Yeats tried to become a painter too, but realized in his teens that his talent was for verse. John Yeats was a brilliant conversationalist and once admitted, "I had within me a certain power of statement." In his case, literature may have lost out to portrait painting. JohnYeats did give some credit to his wife's side of the family for his son's talent. "They had not the poetical mind, but they had the poet's ear." Willie inherited both faculties. As a young man, he hoped to transform into melodic poetry the Irish legends and folklore that he heard when he visited his mother's family in County Sligo.

Father and son were close. When Willie was in his teens, he and his father, John, would take the train from their home in Howth to John's studio in Dublin. There they would have their breakfast, and then they would read poetry together and passages from plays. John taught Willie, "Emotion is the first thing and the last." Surely, John's encouragement greatly helped to promote Willie's creativity.

In addition to WBY's natural gift, his environment greatly affected his poetry. Yeats loved Ireland, felt deeply the tragedy of its warring sides and the injustice it had suffered. He wanted Ireland to take its rightful place in the world. Furthermore, the beauty and sadness of his native land also inspired his lyricism. Ireland, more than any other place, seemed to have a connection with the invisible world. The old people talked of magic and spirits, and told stories of enchanted places. Yeats himself was convinced that he had seen fairies by a cave on a beach near County Sligo. He became interested in the occult and in Theosophy, a non-Christian philosophy, which advances belief in eternal existence. He was drawn to thoughts of a spirit world. On their honeymoon, his wife, George, demonstrated automatic writing and later became something of a medium. She and Yeats sometimes did psychical experiments together. In an emotional letter he wrote of "the very profound, very exciting, mystical philosophy coming in strange ways to George and myself."

The physical body and mind that Willie inherited made him the very model of a poet. He wore long coats and flowing ties with his glasses attached to a ribbon. He had poor eyesight, which may have contributed to a startled, wide-eyed expression. His tall, lank body and black hair worn rather long created a striking appearance, not too out of the ordinary for the style of his era. His personality traits were paradoxical. He was shy but could be arrogant. He was highly intelligent but had an exaggerated respect for the academic achievement of others. He wanted to be respectable, and yet was drawn to mystical phenomena sought by some unorthodox people. John McNeill, his teacher said, "He was a poor speller but in essays, at every turn, showed signs of unusual genius." His teacher also said, "He was tall for his age, dark and good-looking and a thoroughly good boy."

The women in his life, particularly the tall and extremely beautiful Maude Gonne, brought him much joy and pain. Maude and WBY, both members of the Nationalist Party, appeared in some ways to be soul mates. Maud's passion, however, was for the political freedom for Ireland and not for Yeats. After many years, he finally accepted that his love was not returned. She married another man and he married another beauty, Georgie Hyde Lees, "George."

There were other women in his life, before George, and all were beautiful. The other most significant woman in his life was Augusta Gregory, best known as Lady Gregory. Her husband on his death left her Coole Park, a lovely Irish estate. When she met Willie, she found him "full of charm and Celtic revival." Lady Gregory's goal was to bring back dignity to Ireland. Willie's was to establish an Irish National Theatre. Their greatest hopes meshed. He stayed long periods of time at Coole; for thirty years he spent his summers there and sometimes winters too. She was forty-five when they met, and she became his friend and confidant in a platonic relationship. Soon after their first meeting, Willie's spirits were at a low ebb, but her hospitality and her encouragement helped him to regain his equilibrium. The two of them plus Edward Martyn must be given credit for The Irish National Theatre, which became the famous Abbey Theatre. On opening night the first productions were Yeats' *Countess Cathleen*, which was based on the personality of Maud Gonne, and Lady Gregory's *Spreading of the News*. One of the greatest playwrights of the Irish movement was J.M. Synge, who is most famous for his masterpiece, *The Playboy of the Western World*. It was first performed at the Abbey. Sean O'Casey was another luminary there.

The stagecraft of the Abbey was in great contrast to the British and the American style. There was stillness about the production, with a minimum of gestures. The cast remained motionless while they said their lines. Gradually the techniques of the Abbey became realistic, which was not what Yeats wanted. He became interested in the Japanese Noh play with mime emphasized instead of acting, and accompanied by chanting, flute, drum and gong. This style was more suited for the drawing room. His *Plays for Dancers* is an example of this type.

Yeats' interest in drama did not prevent his flow of poetry, but its style changed from the dreamy, romantic and decorative quality to one at once more terse, astringent and masculine. *The Green Helmet and other Poems and Responsibilities* came from this period. *Words upon the Window Pane* became one of his most popular plays.

After spending some time in Italy (Rapallo), what was there left? A poet's tower! They found it in Galway, not far from Coole Park. It was a Norman tower, "Thoor Ballylee."

In his early days, he was a Romantic, valuing imagination and mysticism. When older, he believed poetry should deal with the problems of the modern world. To this end, he simplified his style, using language closer to everyday speech and its rhythms. He never abandoned his immersion in the mystical, which he considered the core of his being.

He became a senator in the Irish Free State. In a photograph, he is shown with six other people. Yeats alone is wearing a frock coat, silk top hat, his knees crossed with his hands holding a pair of gloves. The picture suggests several of his personality traits of this era—eccentricity, formality, dignity, gravity with, as his biographer says, "never...humorous warmth of intimacy." Does it matter what impression his outward demeanor gave to his contemporaries? The important thing is the poetry he left to them and to succeeding generations.

Thinking Place   Yeat's Tower

The towers of Ireland are mute reminders of the warring sides, the native Irish and the invading English who clashed over both land and religion. Norman or Anglo-Norman families moved into Ireland, bought or cleared the land in large areas during the thirteenth and the fourteenth centuries and built castles or keeps to protect themselves from neighbors or raiders from the North.

The Norman family de Burgo or Burke had extensive landholdings in the region on the borders of County Clare and Galway. They erected thirty-two fortified residences, castles, towers or keeps in this area. The Burke family members proliferated, but by the nineteenth century, wars and power plays by their enemies, had eliminated most of them. The towers gradually fell into other hands and deteriorated.

Yeats bought his dilapidated tower in 1917 and hired an architect and builder to do extensive renovation. The tower itself had much symbolism to Yeats, as reflected in his poems. The tower's ascending stairways represent spiritual ascension. In his mind, Yeats could hear "the clanking of armies of yesteryear," echoing in the ancient chambers. Yeats was attracted to the beauty of the remote site, next to a small river. Also, he could tramp through the woods to the homes of two, good friends, Lady Gregory at Coole Park and Edward Martyn.

After renovating the tower and the adjacent old cottage, he occupied the tower in 1919, with George, his wife of two years, and their young daughter. On the ground floor of the tower was the dining room. Bedrooms were on the second and third floors. The fourth floor, a renovation never completed, was reserved for Yeats' meditation.

Yeats often wrote his poems on the first floor, near a large window at a desk, which overlooked a stream. He also wrote late at night with a candle flickering in the darkness. At other times, he sat in the darkness by his wife's bed, watching her sleep while he wrote his poetry. Needless to say, Yeats often lived in a different world from most mortals. Frequently, during the day he walked in the woods in a dream state, to the alarm of the locals.

The Irish Civil War shook the country in 1922, and shocked Yeats' life drastically. One night the bridge at Ballylee was bombed. Yeats moved out for a period. He did spend some time intermittently in his beloved tower (until 1925). He did not visit the tower again after 1928. In 1932, his friend, Lady Gregory died, finally ending his ties with the area. The tower settled into decline, predicted by Yeats in a poem he wanted carved in a stone at Thoor Ballylee:

> I, the poet William Yeats
> With old millboards and
>   seagreen slates
> And smithy work from
>   the Gort forge
>
> Restored this tower
>   for my wife George
> And may these characters
>   remain
> When all is ruin once again.

The stone with the above inscription was not erected until 1948, after Yeats' death, by the board of the Abbey Theater. By 1958 the Kiltartan Society started restoration of the old tower. Time and wars have taken their toll on Thoor Ballylee, but today it stands tall, solid yet graceful, by the peaceful river it has guarded for centuries.

Lagniappe   County Galway

Our journey to County Galway was centered on Yeats' tower, Thoor Ballylee, but, as is so often the case, our search led to other equally interesting sites and subjects. Ireland West

Tourism describes, "the counties of Galway, Mayo and Roscomin are endowed with great natural beauty and the region has a living Gaelic culture, with strong Irish speaking communities in Galway and Mayo and the lovely Aran Islands." Our one-day boat trip to the Aran Islands, with its hundreds of stone fences enclosing rocky little farms and fields was like boarding a time machine and being transported back centuries in time. We talked with the sturdy people there, mixing their accents with ours, and saw how many generations must have eked out a living, yet endured proudly.

Our journey to the area and to Coole Park gave us a better understanding of why Yeats was drawn to the magical spell of this landscape and heritage, and identified so closely with its culture and mythology.

The former home of Lady Gregory, Coole Park is now a wildlife park. It is located a few miles north of Gort and is near Thoor Ballylee and, also, near Kiltartan Gregory Museum at Kiltartan Cross, County Galway. Sadly, the ruined, stately old Coole Park home, occupied by generations of Gregories, was demolished in 1941 by the Department of Forestry. The gardens of the house are preserved with the long walk bordered by many tall yew trees.

The famous "autograph tree" on the grounds is carefully protected. Lady Gregory hosted not only Yeats but many other artists, actors, statesmen, Irish language enthusiasts, folklorists and traveling musicians. Signatures or initials carved by some of her renowned visitors on the magnificent copper beach tree include: George Bernard Shaw, John Masefield, Sean O'Casey, John Millington Synge, George Moore and Douglass Hyde, Ireland's first president. Today, the Coole Park Visitor Centre has exhibits and audio visual presentations, "The Magic of Coole" and "Lady Gregory of Coole." There are tearooms, nature trails and walks around the lake. The Park is a fitting tribute to the significance of this historic thinking place.

Lady Gregory, widow of Sir William, was indeed a very caring person. According to all reports, she lived a life of service with her inherited home, wealth, and position. She took an active interest in the welfare of her tenants. She and her son,

Robert, were held in high esteem by local people. She not only hosted and encouraged many groups and individual writers and artists, she herself was a writer. Her *Selected Writings* are used in college courses today. She wrote several plays which were performed at the Abbey Theater, an outgrowth of the Irish Literary Society which Lady Gregory, W.B. Yeats and Edward Martyn founded in 1896. The Annual "Lady Gregory Autumnal Gathering" was established with a weekend of lectures, plays, music and walks in Coole Park, celebrating the life and contributions of this creative lady.

Our special gift in Galway, our Irish Lagniappe, was a deeper appreciation for the major roles and continuing influence that Yeats and, especially, his friend, Augusta, Lady Gregory, had on reviving and stimulating interest in Celtic history, Gaelic culture and Irish mythology.

Cottage attached
to the tower

One of Yeats' thinking places in the tower

Beatrix Potter

1866 – 1943

Hill Top at Sawrey, Cumbria,
England and a Thinking Place

Beatrix Potter

"Once upon a time there were four little rabbits, and
their names were--Flopsy, Mopsy, Cottontail and
Peter."

The Tale of Peter Rabbit

"I am worn to a raveling. I am undone and worn to a
thread-paper, for I have no more Twist."

The Tailor of Glouster

Journey

Three of our most memorable experiences occurred on our
journey to England's Lake District—or Lakeland—in Cumbria:
the striking panorama of the lakes and mountains;
"Wordsworth's country" and his homes at Dove Cottage and
Rydal Mount; and our visit to the home of Peter Rabbit's creator,
Beatrix Potter at Hill Top, and environs. Lakeland is filled with
charming villages with such names as Near Sawrey and Far
Sawrey, Low Wray and High Wray, Cockermouth, Hawkshead
and Bowness-on-Windermere.

Beatrix's home at Hill Top is like a picture from one of her
books with a path through a garden overflowing with flowers
leading to her front door. We were able to go into the house and
see Beatrix's collection of antique furniture and her other
distinctive home furnishings, including a chair and desk at a
window, which may have been one of her thinking places.

In the small village of Sawrey we had the traditional English
Cream Tea in one of the attractive tearooms. As we walked a-
long the colorful streets we saw flowers filling the gardens
everywhere. Subtle reminders of Beatrix's characters were noted
throughout the village.

The entire Lakeland area is a joy to the eye—and to all the
senses, especially, Wordsworth's points of interest at Grasmere
and near Ambleside. But the principal Beatrix Potter places to

visit include: Hill Top, in Sawrey; Beatrix Potter Gallery and Museum, in Hawkshead; Armitt Museum and Library, at Ambleside; and the "World of Beatrix Potter TM Attraction" in Bowness-on–Windermere.

Beatrix's relationship to Lakeland began as a young girl when her family spent their holidays there in the summer; they returned to Lakeland for the next twenty-one years. By 1903, at age thirty-seven, Beatrix had received income from her publications and bought her first land, a field at Near Sawrey. In 1905 she bought a small farm, Hill Top, in Sawrey; then, she bought Castle Farm, which later became her Lakeland base. In 1923 she bought Troutbeck Park Farm, and she developed expertise in breeding Herwick sheep. (Eventually, she was the first woman to be elected President-designate of the Herwick Sheepbreeders' Association.)

When Beatrix Potter died she left fourteen farms, with 4000 acres, as well as her large flock of Herwick Sheep to the National Trust. The Trust properties have increased in value and, with other donations, the National Trust owns 91 hill farms and 25,000 sheep. The National Trust's Beatrix Potter Gallery in Hawkshead is located in the former office building of her solicitor husband, William Heelis. One may see displays of Beatrix's paintings there and obtain appropriate educational materials, books, and prints.

Of the many books about Beatrix, one of our favorites is *Beatrix Potter's Lakeland*, by our friend, Hunter Davies with photography by Cressida Pemberton-Pigott. This book tells of the relationship of the beautiful Lakeland countryside to a very private woman who "received inspiration from the area, painted many aspects of it and helped to preserve it for future generations." *The Real World of Beatrix Potter*, published by the National Trust, includes interviews from people who knew Beatrix; it also tells of her support and her influence on farm policy of the National Trust.

The Armitt Museum and Gallery at Ambleside on Rydal Road displays many of Beatrix's watercolors and drawings of fungi, mosses and fossils. Beatrix had been a supporter and benefactor of the three Armitt sisters and their concern for the study of Natural History as well as the safeguarding of the Lake District countryside. All of this resulted in a small but worthwhile museum. On our return visit we enjoyed "The World of Beatrix Potter TM Attraction" at the Old Laundry, Bowness-on-Windmere, Cumbria. It is described as "A magical day out for the family, young and old" and has many theme attractions and events including the Peter Rabbit Tea Garden, puppet shows, story telling by a "Beatrix Potter," and picnic teas, as well as meeting many of the characters created by Beatrix.

Beatrix Potter is one of our favorite creative people. Her story of personally making the best of what could have been a disastrous suppression of her spirit and talent by well-meaning but overbearing parents is a tribute to her persistence and integrity. The pleasure and positive influence she brought to millions of readers by her stories and art, as well as her enormous contributions to the development and conservation of her beloved Lakeland make her one of the most admirable of all writer/artists.

Vignette   Beatrix Potter   1866-1943

Beatrix Potter, born in 1866, had written, illustrated and sold millions of copies of *A Tale of Peter Rabbit*, long before Walt Disney built an empire around a rodent named Mickey Mouse. Creatures named Peter Rabbit, Apply Dapply, Jemima Puddle-Duck, Squirrel Nutkin, and many others in subsequent books, have been as real to children as their actual playmates. Five generations of children, from Victoria's reign to the space age, have passed through childhood in the company of imaginary personages who seem both timely and timeless.

At first Beatrix self-published with immediate success, but in 1902, Frederick Warne, Publisher, brought out *The Tale of Peter Rabbit*. Within ten years a million copies had been sold. Beatrix Potter did it all by herself—with no empire, staff or even a secretary. How did she do it? In addition to her own unique talent and business acumen, Beatrix herself would probably give credit to a favorite uncle, a pet rabbit, a canon in the church and a little boy named Noel. In these we see four of the qualities so important in the nurture of her creativity—encouragement, stimulus to the imagination, support and favorable situation. (Without all of the four, she might have proceeded earlier to her second career, sheep-raising, which was also successful.)

Her favorite uncle was Sir Henry Roscoe, who noticed her illustrations and encouraged her to sell them to a card publisher for Christmas cards. Success emboldened her to write and illustrate a story. The pet rabbit was Benjamin Bouncer, whom Beatrix led around on a leather leash. He had been her model for the Christmas cards and now stimulated her imagination. She wrote his story with her typical humor. She was so elated over her sale of the rabbit Christmas cards that she gave Bouncer a cupful of hemp seeds in gratitude. The seeds made him drunk and unmanageable. "Then I retired to bed, and lay awake chuckling till two in the morning, and afterwards had an impression that Bunny came to my bedside in a white cotton night cap and tickled me with his whiskers."

The church canon was Hardwicke Rawnsley, a published writer among other accomplishments, who gave support and guidance in finding a book publisher.

And the little boy Noel? He was the son of Beatrix's last governess, Annie Moore. An illness had confined him to his bed and provided the situation that began the list of twenty four books that Beatrix would eventually write, two published posthumously. She was thirty when she wrote Noel the letter that started her writing career:

> "My dear Noel,
>   I don't know what to write to you, so I shall tell you a story about four little rabbits whose names were Flopsy, Mopsy, Cottontail and Peter...."

After reading the delightful letter, Annie Moore, Noel's mother, suggested that the story should be published.

In a negative aspect, credit for her success could be given to her Victorian childhood, a sometimes dour and repressive age for children. Beatrix needed large amounts of imagination and self-sufficiency to flourish. Her dearly beloved father was a lawyer whose hobby was photography. Her mother, remote and forbidding, allegedly, spent more time making social calls and entertaining than she did with her children, Beatrix and Bertram, who was five years younger than his sister. This circumstance was too often the norm in many affluent families. The period was the age of the governess, and the governess raised the children, with varying support from the parents. The amiable, sensible Beatrix did not seem to show any ill effects from this situation, and she took responsibility for her mother when she grew old. (Sad to say, the mother's disposition, so it was said, never improved.)

Another custom of her time had a positive effect on Beatrix. Her family moved from their house during the two weeks of spring-cleaning. Then later in the season, the family, accompanied by the household staff, spent three months in Scotland. After many years, when their rented house in Scotland was no longer available, the Potters spent their vacation in the Lake District of England. Away from the city, the observant and sensitive Beatrix was more aware than ever of the wonders of nature. She did what she liked to do more than anything else in the world. She drew in great detail—or painted—rabbits, mice, cats, caterpillars, guinea pigs, dormice, flowers, owls, or fungi, interiors of favorite rooms, furniture, a scene she wanted to remember. From a young age, she displayed a mature talent, and practice only made her better.

Beatrix had another talent that boded well for her writing career. Her imagination, like an artesian well, never seemed to stop. And, she had a credulous, accepting nature. Like William Butler Yeats, she believed in fairies. According to Susan Dryner in *At Home with Beatrix Potter*, Beatrix once wrote: "I remember I used to half-believe and wholly play with fairies when I was a child. What in heaven can be more real than to retain the spirit-world of childhood, tempered and balanced by knowledge and common-sense, to fear no longer the terror that flieth by night, yet to feel truly and understand a little, a very little, of the story of life." Young readers were in safe hands when they read Beatrix Potter's books.

As Virginia Woolf pined for "some money and a room of one's own," so Beatrix Potter also hoped for a little money to secure her independence. "It is pleasant to feel I could earn my own living," she said. When she did amass enough money, she bought Hill Top Farm in Sawrey in the Lake District. She asked the tenants to stay on in the house in a wing that she designed and had built. She would remain in the main part of the house. She began to fill it with the carved, substantial period furniture that she had always admired. Parental demands prevented her from staying in Hill Top House as much as she would have liked, but her dream had come true. In time, she would add other houses that she had built. Later Beatrix would become a lady farmer.

She would even become politically involved in issues that affected the farmer. Were there other dreams? Romantic dreams? They came late, and the first was bittersweet. In the firm which published her books, Frederick Warne, she had met and known Norman Warne for five years. He admired the plucky, vibrant woman and he, being shy, wrote and proposed marriage. She was overjoyed. There was one problem. Her parents, particularly her mother, did not want her thirty-nine-year-old daughter to marry "into trade." Beatrix accepted anyway and wore Norman's engagement ring, but out of deference to her parents, suggested they not announce their plans immediately. Little did she imagine that "immediately" was all the time they had. She left for Wales on holiday with family, concerned that he was not well. She wrote him a "silly letter" about rabbits and "the walking stick I was going to get him to thrash his wife with." Norman never read the letter. He died of acute leukemia slightly more than a month after its onset, the length of their engagement.

Beatrix was heartbroken. She busied herself in matters at Hill Top. As time passed, she continued to wear his ring, but she made herself become even more involved in the beautiful land that she owned. She made Hill Top Garden a reality. She began to raise sheep and other farm animals. She wrote books. Her old friend and admirer, Canon Rawnsley and his son, Noel, persuaded her to raise Herdwick sheep, a breed appropriate for the area. Together they founded the Herdwick Sheepbreeders' Association. She worked for tariff reform.

Beatrix had a new concern—hydro-aeroplanes. Across the Atlantic, Glenn Curtiss was building planes and setting new records for flying, and Britons, too, were building all sorts of airships and flying machines. But Beatrix considered the new-fangled aeroplane a nuisance on Lake Windermere."... it makes a noise like ten million bluebottles. It has been buzzing up and down for hours today, and it has already caused a horse to bolt & smashed a tradesman's cart." The newspaper agreed with her, and she successfully collected signatures on a petition. The proposed aeroplane factory was not built, and the noisemakers left Windermere.

In 1909, Beatrix had bought Castle Farm, and she kept an eye on what it produced. The significant relationship, however, was one she had with William Heelis, a local solicitor, who advised her on her real estate transactions. They had known each other for six years when he proposed. She accepted him in spite of the usual parental objections. They were married in London with plans to live at Castle Cottage, which was receiving a large new room. He was forty-two. She was forty-seven. In the same month of her marriage, she published *The Tale of Pigling Bland*. Pig Wig in the story was in real life a Berkshire pig, but unacceptably black. When the farm manager refused to let Pig Wig stay with the pedigreed pigs, Beatrix let it sleep in a basket by her bed and bottle-fed it. All her life she had shown love to animals, handling them, diagnosing their ills, even taking them with her on holiday. They repaid the debt by inspiring the heroes of her stories.

There is a footnote in the romance department. When his wife died, Canon Hardwicke Rawnsley, according to his family, would have married Beatrix, but she had been married for two years to William Heelis, so he married another. And so the world turns. Interestingly, Rawnley, in 1895 was one of the founders of the National Trust. From the beginning, Beatrix planned for the National Trust to take over her properties after she and her husband died, and that is what eventually happened. Beatrix, who believed in conservation, had the pleasure of knowing that thousands of acres would be protected from development.

With handsome royalties from her books, Beatrix continued to buy land in the Lake District. During World War II, she made a house available for a family whose house had been commandeered by the Government. She allowed a friend to live in another one, and she enjoyed having the Girl Guides camp on her property. She always felt that her property was too isolated and remote for threats from enemy planes, but she did suggest to the Girl Guides during war time that they pitch their tents under the trees for camouflage purposes.

Even as she continued to write, Beatrix was becoming a specialist in sheep raising, in judging at fairs and generally promoting the Herdwick breed as a suitable breed for the climate and geography of the Lake District. She could now financially indulge her fondness for old oak furniture and fine examples of pottery and china. Examples of these may be seen when visitors come to Hill Top House. Her collections served a two-fold purpose, her own enjoyment and conservation for the future.

Once again, a smart move on Beatrix's part predated Walt Disney's business ideas. Early on she had a Peter Rabbit doll manufactured for sale. Other dolls followed, then painting books, dinner mats, china, cards, a magazine and many other items for children became licensed merchandise. They are available for sale today. Items of special value were bequeathed to the National Art Library of the Victoria and Albert Museum. A Peter Rabbit postage stamp was issued in 1979. Her books were translated into six languages, reaching thirty languages at last count. An exhibition was held at the Tate Gallery in London and at the Pierpont Morgan Gallery in New York. The Beatrix Potter Society, founded in 1980, has members all over the world.

Beatrix Potter had a special gift that transcended her outstanding draftsmanship that depicted all the animals that she so sincerely loved. She was able to convey emotion that made the animals seem human. In one greeting card, a mother rabbit is spooning a dose of medicine into the little rabbit whose head is barely seen above the cover. At the foot of the bed, two rabbit playmates sit upright on the floor as they peer up at the patient. Almost palpable compassion and concern radiate from their up-turned ears to their fluffy tails.

The effect for good on millions of Beatrix Potter readers is incalculable. Although Beatrix had to endure sadness, loneliness at times and difficulties, she would probably say that she was more than repaid by a life that was both happy and fulfilled.

Thinking Place

Beatrix Potter, while growing up had plenty of time to think—and to be creative—in her Victorian household. She never went to school, but she had governesses who must have been good teachers or, at least, did not suppress the child's natural inquisitiveness and growth of artistic talent. Beatrix's love of animals and all of nature nourished her imagination while in London or Lakeland. Obviously, she had many thinking places over time. Her most productive years for publication were considered to be from 1905, the year she bought Hill Top, to 1913, the year of her marriage. Because of family pressures she did not live permanently at Hill Top, but apparently she did spend much time there furnishing and decorating the home and possibly, writing some stories during this most creative period of her life.

Lagniappe

How often does memory converge on reality? How often does something look just like you expected it to look? Beatrix Potter's Hill Top, the first house she bought in Sawrey, came up to every expectation. We half-expected to see Peter Rabitt scurry away from Mr. McGregor's uplifted foot as we walked up the garden walk. A profusion of summer flowers in many colors nodded with a breeze and almost obscured the path in places. The disarray was charming. And there were hollyhocks! One of us had not seen a hollyhock since childhood nor gathered up the folds of a blossom, imprisoning a bee before letting the bee fly away. We had not been stung by a bee in years.

When we walked into the house, we experienced déjà vu. How could that be? We had been here before. How? When? Through the Beatrix Potter books, most likely. Young memories, some of our first memories, that is, seem to last longer, to be more concentrated in lingering effect. We had not opened a Beatrix Potter book in years, but the characters and the stories were more vivid, more luminous in our mind than yesterday's newspaper.

And so we received our lagniappe. It was no less real for being abstract. We would carry away from our visit to Hill Top and Hill Top Garden, a feeling of reassurance and a feeling of connectedness. It was comforting to be shown that the past has not passed. It's still with us. Those grown-ups who once read to us Beatrix Potter books are as connected to Beatrix as they are to us, and we are to her. As we admire this beautiful country, we feel a kinship with Beatrix who loved it too, and saved it for all of us who follow in her train. A silent "thank-you" seems inadequate until we reaffirm that words are frequently just inexact symbols for thoughts that we cannot express.

Photographic credits:
Picture of Beatrix Potter at Hiltop © NTPL is courtesy of The National Trust.

Peter Rabbit model at the World of
Beatrix Potter's at Bowness-on-Windermere

©NTPL

Beatrix Potter at Hiltop

Virginia Woolf

1882 - 1941

Virginia Woolf's house in Rodmell
and her Writer's Hut or Lodge.

Virginia Woolf

"The beauty of the world has two edges, one of
laughter, one of anguish, cutting the heart
asunder."

A Room of One's Own

"Women have served all these centuries as looking
glasses possessing the magic and delicious power
of reflecting the figure of man at twice its natural
size."

A Room of One's Own

"She bore about with her, she could not help
knowing it, the torch of her beauty; she carried it
erect into any room that she entered; and after all,
veil it as she might, and shrink from the monotony
of bearing that it imposed on her, her beauty was
apparent. She had been admired. She had been
loved."

To the Lighthouse

Journey Monk's House, Sussex

Our first journey to Virginia Woolf's house in Rodmell,
Sussex was toward the end of a day when we had visited the
home site of Henry James at Lamb's House, in Rye. Before our
visit we knew that James' vividly described garden house, one
of his favorite thinking places, had been demolished by a bomb
during World War II. We wanted to see the house itself, but we
learned that it could be visited only by appointment.

When we arrived at Monk's House, located close to the main
road outside of Rodmell, it was off-season, and we could only
look through the windows of the house. No one was there. It
was quite a blustery day—dark, cool and damp; rather fitting,

remembering the many bleak days that Virginia Woolf must have had toward the end of her life. On the other hand, we knew that some of her happiest, most productive days were spent here at Monk's House, her choice of thinking places. In the backyard the gardens were unkempt and awaiting the renewal of spring. But in the back of the garden area, like a shining star, was our prize, what we had come to see on this wintry day. Woolf's little gray writing hut or "lodge" as she called it, and its setting, was everything we had expected it would be, a remote, secluded place for Virginia's solitude and creative work.

When we returned to Monk's House years later on a sunny October afternoon, we joined a large number of visitors. We toured the downstairs rooms, including Woolf's bedroom opening onto the gardens. The room had the hallmarks of the artful decorations of Vanessa Bell, Woolf's sister, and Duncan Grant; evident to us since on the day before we had just seen Vanessa's colorful Charleston Farmhouse nearby.

Vignette   Virginia Woolf   1882 – 1941

There is a mythic quality about the life and personality of Virginia Woolf. It's as if she is the fair princess of a fairy tale. Her fairy godmother bestows upon her many gifts – striking beauty, unspoiled by her eccentric dress, high intelligence, a caring husband, admiring friends, and a rare talent for creating stories in a new, powerful manner, uniquely her own. Then, in a perverse turn, the godmother causes a blight to fall upon the rare creature she had previously endowed. A chain of misfortunes befalls the princess. Early in her life, her mother dies, then her stepsister who cared for her. Her father, and her brother die within a few years of each other. Her stepbrothers abuse her; only her sister, Vanessa, remains forever loyal. Finally, the most terrible blow of all comes in the form of an illness of her mind. Four times the illness strikes her down, threatening the very source of the princess' greatest gift – her power to create.

The fairy godmother grants her one boon, similar to the love of the loyal but sometimes competitive sister; this special gift is a husband who will love and sustain her throughout all her trials. His presence strengthens her resolve to conquer the enemy of the talent that she knows resides within her, and also to measure up to the achievement of her father, Sir Leslie Stephen, the well-known editor famous for *The National Dictionary of Biography*. The power of the terrible blight begins to fade as the princess finds that she can still tell her stories. Alas, she is ultimately unable to conquer the dreaded illness, but she is rewarded for her constancy in persevering. By the rules of the Kingdom of Fairness, her stories and her varied writings are destined to endure and to have a life of their own.

Although Virginia Stephen Woolf's life did not have the "lived happily ever afterward" ending of a fairy tale, in her lifetime she did have compensations. The first came when she, Vanessa and their two brothers moved to a house in Bloomsbury, a section of London. On Thursday evenings, a group of artists and authors would meet for discussion at their house. They became so well known that they acquired the name, "The Bloomsbury Group." In the midst of this highly charged and gratifying time, Virginia made a decision to marry Leonard Woolf, a writer, editor and critic, then publisher, whom she met soon after his return from India. She had been hesitant about marrying, perhaps fearful of surrendering her independence or concerned about her previous mental breakdowns. In any case, the Woolfs were happy together in what was, in some ways, an unconventional marriage. They had good friends who visited them, and they shared interest in publishing.

Their life in London was stimulating but they loved to retreat to Monk's House, a holiday house of Virginia's own choosing. The house had no running water, heat or electricity. As their finances allowed, they gradually converted it to their permanent home. At first, life was difficult in Monk's House, sometimes so cold that Virginia could not hold a pen. The Woolfs gamely put up with the inconveniences in return for the natural beauty of the surrounding Sussex downs. They had other homes before Monk's House, but this was probably their happiest location. Virginia found she liked to cook and made buns, bread and cake for relaxation. Leonard converted the back yard into gardens and filled the house with flowers and pot plants. Virginia asked her sister, Vanessa, a fine artist, and fellow artist-friend, Duncan Grant, to do the decorating, but Virginia herself insisted on a special color of green paint that she liked for the living room. (The accurately matched color, a bright, light green, may be seen in Monk's House today.)

A mutual project with Leonard, Hogarth Press, was first started in a former house in London. It shared space with her writing studio. In the beginning, their kitchen table held all of the press, but it grew and eventually published such luminaries as T.S. Eliot, Sigmund Freud and others, including Virginia's own work.

Virginia Woolf deeply regretted her lack of a University education, which few women achieved in her day. This situation led to her growing support of feminism. *A Room of One's Own* is an eloquent expression of her belief. She was also a pacifist and a socialist.

She was prolific in writing with many novels and over 500 essays to her credit, as well as five volumes of memoirs. Her fame rests on her distinctive style, the use of stream-of-consciousness or interior monologue, which she employed in her novels. Her writing could be clear, logical, precise; at other times it was poetic.

To evoke women's experience and to get beneath the surface, she abandoned the more traditional linear narrative. She developed characterization by revealing the thoughts of her characters in place of plot action. She began this technique tentatively in *Jacob's Room*, then more expertly in *Mrs. Dalloway* and *The Waves*. Many consider *To the Lighthouse* her best work. *Orlando*, humorously conceived, shows her fascination with the problems of time and history. The hero starts out as a young man, and then changes sex four centuries later. It is based on Knole, the Sackville family palace, and most especially, her friend, Vita Sackville-West, who is the subject of photographs that illustrate the book. (For some years Virginia had a Sapphic relationship with Vita. Such a friendship was not uncommon among the Bloomsbury group to which she and Leonard had belonged before their marriage.) *Orlando* demonstrates Woolf's concern with spiritual, social and sexual ambiguities of modern life.

Today, more than ever, Virginia Woolf is "in style." Recently, *The Voices*, both a novel and a movie, brilliantly re-created the story of Mrs. Dalloway. Woolf comes to life in *Recollections of Virginia Woolf* (by her contemporaries), edited by Joan Russell Noble. All the memoirists agree that she was a genius. "She was a perfectly poetic creature, all of a piece, with-out and within." Her friends recall her sitting by the fire (she hated, was almost afraid of the cold), her long, thin but lovely hands, moving through the air or often at other times hugging herself in her folded arms as she rocked her body from side to side, carried away with her own argument. An observer was usually conscious of Virginia's beauty—her finely sculptured face with its aquiline features, deeply sunken green, sometimes gray eyes that had a luminous quality, all adding up to an air of refinement with almost an ascetic quality. Probably Virginia gave this impression when she was discussing the issues that intrigued her most: the passage of time, perpetual change and flux, order and chaos.

She had a lighter side. She loved to just talk, even to gossip. Her friends remembered her asking innumerable questions, giving nicknames, type-casting people. She was humorous, sometimes malicious, though not cruel. She wanted to know all the details about a newcomer and frequently would fantasize a story about the person, which she would then relate to the assembled company. She was single-minded, so her friends said, and not at all afraid to voice her own opinion. "She was the most enchanting conversationalist I've ever known," one friend concluded.

Some of the things she valued most were: the awareness of physical sensations, the intellect and knowledge, the privilege and power of a university education. She was also a social person who liked fancy dress parties (her own clothes were sometimes like loose draperies), charades, traveling with family or friends and surprisingly, walking, her favorite pastime, her joy. She did not drive. She had many friends but closest to her were her husband, Leonard, and her artist-sister, Vanessa, another beauty in the Stephen family.

When she was fifty-nine, Virginia Woolf committed suicide by walking into the Ouse River, with her pockets weighed down with heavy rocks. Possibly it was her second attempt within a short time. In early life she had had four breakdowns. From 1913-1915 she suffered so much from manic-depression, accompanied by migraines, that eventual insanity was feared. Miraculously, she rose above her illness and produced her best work.

In 1941 she left a suicide note for Leonard, telling him that she was hearing voices, could not read nor write and could not bear the thought of madness. She thanked him for giving her the happiest part of her life. Her readers owe a debt to Leonard too. For a long time he had loved and cared for his wife so that she could function and become, many considered, the foremost woman writer of her century.

Thinking Places   The Lodge

It was a small building, weather-boarded and plain and situated in the rear of the garden. On adjacent property an old church seemed to hover over it. Virginia Woolf loved the silence and the solitude. She used it mainly in the summertime. It was not built for cold weather.

The unusual glassed-in eave and glass on the doors gave plenty of light in the sparsely furnished room. When we looked inside, through the window, we could see the writing room with her desk, piled with the blue writing paper that she favored—a ghostly reminder. In earlier years, Virginia had the habit of standing up while writing at a tall architectural table. When the Woolfs acquired Monk's House in 1919, she frequently sat at the desk in the Lodge. Early in the morning, she would seclude herself for hours. Using a metal pen dipped in green ink, she was meticulous as she wrote in her distinctive hand-writing.

In 1928, the Woolfs built a wing on Monk's House. Downstairs was "Virginia's green" living room. Upstairs was a bedroom. All of this was financed by sales of her successful book, *Orlando*. The installation of electricity in Monk's House was paid for by *The Waves*. Virginia did some of her writing in the new addition's living room, but the Lodge was her special thinking and writing place, weather permitting.

Lagniappe   Monk's House

Seeing Virginia Woolf's lodge or writing hut was not only a "bull's-eye" as an ideal example of a secluded, thinking place, but lagniappe on a bleak day on our first visit. On our second visit, in the sunshine of a bright autumn day and amid the striking colors of the interior of the home and of the garden, we could appreciate more keenly the Woolfs' attraction to their beloved Monk's House.

More important, we were stimulated by our visit to Virginia and Leonard's house to learn more about their relationship — and to re-visit Virginia's books—and to re-read the stories of Virginia's ups and downs, sometimes joyous, sometimes tragic, always with creative flair. Our special gift, our lagniappe, from Virginia was her last written expression of love and appreciation for her husband. In spite of some tempestuous pressures on their relationship, and her feeling that she was "going mad again," the bottom line of her feelings were expressed in her final note to Leonard: "...what I want to say is I owe all the happiness of my life to you."

The Woolf's backyard," The Lodge" and an adjacent church steeple.

Interior of "The Lodge", Woolf's writing hut-thinking place

Busts of Virginia and Leonard in the Woolfs' garden area

Vita Sackwell-West

1919 – 1953

Sissinghurst Castle and
Vita's Desk and Study

Vita Sackwell-West

"The greater cats with golden eyes
  Stare out behind the bars.
Deserts are there, and different skies
  And nights with different stars."

"The country habit has me by the heart,
  For he's bewitched forever who has seen,
  Not with his eyes but with his vision, Spring
Flow down the woods and stipple leaves with sun."

The King's Daughter

Journey   Sissinghurst Castle

After visiting Churchill's home, Chartwell, in Surrey on a beautiful and sunny day, we had no hint that the next day's journey to Sissinghurst Castle and gardens, might be totally canceled by unexpected circumstances. Vita Sackville-West and her husband, Harold Nicolson, had developed their home into a place of beauty. This was our second attempt to see this National Trust property.

We had stayed at a charming inn in Tunbridge Wells the night before. On the following pleasant morning we had visited the exhibits and museums of the popular spa of the wealthy gentry during the Georgian era.

As we drove in the rain that afternoon toward Sissinghurst, the traffic became slower and slower and then came to a complete stop. We learned that the village beyond us was marooned by the flooding of a river. (Later we heard that much of Tunbridge Wells was also under water just hours after we had left.) According to police, there was no way to drive further toward our destination. Luckily, a young woman stranded nearby in the long line of cars, said she needed to go our way too, and that she knew some back roads, some of which were not on the map. We decided to follow her, but keeping up with her on those narrow country roads was not easy. What should have been vistas of green pastoral England was now nothing but brown, moving water, marked in places by swift, dangerous currents. Fields, meadows, even buildings were covered by the growing flood.

Finally we made it through the high waters. Our anonymous guide showed us the entrance to the grounds of Sissinghurst and went on her way. We had left the flooding behind us. Much to our disappointment we read a sign on the gate that said," Closed because of flooding," but someone working by the entrance waved us in. The long road toward the castle clearly was open so we drove cautiously, hoping to get just a peek of the place famous for its gardens and its literary association. Near the front of the castle, a distinguished-looking, older gentleman was bidding good-bye to an attractive, young couple as they prepared to drive away. When the couple left, Carolyn apologized and explained that we had come a long way to see the gardens and Vita's writing and thinking place. "Of course, you can come in," he said, "I live here. I am Vita's son, Nigel Nicolson!"

Sir Nigel took us into the tower and to the second floor where Vita's desk and thinking place was still intact. When we visited him, Sir Nigel's own desk and office were very near Vita's desk in the tower. It was ironic since he had written that as boys, growing up in the Castle, he and his brother, Ben, were allowed in his mother's sanctum only a few times; during the thirty years prior to her death he had entered his mother's sitting room only a half dozen times. Nevertheless, when we saw him he was ensconced in the tower, and he demonstrated the greatest respect for both of his parents.

He invited us to take pictures inside the tower and of the castle gardens. Indeed, he offered us several original pictures of Vita, his father and of Vita's thinking place. He simply asked that we return them after we made copies. (We did!)

Needless to say, the experience further underscored our conviction that the journey may be even more important and gratifying than the destination—and that the journey is enriched by getting to know better old friends we read about purposefully and new friends we meet by chance.

Vignette   Vita Sackwell-West 1919 – 1953

She was born in a palace, one of the largest in England, and she died in the restored remnant of a small castle with a fairy-tale tower.

Victoria Sackville-West loved Knole, her family's majestic palace, and a village in itself. She gloried in the vast parklands, the huge structure containing 365 bedrooms, one of the most valuable collections of furniture in all of England, and the abundant spaces where she had played as a child. Her imaginative and poetic nature cherished Knole most for its long history and for its family associations. Elizabeth I had given Knole to Vita's ancestor, John Sackville. In advantages, Vita was almost a princess to the purple born, but in order to hold on to Knole she should have been born male. Perhaps she was trying to compensate when she emphasized masculine traits, and in later life chose jodhpurs and half gaiters as her daily uniform. Nothing could prevail against the laws of primogeniture. A female could not inherit Knole. The stately palace went to a male cousin, a psychic wrench from which Vita never fully recovered.

Another forebear was Vita's colorful grandmother, Pepita, a Spanish dancer. Vita's biography of her is aptly entitled, *Pepita!*

Vita's good friend, Virginia Woolf, a groundbreaking novelist of the twentieth century, wrote a very strange book starring Vita and set at Knole. Entitled *Orlando,* the title character who lives at Knole, is born a young man but, later in the book, becomes a woman. In her life and work, Vita showed brilliance and rare creativity, blended with paradox and tinged with the bizarre. She was known for her beautiful speaking voice and could have been the center of attention anywhere except that she was shy and much preferred her own private world.

Standing six feet tall with classic features and dark coloring, she must have been a stately bride when she married Harold Nicholson, a diplomat, member of Parliament and noted writer, one of the ablest of the twentieth century. They had two sons. After the deaths of his parents, their son Nigel, our hospitable host, later wrote *Portrait of a Marriage*, a record of their unusual but happy union. However, this is Vita's story.

To illustrate Vita's brilliance in writing, which she began in childhood, continuing later with a verse drama written when she was seventeen, this paragraph may sound like the *Encyclopedia Britannica*. Keep reading. It will soon morph into *The National Enquirer*. Vita considered herself primarily a poet with twelve volumes of poetry to her credit. *The Land*, a long pastoral poem won the Hawthornden Prize in 1927. In addition, she wrote thirteen novels (*The Edwardians* and *All Passion Spent* generally considered the best), thirty-four short story collections, nine biographies, three volumes of letters, eleven books on gardening, seven unclassified works, of which four are on travel, and many periodical features on gardening.

The disappointment over losing Knole was ameliorated when the Nicolsons discovered Sissinghurst, a dilapidated castle in need of much repair, which they vowed to give it. Sir Harold designed the gardens and Vita chose the plant material and presided over their cultivation.

Today Sissinghurst has become synonymous with the beauty of its gardens, and many visitors make their way to the most famous garden in England. Even Royalty comes calling. Ironically, Vita's literary output is not currently popular, but she is still justly famous, especially, for her "white garden." Perhaps, as she worked in them she found recompense for the loss of an enormous palace, falling heir instead to a charming castle with a tower and her very own thinking place.

During much of their lifetime, Harold lived in London, the center of his public interests, and joined Vita at Sissinghurst on the weekends. Harold also spent time overseas as a diplomat.

At one time in their marriage Vita eloped to the continent with another woman. She was Violet Trefusis, married daughter of Alice Keppel, who was mistress to King Edward VII and grandmother to Camilla Parker-Bowles, later Princess of Wales. The two husbands, accompanied at every turn by the tabloid bloodhounds, pursued their wives who finally came home. Violet, especially, did not give up easily. Later Vita and Virginia Woolf also had a close relationship.

As the story nears its end, we discover that both Vita and Harold were bisexual, but were truly devoted to each other. The couple continued together their gardening, which had first begun in muddy, weed-filled fields. Vita, honored by the Royal Horticultural Society, was said to have done much to change the face of gardening in England. She was named a Companion of Honor.

Vita should have the last word, and she expressed it in a letter to Harold:

"I thought the other day, in the night, that you were the only person I have ever really loved. I thought this out rather carefully, and analyzed my feelings, and came to that conclusion. I won't say that I haven't been in love with other people, but you are the only person that I have ever deeply and painfully loved. That is true...I love places (Sissinghurst, the Dordogne, Florence...And of course Knole...) but that is a separate thing I can't speak about. That goes too deep."

Thinking Place

The tower was enchanting to Vita; she made it into her thinking place. A curving stairway led to her chosen sanctuary, centered by a desk and filled with books, pictures and object d'art. Through the windows she could see her beloved gardens. Her privacy to think, and to write, was respected by her family.

Like Thomas Carlyle, Vita needed the quiet of solitude, and like William Faulkner and Mark Twain, she craved privacy. A tower retreat must have answered her poetic requirement, as it did for William Butler Yeats at Thoor Baylee. With all these conditions fulfilled, her literary output was prodigious. In addition, consider the correspondence between Vita and Harold. It totaled 10,500 letters, which helped span the distance when they were apart. No wonder she loved her very own tower retreat!

Lagniappe

We received many extras from our journey and visit to Sissinghurst Castle. One was discovering once again the innate decency of most people when they perceive a need and try to respond to it. Certainly on that day of the floods in southeastern England, we were dependent on the kindness of strangers. A stranger led us through the flooded area to our destination. A caretaker took pity when he saw our disappointed faces and waved us through the gates that were marked "closed". Sir Nigel's warm welcome brightened what would have been an otherwise gloomy day.

We knew already the name, "Nigel Nicolson," as an ac-claimed editor and writer. After meeting him, we would remember him for his graciousness, helpfulness and generosity in allowing us to roam the castle tower and grounds, and for lending family pictures.

A pleasant surprise was discovering that the many gardening books and articles authored by Vita, are still available. This cooperative effort by the Nicolsons in gardening was an example of the compatibility of two people who had an uncon-ventional marriage but, nevertheless, were deeply devoted to each other.

Finally, and most important, in seeing the home that Vita and Harold made together, we had a better understanding of two people who were good stewards of the talents with which each was richly endowed. Lagniappe, yes, but even more richly in-creased by our meeting Sir Nigel!

On our return visit in 2004 we were able to see the gardens in full bloom – but we learned, sadly, that Sir Nigel had died a fortnight prior.

Photographic credits:
The picture of Vita below at her desk in her tower thinking place was lent to us by her son, Sir Nigel Nicolson.

Vita Sackville-West   Sir Nigel Nicolson , Vita's son

View of the Sissinghurst gardens from the top of the tower

Dylan Thomas

1914 - 1953

Dylan Thomas' home, the Boat House near Laugharne,
Wales, and "The Garage", his thinking place

Dylan Thomas

"Do not go gentle into that good night
Old age should burn and rave at close of day
Rage, rage against the dying of the night."

"Do Not Go Gentle into That Good Night"

"My poems are written for the love of man and the praise
of God—and I'd be a fool if they weren't."

-Dylan Thomas' Poetic Manifesto

Journey   Laugharne, Wales

It did seem to be a long distance from Dorchester to the southwest coast of Wales, but the vision of Dylan Thomas' little blue writing hut, isolated and clinging to the side of a cliff, led us on our quest. Pictures of this colorful shed represented a typical example of a special thinking place of a very creative person.

Laugharne is a quaint, seaside village with an ancient castle nearby, some interesting shops and tearooms and, as Dylan attested to, a liberal number of pubs. The house in which Dylan and his family lived in his later years is a short distance from town. The old boat house, positioned at the edge of the sea, was remodeled as a comfortable home and provided to Dylan and his family by a literary admirer and supporter. It was a steep climb for Dylan from the house to the writing hut on the side of the cliff, but today the paths are quite well paved and accessible. The writing hut, or "garage", is described in the section below.

When we completed our visits to the boat house, hut and village we were quite pleased and felt that the long journey was more than worth the effort. We turned our thoughts to looking for a place to stay that night. Suddenly, our warm feelings and composure came to an abrupt halt as our rental car sputtered, stalled and stopped. We did not know then that this emergency situation would lead to one of our most cherished musical adventures.

Vignette   Dylan Thomas   1914 - 1953

Dylan Thomas never mastered Welsh but many would say that he created his own music in his use of the English language. His sonorous lines, rich in rhythm, symbolism and imagery were well-crafted, lyrical and romantic with an occasional touch of the primitive. They propelled him into recognition as one of the major poets of the twentieth century. His ear was finely tuned to sound and music. The sounds of words themselves had great meaning for him. In fact, he believed that poetry is best read aloud. He became equally famous for his readings of his own work, especially to American audiences, which delighted in his poetry and stories. Some of his poetry can be difficult to understand.

Dylan Marlais Thomas was born on October 27, 1914 and died in New York City on November 9, 1953. In his short life of thirty-nine years, he produced collections of poems, short stories and film and radio scripts, the most famous of which is *Under Milk Wood.*

Life was not completely bleak during childhood, as a reader of *A Child's Christmas in Wales* discovers. In order to find work he had to move away as a young man. Probably Dylan's happiest years came later when he was able to leave London and Oxford. It's easy to imagine the joy he felt to be back again in Wales. To be in Laugharne, a small village on the sea; to live in the Boat House, surrounded by water, almost moored to the shore like a ship; to hear again the Welsh language—all of these were beneficent influences that led to the most productive period of his life. He called their new home, "this place I love." It was made possible by the purchase of the Boat House by a patron, Margaret Taylor, whom he thanked with these words, "You have given me my life, and now I am going to live it."

The Boat House, anchored to a cliff, had a penetrating dampness that in wintertime, especially, was detrimental to Dylan's weak lungs. Caitlin, pregnant with their third child, set about to make the Boat House a cheerful home, and she accomplished her aim with bright rugs, family photographs and fires burning in the grate.

Life was seldom easy for Dylan or Caitlin and their three children. Most of his life Dylan endured poverty and hardships that would have thwarted a person of less creative genius.

In the latter years of his life he made three lecture tours in the United States, hoping to bolster the meager resources of his family. His deep, Welsh voice, his charm and wit made him even more popular with the public, especially college students. Dylan's extensive touring was prompted by the previous action of one of his heroes—Charles Dickens, who also undertook lecture tours in America. The two authors had much in common. Both knew poverty. Both liked to walk the city streets at night, believing they could tap into a special inspiration. Both were performers of outstanding merit. Both had most successful tours with enthusiastic audiences.

Dylan's American tours raised more money than the Thomases had ever had. Ironically, profits of the tours, although financially successful, were canceled out by taxes. Dylan had been naïve about this, never having had to pay taxes before. And in Dylan's case, his lengthy times away from his family and from Wales, proved disastrous to his health. His lifelong but controlled habit of pub-drinking with friends escalated into a drinking problem that eventually took his life.

Today visitors from all over the world come to see the Boat House and the "Garage," Dylan's thinking place. Some may have a simple hope as they view the stark surroundings and the encircling sea. Perhaps they will catch something of the spirit that stoked Dylan's creative powers. Certainly the place exudes something extraordinary. Many people can also identify with his words, "My poetry is the record of my individual struggle from darkness toward some measure of light."

Thinking Place

The greatest boon to Dylan was the creation of his Thinking Place. It was originally a storage house, a small, one-room space that overlooked the Boat House below. The hut clings to the edge of the wind-swept cliff. It's no wonder that he viewed it as "the long-tongued room, his slant, rocking house." The windows look out on both the estuary and the bay. He called the simple shed "this water and tree room on the cliff." He was home, appropriately surrounded by water since the name "Dylan" means "sea." Here for five hours every afternoon, he continued to work on *Under Milk Wood*, his "play for voices," written for radio. Here he also completed other material for radio broadcasts and several poems.

Today a visitor can look through a window and see the inside of Dylan's thinking place, presumably kept just as he left it with untidy bits of crumpled paper, a small rough bookcase haphazardly filled with books, clippings and a few pictures on the walls, a single wooden table by the window, four straight-backed chairs, a small cast iron stove and a faded rug.

Lagniappe and Serendipity   Wales

Our misadventure, the breakdown of our rental car in Laugharne, was followed by one of our richest experiences! The very courteous and efficient AA roadside emergency technician repaired our car promptly, and then led us to a nearby village to the Golden Grove Arms, a picture book version of a rural, village inn. The brochure described the surrounding towns and villages with their interesting and melodious Welsh names: "situated 7 miles from the county town of Carmathen and about 6 miles from the delightful town of Llandeilo. It is within easy reach of historic Dryslwyn, Dinefwr and Carreg Cenne Castles, conveniently situated for visiting the West Wales coastal resorts: Llansthephan, Laugharne, Pendine, Amroth, Saundersfoot and Tenby."

We settled into our chairs in the substantial, timbered dining room of the Inn, ready to enjoy the warmth of the roaring fire in the huge fireplace and a good meal. Our waitress said if we liked music we should go right away across the highway to the local elementary school's annual singing and harp music concert. We would not have time to eat very much, since the program would start very soon. We gulped down coffee/tea and a serving of sticky toffee pudding and headed across the street. Welsh music, especially men's choruses, had long been an interest of ours. What an unforgettable musical evening: young children and teenagers singing solos, duets and joining in choruses; all of it frequently accompanied by harp music and other instruments!

The guest star for that night was an adult, a baritone soloist who was introduced as the winner of last year's National Eisteddford, an annual event when hundreds of singers, dozens of village choruses and many, many harps are brought together in a giant music festival and fair. (This introduction led us to attend an Eisteddfod Festival a year or two later—a golden experience.) Before singing, the baritone spoke,"I will speak to you first in English, but when I sing, it will be in the language of heaven—Welsh!"

When we returned to the Inn the dining room was closed, and there wasn't any sticky toffee pudding. Nevertheless, we felt quite satisfied after our bountiful banquet of joyful music and warm, Welsh fellowship—lagniappe after a most fulfilling day.

In case we have made you hungry, here is a recipe for Sticky Toffee Pudding from *Golden Grove Arms, Ann and Paul Jaycock, Proprietors, Llanarthne, Nr. Carmarthen Dyfed, SA32 8JU1:*

Sticky Toffee Pudding

1 lb. (4 cups) self rising flour
3 teaspoonfuls baking soda
1 lb. (2 cups) castor (granulated) sugar

1 lb (4 sticks) melted butter
6 eggs
2 teaspoons vanilla essence (extract)
10 oz. chopped dates covered with 3 1/4 cup boiling water

Method:
Heat oven to 350 degrees.
Grease a 10- inch pan or pudding basin. Chop the dates fine.
Place in a small bowl and add the boiling water; set aside.

1. Cream sugar and butter.
2. Add eggs, beaten until light-colored.
3. Add vanilla.
4. Sift flour with 3 teaspoons baking soda.
5. Mix with butter and eggs.
6. Add dates, and water mixture. Blend well. Pour into pan.
8. Cook for 35-40 minutes or until pudding is firm on top.

Toffee Sauce
7 ounces soft brown sugar (14 T)
1 pint double cream (whipping cream)
4 1/2 ounces melted butter (9 T)

Combine all ingredients in a boiler and heat to boiling, constantly stirring. Cook over medium low heat until thickened, about 7-10 minutes. Spoon about 1/3 cup of the sauce over the pudding, spreading evenly on top. In a pre-heated broiler, heat sauce-covered pudding until sauce begins to bubble for about 1 minute. Careful! It will burn quickly. Serve in bowls, topping each serving with toffee sauce. Serve with a pitcher of double cream (whipping cream), beaten stiff. Alternatively, a pitcher of the sauce may also be passed, so that each person may measure his own sauce. Very rich. Very good!

Photographic credits: Picture of Dylan Thomas is from the Jeff Towns collection

Dylan Thomas

Dylan Thomas

"Each day since coming into this place I love and where I want to live and where I can work and where I have started work (my own) already I have been saying to my contemptible self. This is it: the place, the house, the workroom, the time."

Interior of Dylan's writing hut

Thinking Places

of

Creative People

in

America

Thomas Alva Edison

1847 – 1931

Glenmont, the Edisons' Home in West Orange New Jersey; and Edison sitting at his "Thought Bench" in a room adjacent to his bedroom where he sometimes secluded himself over the weekend in a "visionary fugue state" until he completed elaborate new plans.

Thomas Edison

"There is no substitute for hard work."

-Edison

"Genius is one percent inspiration and ninety-nine percent perspiration."

-Edison

Journey   West Orange and Fort Myers

We had visited the Edison laboratory and home in West Orange, New Jersey long before we thought about thinking places. At the time, we learned that no one has contributed more to the world in making available energy, light and sound. We wanted to know more about the man responsible.

At the Edison National Historic Site this enclave "epitomizes the schism in Edison's psyche." On the one hand is the long, brick-walled machine shop with its huge engines and machines, ponderous and heavy-duty parts of Edison's enterprises. Attached to it is the essential stock room with its hundreds of pigeon holes and drawers from floor to ceiling.

On the other hand, consider the building where the library is located. The walls are forty feet high. The cathedral-like windows give light to the large room with its pine-paneled ceilings and parquet floors. The three levels of book-lined shelves, with railings, encircle the room, and a staircase connects all levels. A large clock centers the mantel over the open fireplace. A large pipe organ at one end is an imposing feature.

Visitors to the Edison Center may see, as we did, the first motion picture production studio in America, called the Kinetographic Theatre, or informally, "The Black Maria." It is an oblong, irregularly shaped building, some fifty feet long. A pivoting top allows natural light into the area. Painted black, it was probably very hot during filming in warm weather, many years ago.

Nearby in West Orange is the Edisons' home, a Victorian mansion with Queen Anne architecture. Edison bought it furnished just before he married Mina. Today the house is open for tours.

We also visited the Thomas Edison Winter Estate, which is operated and maintained by the City of Fort Myers, Florida. The two spacious houses, with wide verandahs, are furnished as they were when Mina and Tom lived there in the winter. One may visit the reconstructed laboratory, where Edison had worked on synthesizing rubber from goldenrod plants. Other interesting features are the fourteen acres of landscaped grounds, the still-operative swimming pool, the extensive Botanical Gardens and the interesting Edison Museum, containing a large collection of Edison's inventions and his own automobiles. Edison's close friend, Henry Ford, had an estate nearby, now open to visitors.

Journeys with Edison to West Orange and Fort Myers are journeys to yesteryear, and a most significant era when light and sound were first activated by the hard work and genius of the "Wizard of Menlo Park."

Vignette   Thomas Alva Edison   1847-1931

Many have called him "The greatest inventor who ever lived," and during his lifetime he was honored by many nations in addition to his own. This giant of a man was once the same little boy whose teacher sent him home because he was "addled" and incapable of learning. What a strange judgment about a genius who never stopped learning. At age eighty, Edison took up the study of botany. He studied over 17,000 different plants in an effort to synthesize rubber. He successfully did it with goldenrod within the four years remaining before his death at age eighty-four.

By the end of his life, Edison owned 1,328 patents for a list of inventions and discoveries that fill many pages. With only a third grade education, he relied on his native intelligence, the thousands of books and papers he researched and the 2,500 notebooks that he kept. He was unhampered by barriers that said, "It can't be done." or "It never has been done." One of Edison's greatest natural gifts was curiosity, coupled with ingenuity, patience and perseverance. "Interested in every-thing," he wrote on a business card when he first visited Luther Burbank. He also said, "Genius is one per cent inspiration, ninety-nine per cent perspiration. Yes sir, it's mostly hard work."

Edison was indeed super-intelligent, but, like most human beings, he had his own eccentricities. He was a talented entre-preneur and great promoter, but sometimes he was a poor businessman, frequently investing more in an investigation than a finished invention would pay off. He was habitually short of cash. In fact, he often had trouble paying his debts. He believed that we sleep too much. He existed on four or five hours of sleep a night. Many times he slept on the desk at the lab with books as his pillow. He could wear a formal top hat if he had to, but most of the time he wore a suit that was badly rumpled and stained with chemicals. He replaced his suits by ordering them through the mail, according to measurements on file. He was his own barber. Quite modest, he said once, "I have tried a million schemes that will not work. I know everything that is not good. I work by elimination."

Edison had a very understanding mother. Perhaps his mother, Nancy, was his first reason for success. In spite of the teacher's "addled" label, Edison's mother recognized his abilities. She taught him at home and gave him many books to read, books that would be considered too advanced for a child today. Besides the Bible and Shakespeare, she assigned Gibbons' *Decline and Fall of the Roman Empire*, Sears' *History of the World* and Paine's *Age of Reason*. For the remainder of his life, Edison was a voracious reader. His favorite book of all the many that Nancy had given him was *A School Compendium of Natural and*

Experimental Philosophy. His abiding interest became chemistry. Strange to say, he was not proficient in math.

At twelve, he was out of school and eager to make money to pay for the chemical elements he was collecting. He became a "candy butcher" on a train. He not only sold candy and other sundries as he walked down the aisle, but he peddled fresh vegetables to housewives along the route. Hiring other boys, he also set up a shop for periodicals, but he had employee troubles and had to close it. The train was his main business address. In an empty baggage car he set up his own laboratory for experiments and, with a small press, he published a newspaper, *The Weekly Herald,* the first newspaper ever printed on a moving train. When the train had long breaks in its schedule, Edison went to the public library and spent his time reading.

An accident propelled his career forward. A small chemical spill caused a fire in the baggage car, and according to legend, Edison and his lab were thrown off the train, resulting in an injury that led, not only to a new occupation, but also to his lifelong deafness. Not true, Edison said. The trainman actually saved his life, he said, by pulling him up by the ears when he was falling from the moving train. Edison was partially deaf from early childhood, which may explain why he did not do well in school. His disability worsened through the years, but his wife, Mina, would sit by him and tap on his knee a Morse code version of conversations and banquet remarks that he could not hear. Strange to say, his favorite invention was connected with sound–the phonograph. Edison explained that he could hear through his skull and through his teeth. He sometimes "bit" the piano to hear the tones. Later when he auditioned singers to record on his records, he determined that a "straight" voice sounded better for recording than one with a tremolo.

When he was fifteen, Edison snatched a young boy from the path of an oncoming train. In gratitude for his saving the life of his son, the father taught Edison telegraphy. This ability supported Edison until he was ready to set up his first lab.

How he combined his knowledge with ingenuity and resourcefulness was an early secret of his success as both an entrepreneur and an inventor. After the Battle of Shiloh during the Civil War, Edison persuaded a telegraph operator to wire the news of the battle to railroad stations all down the line. Knowing readers would be eager for background news, Edison bought on credit 1500 newspapers instead of the usual 100 that he bought for resale from the train. At each stop, he increased the price of the newspaper and still sold every one. He was only fifteen.

The next six years, he moved about from job to job. He was frequently hungry, always shabbily dressed, and poor, or worse, broke. In New York, he set himself up as an inventor and was hired by Western Union. He invented an improvement for the telegraph, and Western Union paid him eight times more than he had planned to ask. With capital in hand, he moved to Newark and assembled a team of like-minded men. A year later he was able to marry pretty Mary Stilwell.

In 1876, he moved his lab from Newark to Menlo Park, New Jersey, where he set up the first laboratory for organized industrial research. Soon he would be called "The Wizard of Menlo Park." British newspapers referred to this lab as "the inventions factory." As mentioned previously, it did have some unusual features—at one end was a pipe organ, which Edison would occasionally play with two fingers. The lab also featured a library that occupied two levels and contained 10,000 books. He started a habit of requesting every publication on a subject before he started experimentation. Two pets were part of the scene—a St. Bernard dog and a raccoon that spent his time fruitlessly trying to pick up mercury droplets.

Two of his personal characteristics served him well during this period. Edison was an optimist who liked to look on the bright side of things, and he believed in work. His employees liked his winning ways and manners. No one could complain about the workload because Edison worked harder than anyone else. He enjoyed the six day, ten hours plus a day work-week, which sometimes was longer than that. He probably resented having to sleep, but he could sleep anywhere and did, soundly.

His first invention was patented as the "Electrical Vote Recorder" for political bodies. The device had one problem—the politicians didn't want it, so Edison moved on to something else.

In 1884, his first wife, Mary, died of a probable brain tumor. They had one daughter and two sons. Two years later, he married Mina Miller, whose father, Lewis Miller, had improved on the agricultural reaper and had co-founded Chautauqua Institution, where the Edisons would spend many happy summers. They spent their honeymoon at a winter home Edison owned in Fort Myers, Florida. Tropical and exotic flowers and trees surrounded the two charming Victorian houses joined together. Its wood had been precut and shipped from New England. The grounds soon sported a separate building, a laboratory. Here Edison would later conduct his experiments on the use of golden rod in the synthesizing of rubber. Here he built the first swimming pool in Florida. It was built of Edison Portland cement and has never had a leak. Every day "on vacation" Edison read several newspapers, an easy feat for him since he had taught himself speed reading.

The number of his inventions kept increasing. He made improvements on Bell's telephone to make it more practical. Other inventions followed: the automatic telegraph; the "electric pen" (mimeograph); the microphone; the phonograph; the incandescent electric light; the "Edison effect," the fundamental principle of the modern science of electronics; the first commercial, central electric power station; the motion picture camera and projector; the first movie studio (called "black Maria"); an iron ore concentrating plant; the first electric semaphore signal; the first fluorescent electric lamp; the alkaline storage battery; the kinetophone for talking motion pictures; safety lanterns for miners; the process for the manufacture of synthetic carbolic acid, in short supply due to World War I; the manufacture of an improved cement, with pre-fabricated houses to follow. This is only a partial list.

Edison chose not to patent one of his important inventions. In experimenting with the X-ray discovered by Roentgen, he developed the fluoroscope. Because of its significance in the practice of medicine, he chose to leave it in the public domain. He received many requests to invent a solution to deafness. He never did. He may have had a special reason. He once said, "In my isolation (insulation would be a better term), I have time to think things out. Most nerve strain of our modern life, I fancy, comes to us through our ears."

Then came December 9, 1914! On that date his plant at West Orange burned. Five buildings were destroyed; seven others were gutted. The loss (uninsured) was five million dollars. Edison's comment was typical. "No one is ever too old to make a fresh start." He was sixty-seven at the time. Within thirty-six hours, the rebuilding began.

Honors piled upon honors. He was given a special Congressional Medal in 1928, and the following year, President Hoover and other world leaders honored him on the fiftieth anniversary of the incandescent lamp. From France he received the Legion d'Honneur, followed by the Commander of Honor. At the Centennial Exposition in Paris, his exhibits took up one-third of the space allotted to the United States.

At the request of Secretary of the Navy Josephus Daniels, he became President of the Naval Consulting Board. There is a long list of his honors. One of his pleasures, besides his work and devotion to his wife, Mina, was his long friendship with Henry Ford, Harvey Firestone and naturalist, John Burroughs. The foursome enjoyed camping trips and, on occasion, took their wives along.

Much more could be written about Thomas Alva Edison. Henry Ford probably said it best: "To find a man who has not benefitted by Edison and who is not in debt to him, it would be necessary to go deep into the jungle. I hold him to be our greatest American."

Thinking Place

Thomas Edison's work habits validate the concept of the "thinking place." In his labs he had a moveable thinking place, which he moved from one of his several labs to the next one. It was a small, simple, two-drawer worktable. Its placement was significant. It never faced outward in view of other men working. Instead it was placed so that it would face the wall. Edison did not like distractions. On the other hand, he also placed his routine working desk in the middle of the huge library-laboratory, in the center of activities. His deafness was an asset in his doing his thinking at work.

At home in Glenmont, the second floor living room, a few steps away from the master bedroom, was often used as a family room for quiet activities. However, in the evenings this became Edison's "favorite retreat, his 'place of quiet repose' where he sat at his 'thought bench'". When Edison was thinking of the cement company, according to Baldwin, he "entered one of his renowned visionary fugue states, secluding himself at Glenmont over a week-end and emerging with a fifty-page handwritten proposal." At Glenmont, Edison, no doubt sat on his "thought bench" a good part of the time that weekend.

When Edison went fishing with his associates, which was probably not very often, he fished without baiting his hook. His companions respected his silence and his concentration. This respectful attitude of family and associates also applied at other times when Edison chose certain chairs or places when he wanted to think.

Lagniappe   Chautauqua

Why something extra in Chautauqua? To some, what is Chautauqua and where is it? To others, what does it have to do with Thomas Alva Edison? Chautauqua Lake is located sixty miles south of Buffalo, New York. Chautauqua Institution on the lake is in a gated town that has grown from its modest camp-like beginnings in 1874 to its present status as a premier center for learning, moral and religious studies, music, dance, drama, recreation and family gathering—just the kind of place that the ever inquisitive Edison would have liked—and did.

Many of the present, colorful, charming Victorian cottages, larger houses, inns and hotels were built before 1900. The five-thousand seat open-air but roofed amphitheater, constructed in 1896, still serves as the nerve center of the many lectures, educational, musical and entertainment programs during the nine-week schedule each summer.

According to Jeffrey Simpson and others, in 1878, four years after the Chautauqua Assembly had started, the oldest continuous book club in America had its beginning—the Chautauqua Learning and Science Circle (CLSC). The Co-Founder of Chautauqua, Reverend John Heyle Vincent stated the purpose of CLSC was: "To promote the habit of reading and study in nature, art, science, and secular and sacred litera-ture...especially, among those whose educational advantages have been limited." Eight thousand individuals signed up for the first class which involved reading a certain number of books a year from a list for four years. By the 1920's three hundred thousand correspondents had signed up.

Reverend Vincent, a Methodist-Episcopal minister, later a bishop, was editor of *The Sunday School Gazette* with a monthly circulation of 100,000. The other Co-Founder, Lewis Miller of Akron, Ohio had made his fortune with the manufacture of a modified McCormick reaper. Miller was also interested in the popular Sunday School Movement of the day. Both had great curiosity, a belief in universal education and enthusiasm for developing avocational programs. They wanted to make it pos-sible for public school teachers to go somewhere affordable in the summertime for a learning and recreational experience, thus, strengthening Sunday School teaching. They were distrustful of the emotionally charged camp meetings, which had been pop-ular since the Great Awakening evangelism of the 1840's. Vincent and Miller stressed the lecture and discussion format. They found an existing campsite on the south shore of Chautauqua Lake, leased it at first, and then bought it for the Assembly.

With the publicity generated by *The Sunday School Gazette*, four thousand people showed up for the first day of the Assembly; over the next two weeks ten thousand had attended!

Each year the Chautauqua Assembly program grew and by 1904 over three hundred independent Chautauqua Assemblies had spread out over the U.S. (About twenty-five persist today.) Eventually, over one hundred units evolved on the independent Traveling Chautauqua Circuits, with programs made up of one-third lectures and two- thirds entertainment. This lasted through the 1920's when more sophisticated forms of entertainment developed, and the Depression occurred. The CLSC movement spread widely in its early years with Circles in over ten thousand towns and cities; a quarter of the towns had populations of five hundred or less. The CLSC is still going strong with annual meetings at Chautauqua, New York each summer.

So what does all this have to do with Thomas Alva Edison? He was born in 1847 and grew up in an era of national growth, ferment of ideas, inventions, and development of new ways of doing things. Certainly, Chautauqua and its several movements fit the pattern of these inquisitive, searching, "can do" times.

More specifically, Edison became personally related to Chautauqua when, some two years after his first wife died, he married Mina Miller of Akron. She was the daughter of Lewis Miller, Co-Founder of Chautauqua. Mina and Thomas spent many summer visits at the Miller cottage near the earliest center of activity in Chautauqua. Tom Edison was a member of CLSC, class of 1930. In fact, his class chose as its name, "The Edison Class." The first class in 1874 had called itself "The Pioneers"; other classes chose names like "Dickens," "Plymouth Rock" and "The Argonauts".

The Miller cottage with features similar to a Swiss chalet has distinctive crisscross boards on the sides and is now painted light gray. Still in excellent condition, it overlooks Miller Park, the site of the original gathering place. The Miller Cottage, renovated and revised in 1922 by Mina Miller Edison, has an illustrious history of its own. It is one of the oldest prefabricated houses in America. Its parts were shipped from Akron and assembled just in time for the summer of 1875 visit and speech by President Ulysses S. Grant. President Grant had been a long-time friend and a parishioner of Reverend Vincent in Grant's hometown of Galena, Illinois. Also, President Garfield visited the cottage in 1880. In 1966 Charles Edison, Governor of New Jersey, the Edison's son, was in attendance for the ceremonies designating the cottage as a National Historic Site.

In 1929 Chautauqua celebrated "The Festival of Light," the centennial of the birthday of Co-Founder, Lewis Miller, and the twenty-fifth anniversary of Edison's invention of the light bulb. There were performances of the Chautauqua Symphony in the amphitheater, an inaugural performance of the opera, *Martha*, and a symposium at which time questions were answered by Edison, Henry Ford and Adolph Ochs, publisher of *The New York Times*.

Through the years, Chautauqua became a platform for many personages, including Presidents William McKinley, Theodore Roosevelt, William Howard Taft and Franklin Roosevelt, who gave his famous "I Hate War" speech in the amphitheater. A partial list of speakers includes: Booker T. Washington, Edward Everett Hale, Susan P. Anthony, Julia Ward Howe, Rabbi Henry Berkowitz, Kate Douglas Wiggins, William James and Amelia Earhart.

Surely, Thomas Alva Edison was one of the most creative geniuses of all times. His life's story is awe-inspiring and, indeed, inspirational. Today, Chautauqua Institute and township, with its facinating roots and history, is one of the most charming and worthwhile spots in America. How delighted we were to realize that two of our favorite subjects, Edison and Chautauqua, are joined here by the little "Swiss chalet" overlooking Miller Park, the place where "Chautauqua" began.

Photography credits:
Pictures of Glenmont in West Orange, New Jersey; Thomas Edison at his thought bench at Glenmont; Mina and Thomas Edison; and of Seminole Lodge, the Edisons' winter home at Fort Myers, Florida are courtesy of The Edison National Historic Site, West Orange, New Jersey.

Picture of Edison's original Florida laboratory is from *Unknown Florida*, Florence Fitz, (1963)

Seminole Lodge, the Edisons' winter
home at Fort Myers, Florida

Edison's original laboratory at Fort. Myers, Florida.

Nina and Thomas Edison

Miller-Edison Cottage overlooking Miller Park at Chautauqua

Alexander Graham Bell

1847 – 1922

The Bell's summer home at Beinn Bhreagh, Nova Scotia,
Canada and his houseboat thinking place

Alexander Graham Bell

"The A.E.A. (Aerial Experiment Association) is now a thing of the past. It has made its mark upon the history of aviation and its work will live."

Bulletin

"Don't keep forever on the public road, going only where others have gone, and following one after the other like a flock of sheep. Leave the beaten path occasionally and dive into the woods. Every time you do so you will be certain to find something that you have never seen before. Of course it will be a little thing, but do not ignore it. Follow it up, explore all around it; one discovery will lead to another, and before you know it you will have something worth thinking about to occupy your mind. All really big discoveries are the results of thought."

A Valedictory Address

Journey

Some years after Alexander Graham Bell's great success with his invention of the telephone and formation of a telephone company and a research institute, he and his wife, Mabel, moved to Washington, D.C. where Bell found the summer heat most uncomfortable. They found a suitable site for building a summer home near Baddeck, Nova Scotia. This "New Scotland" was a reminder of his native land with its rugged coastline and low mountains overlooking the sea. According to local legend, Bell described his reasons for choosing this area, "I have traveled the globe. I have seen the American and Canadian Rockies, the Andes and the Alps and the highlands of Scotland, but for simple beauty, Cape Breton outrivals them all."

Later, the Bells built a magnificent home on a high place at Beinn Bhreagh (Gaelic for "beautiful mountain") located on the tip of a peninsula jutting out into the Bras d'Or, a saltwater inland lake. Here at Beinn Breagh Hall, Bell's energetic creativity and family life flourished. Locals call the house, "The Big House" and family members call it "The Point," according to Dr. Gardiner Myers, Bell's great-grandson.

But how did we get to Baddeck and Beinn Bhreagh? How did our once-in-a-lifetime experience happen? In short, Dr. Alexander Graham Bell is one of the leading characters in our and Allen Pote's musical, *Seaplane*, which includes an account of Bell's role in the history of early flight. (See chapter on Glenn Curtiss.)

Our trip to Nova Scotia was an afterthought and serendipitous. After long months of study and research, we were en route by air to Hammondsport, New York to visit Glenn Curtiss' hometown and site of the prize-winning, first pre-announced flight in America in 1908. This flight had been the brain child of Dr. Bell, Glenn Curtiss and the three other members of the Aerial Experiment Association.

During a layover in Newark, New Jersey, we noticed a posted schedule showing a flight to Halifax, Nova Scotia. Was this near Alexander Graham Bell's home? It was! And we could soon get a seat on a plane, and then drive to Baddeck. Later, we could fly back to Montreal, and then drive across the Adirondacks to Hammondsport. It was a quick–and wonderful – decision! The fall foliage proved to be spectacular, and we were to have an introduction, not only to Alexander Graham Bell's home but also, to Mark Twain's summer home and thinking place in Elmira, New York. What an accidental, serendipitous experience-to-be! What lagniappe!

We did see Beinn Bhreagh and had a most interesting visit and experience there. We met three granddaughters of Dr. Bell, including Mrs. Carol Myers. (For details see section on Lagniappe.) Beinn Bhreagh Hall is now the private property of the Bell and Grosvenor family foundation.

Before leaving Baddeck, we visited the Alexander Graham Bell National Historic Site, locally, called The Bell Museum with the tetrahedron prominent in its architecture and displays. The complex contains the largest collection of Bell artifacts, memorabilia, kites and replicas of his inventions, including the first telephone and the original, as well as a full-scale replica, of the HD-4 hydrofoil craft. Seeing these three exhibit halls was alone worth the trip to Baddeck.

Many months later, we called on Mrs. Myers in Washington, D.C to give her our progress notes and to play for her some of the songs featuring the actor's voice of Dr. Bell. When *Seaplane* finally became a reality with some of Allen Pote's greatest music, we invited Mrs. Myers' son, chemistry professor, Dr. Gardiner Myers of the University of Florida and his wife, Jane, to attend performances over several different years in Pensacola, Florida. Later, Professor Myers gave us one of our most prized possessions, a small tetrahedron unit made over a hundred years ago in his great-grandfather's lab at Beinn Bhreagh. These ten-inch wooden strips in triangular conformity became four-sided units or cells; they were covered with red silk and mounted into huge assemblages, resulting in a man-carrying kite. Dr. Bell hoped this large tetrahedron constructed "wing," assembling 3300 of these "cells," powered by Curtiss's famous motor, would solve the problem of stabilizing flight. This scheme did not work out, but the A.E.A group switched emphasis to glider-type bi-wings (which Bell had previously experimented on in the mid-1890's.) Dr. Bell provided leadership; he suggested adoption of a new idea of small wings (ailerons) between the two main wings to give lateral stability resulting in successful flight!

Actors who played the roll of Alexander Graham Bell in *Seaplane* usually wanted to read more about him in preparation. This role and learning more about the character of Dr. Bell made a profound and positive impression on them. The lyrics below for one of the actor's songs in *Seaplane* were our paraphrasing one of Bell's commencement speeches.(See Dr. Bell's original words for that speech on the introductory page of this chapter.)

"Don't just travel on the public road, Going only where others have gone.

Don't follow each other like flocks of sheep, Go the lone way on your own.

For when you seek to find a new way, to follow a thought of your own, Sometimes you must leave the beaten track, turning into the woods on your own.

As you explore you'll find something more, an idea you've never been taught. Your mind will have something worth thinking about, Discoveries are children of thought!

Don't just travel on the public road, Going only where others have gone.

Don't follow each other like flocks of sheep, Go the lone way on your own.

For when you seek to find a new way, to follow a thought of your own, Sometimes you must leave the beaten track, turning into the woods all alone."

Alexander Graham Bell, "teacher, inventor, celebrity and family man" is one of the creative persons we admire greatly. He was a kind and generous man who gave credit to those who came before him and encouragement to his contemporaries. His contributions to science and to the general welfare are immeasurable.

Vignette   Alexander Graham Bell   1847 - 1922

The telephone was not Alexander Graham Bell's favorite of his many inventions, but Bell's patent for the telephone, #1 74,465, issued on March 7, 1876, is considered one of the most valuable, if not the most valuable, patent ever issued by the U.S. Patent Office. Bell frequently referred to the telephone as a "nuisance." (He was well aware, of course, of its significance.) Bell called the photophone "the greatest invention I have ever made." It was even greater than he imagined since it was the forerunner, by a century, of the laser and fiber optics. Both the telephone and the photophone helped usher in the modern age of high-speed communication.

Bell is credited with many other inventions that helped revolutionize the way we live. The following is a partial list: desalinization of water; artificial respiration or a metal breathing jacket that was a precursor of the iron lung; a metal detector developed to locate the assassin's bullet in President Garfield; today, metal detectors are important in security concerns; the audiometer to quantify hearing loss; design of the tetrahedron, a four-sided triangular structure that provides extra strength and is a boon to architecture; an advance in sheep-breeding that resulted in multiple births of sheep; the hydrofoil, with Casey Baldwin, first advanced as an aid in detecting submarines in World War I and, for over forty years, holder of the water speed record of 70 mph.

Always ahead of his time, he anticipated future needs, so he hoped to develop solar panels, air conditioning, alternative fuels, methods to deal with air pollution and for separating salt from water. Another idea he had was to design a tape recorder and a hard and floppy disc.

"Getting into the air," his term for flying, was his fondest dream. Almost ten years before the Wrights' first manned flight in 1903, Bell predicted that the problem of aerial navigation would be solved within ten years. In 1896, Bell had witnessed the first flight of Professor Langley's unmanned, heavier than air flying machine catapulted from a boat-tower in the Potomac River. Bell later pursued his ideas about flight when he and four other younger men formed the Aerial Experiment Association or the AEA. (See chapter on Curtiss.) The dream became a reality on July 4, 1908, when Glenn Curtiss, one of the five members of the AEA, flew the June Bug to win the *Scientific American* prize for the first public, pre-announced flight by an aeroplane in America. (The Wright Brothers' flights at Kitty Hawk were the first, but there was little public viewing and no press coverage. The world was still skeptical about the meager reports of the Wrights' earlier flight.)

Important as his contribution to flight was, the telephone remains Bell's greatest achievement. The telephone was not only a most valuable patent but also one of the most contentiously fought by other inventors. There were many claimants in the field of the telephone, and later, 600 patent suits, a huge problem for Bell, with other inventors claiming precedence. The telephone itself illustrates the frequent synchronicity in the development of a new idea. (See another example in the life of Charles Darwin.) Thomas Edison was one of many who had been working on similar devices; later, Bell and Edison jointly founded the Oriental Telephone Company. It is generally conceded that Bell, along with Thomas Watson, not only developed the idea for the telephone but also brought it to fruition as a practical, workable invention. In time, others made improvements. The general acceptance of the "decibel," one tenth of a bel, proposed by someone else, as a measurement of sound, further emphasizes Bell's merited recognition.

Bell was a young man of twenty-nine when he invented the telephone. Perhaps our seeing so many pictures of the older Bell with white hair and beard prevents our realizing this. How did he do it? Certainly, he had a large store of persistence, observation, creativity and time spent in meditation and thinking about matters that interested him. In addition, Bell was blessed with an exceptional family that helped propel him on his distinguished career. His father, grandfather and uncle before him were teachers of correct speech and elocution. His father, known worldwide for his writings, authored *The Standard Elocutionist*, which had 168 printings.

George Bernard Shaw in his play, *Pygmalion*, modeled a character, Professor Higgins, after Bell's father and explained who Melville Bell was, in his preface to the play. Melville's most famous treatise was *Visible Speech* in which every sound made by the lips, mouth, tongue and throat could be represented visually and could be applied to any language. Furthermore, the system could be helpful to teach the deaf to speak. (Deaf people often never learned or forgot how to speak after years of silence.) Deaf mutes, using their eyesight, could be taught to articulate words by watching the motions of others' lips.

The young Graham Bell also became a dedicated teacher of speech, utilizing his father's method. Graham's mother was partially deaf, using an ear trumpet for years. This was one of the reasons he became interested in the science of acoustics while he was still in Scotland. All of this was the background for Graham Bell's interest in teaching the deaf to speak and, eventually, experimenting with devices to transmit sounds of the voice, evolving as the telephone!

How did Graham Bell, later known as Aleck, get from Edinburgh, then London and finally to Brantford, a small town in the rolling hills of Ontario, Canada? (Brantford is near Hamilton, Ontario and Buffalo, New York.) After the tragic deaths of two of Bell's brothers due to tuberculosis, the family immigrated to Canada to remove Graham from the polluted air of industrialized Britain. They knew friends in the area and decided to settle at Tutila Heights, a few miles outside of Brantford. Melville Bell was asked to speak to teachers of the deaf in Boston, Massachusetts. Later, when asked to accept a position there, he suggested that his son take his place. Graham Bell was a great success, lecturing and tutoring the deaf, as well as teaching classes at Boston University. While in Boston, and at Brantford, Graham had resumed his acoustic experiments and his work on a device he called a harmonic or multiple telegraph, for sending more than one message over a wire at a time.

Graham came home to Brantford in the summertime and for vacations. He stayed in the same downstairs bedroom which one may visit today, as we did. Here he continued his experiments at Tutila Heights. In the parlor he would sit at the piano for long periods of time with his tuning fork, singing a single note with his foot on the piano pedal while listening for vibrations of the corresponding strings. He continued to think about his device. Eventually, he left Brantford with formulated plans, which would lead to a patent on the telephone. A plaque at the home site states, "In this home, Alexander Graham Bell conceived the idea of the telephone in July, 1874."

While in Brantford, Graham had contact with many of the Mohawk Indians in the area. He spent time with them, learning their customs and studying their language with the Visible Speech System. The Mohawks had high regard for Bell and made him an honorary Mohawk. They presented him with a tribal outfit and taught him their war dance. Later, reportedly, when Bell was happy with good news, he would do a little Mohawk dance and war whoop!

Fate had another deaf person in mind for Bell—his future wife, Mabel Hubbard, who became his sweetheart and partner for life. Mabel had been deaf since a febrile illness at age six. She became Bell's student at the Boston School for the Deaf. Later, when she was seventeen and Bell was twenty-eight, he realized that he was desperately in love with her–in a proper, Victorian way. Counseled by her mother to wait for six months, Bell agreed, but they became engaged on Thanksgiving Day, 1875, her eighteenth birthday. Graham, or Aleck as she called him, was ten years older than she. Her father, Gardiner Greene Hubbard, was a distinguished attorney of Boston and later of Washington, D.C. He encouraged Graham and provided some financial backing for Bell's experimentation, as well as help with later patent disputes. Mr. Hubbard was a founder and first president of the National Geographic Society in Washington, D.C.

Bell's research led him to "think outside the box" or, as he said, "Leave the beaten paths occasionally and dive into the woods." In his teaching deaf students, he used a metal device, a phonoautograph, which responded to voice vibrations and recorded undulations on a smoked glass. An audiologist in Boston suggested that Bell use instead a human (cadaver) eardrum, attaching a stylus to the eardrum (anvil) to make the same type of recordings. This led to Bell's constructing a device in which sounds of a voice caused vibration of a diaphragm; when adjacent to an electro-magnet, movements of the diaphragm produced undulating currents. These electrical signals transmitted by wire to another similar device reproduced sounds of the voice – a telephone.

Bell continued his work at his home in Boston and, on March 19, 1876, made the famous, first successful call to his assistant in the basement, saying into the device, "Mr. Watson, come here, I want to see you!" Excitedly, Watson answered by coming up from the basement to Bell's room! Possibly, Bell did a little Mohawk dance and war whoop! Bell introduced the telephone to the world at the International Centennial Exposition in

Philadelphia in 1876, and a telephone company was organized with the   help of Mr. Hubbard and others. When Mabel and Bell were married in 1877, Aleck's wedding presents to Mabel were a pearl cross and 1,497 shares of Bell Telephone stock. He kept ten shares for himself. When Aleck and Mabel traveled widely soon afterwards, they discovered that Bell had become famous. They lived a year in London with Bell helping to establish a telephone company, then moved to Washington, D.C. where the company was based.

The Bells did not become immediately wealthy, but in time, they were more than comfortably fixed. They held forth in a society that was more scientific than social. They enjoyed the company of associates at the Smithsonian Institute. Bell found the humidity in Washington stifling in the summertime and the continuing patent disputes a terrible burden. However, he never lost a patent case, due in part to his meticulous note-taking as he experimented.

They searched for a suitable site for a summer home and decided on Baddeck, Nova Scotia. At the Bells' magnificent summer home, the climate was bracing and, as Mabel desired, their two girls could play in "trousers". They named the large, Victorian house, Beinn Bhreagh Hall. From its high promontory, it overlooked surrounding waters below and a primeval forest. Here they raised their two daughters. Their infant son, Edward, had died of breathing problems. In response to this tragedy, Bell invented the vacuum jacket, a device put into use many years later. At Beinn Bhreagh, a sheep was pulled unconscious from the water. The sheep was revived after he was fitted with the jacket.

Life was pleasant in Nova Scotia. Mabel relieved Aleck of all the practical considerations in running a household and in raising a family. Both became interested in the Montessori method of teaching. Bell believed in a method that "brought forth from the student rather than pouring in." Mabel later provided funds to start the program in Washington and became president of the Montessori Educational Association.

In the last ten years of his life, Bell remained as busy and involved as ever. Since the 1870's, he had been an advocate of women's rights, including the right to vote. He was pleased to discover that women made better telephone operators than men.

He named, described, and was concerned about the "greenhouse effect." He believed in equal rights for all races. One of his closest associates was Charles Thomson, their African-American butler, who passed up the opportunity to be a steward at the White House in order to stay with the Bells. According to Thomson, Bell would go anywhere and speak anywhere to help the hard of hearing. Bell was also concerned that "we are spend-thrifts in the matter of fuel...we can take coal out of a mine but we can never put it back. What shall we do when we have no more coal or oil?" He experimented with solar energy. He served as president of the National Geographic Society and helped make it more successful with a change in the format of the magazine more favorable to the general reader. He was a founder of the Cosmos Club in Washington. New ideas continued to come and Bell nourished his long-time habits of inquiry and learning.

At night, he would take off from his laboratory work to play the piano for his children and grandchildren to sing. Mabel would stand with her hands on the piano, feeling the vibrations to catch the rhythm, so that she too could join in. Aleck's rich baritone voice would lead the group. He probably did not even remember that in his youth he had planned to become a concert pianist. He demonstrated the well-known fact that a genius frequently has multiple talents.

Bell did not like controversy and was always the peacemaker. Once, inadvertently, he invited two famous scientists with known opposing views, to visit his home, Beinn Bhreagh, at the same time. Dr. Samuel Langley, honored Secretary of the Smithsonian Institute, and close friend of Bell, had launched in 1896 a heavier-than-air, unmanned "aerodrome" and was planning a manned flight just before the time of the Wrights' successful flight in 1903. His nemesis, Dr. Simon Newcomb, internationally famous as a mathematician and physicist, had published his "proof" that man could never fly. Both men were contentious and disagreed on every subject. Bell seized the opportunity to bring some levity to the occasion when

Langley asserted that a cat, held in any position before dropping him, would always land on his feet. Newcomb strongly disagreed, saying that cats would need a reference point to touch in order to right themselves. Bell asked Charles Thomson to round up some of the twelve or so cats around Beinn Bhreagh. Three of the world's most eminent scientists spent the rest of the late afternoon dropping cats off the porch to a mattress and cushions ten feet below. Dr. Langley was right about cats–and, later, about predicting man's ability to fly! His own manned aeroplane crashed accidentally on take-off, shortly before the Wrights' first flight. Ironically, the catapult device, similar to the one which had successfully launched Langley's un-manned flight in 1896, possibly was faulty or snagged the aeroplane. Many years later, Glenn Curtiss reassembled the Langley plane and with modifications, including additions of pontoons, the Langley plane did, indeed, fly a short distance.

After a gradual decline in health, Alexander Graham Bell died in his sleep of anemia and kidney failure on August 2, 1922 at Beinn Bhreagh. He was buried in a clearing on the highest point of his beautiful mountain, a site he had chosen. Many attended his funeral service. His daughter, Daisy, described the details. The American and British flags at each side were at half–mast on short poles. The wooden coffin, built by his co-workers, was followed by a procession of thirty men working at Beinn Bhreagh. One simple wreath of laurel, wheat sheaves and pink roses was placed on his coffin. A few verses were read from the 90th Psalm. "Bringing in the Sheaves" and "Crossing the Bar" were sung. Passages from Robert Louis Stevenson's "Requiem," Longfellow's "Psalm of Life," and "The Lord's Prayer" were read.

Although born in Scotland, his epitaph proudly proclaimed his American citizenship. Mabel died of cancer some five months later on January 3, 1923. Her ashes were placed in the grave beside him.

Bell, from his earliest years, had been committed to teaching, investigation and learning. "Self-education is a life long affair," he once said. "There cannot be mental atrophy in any person who continues to observe, to remember what he observes, and to

seek answers for his unceasing hows and whys about things."
To this driving force in his life was added humility, respect for
all people, generosity and kindness.

Thinking Places

Alexander Graham Bell was always thinking of new and
practical ways to solve everyday problems. He put thinking and
theory into action. Also he kept looking for better thinking
places wherever he found himself. At his parents' home at Tutila
Heights near Brantford, Ontario, Bell did much thinking at his
desk and by the river below the house. A tree with a hollowed
out area had fallen over the river. Graham nailed boards in the
hollow area and placed a chair on the "flooring" where he
would sit for hours in what he called his "dreaming place."

In Washington, D.C. his Scottish background led to his
physical intolerance of the hot, muggy weather in the summertime. He and Mabel had built one of the first private swimming pools in Washington. Bell decided that an underground
room would be a cooler thinking place than anywhere else. He
had the pool drained, and with a top over it, he set up his office
in the deep end of the former pool. It must have been a sight to
see him dictating to one of his secretaries in this "subterranean"
room.

Later he built a canvas tank in the attic of his home and had
it filled with ice. A canvas "windpipe" extended to his study,
bringing cool air to his get-away place in Washington. A better
solution came when the Bells built Beinn Breagh, in cool Nova
Scotia, where they spent their summers. Bell was supremely
happy in his spacious home and grounds. He and his family
thrived in the pleasant weather and beauty of this special place.
As related by Dr. Gardiner Myers, Bell's laboratories and
warehouse were near his home, and the Kite House and kite-
flying meadow were also nearby in a clearing on the mountain.
His principal office was in the Kite House. He was experi-

menting and thinking all the time in all of these places. He kept an extensive series of notebooks, which he called his "thought books." He was obsessive about recording every idea and observation.

The Bell's houseboat, *The Mabel of Beinn Bhreagh*, brought a great deal of pleasure to the family. They explored the waters and coastline of the Bras d'Or Lakes, often on overnight excursions. Eventually, the boat was no longer seaworthy, and it was put on blocks on the beach at quite a distance from Beinn Bhreagh Hall. Bell often used the docked houseboat as an office. Like so many creative persons, Bell needed a place to get away, and to escape the interruptions and busy life of the family, particularly on week-ends.

Bell often retreated, usually alone, to the houseboat, "his place devoted especially to thinking." At those times the only people allowed on the houseboat were Mabel, who would often show up for lunch, or his trusted friend and employee, Charles Thomson. According to Dr. Myers, the houseboat was, indeed, "a do-not-disturb, weekend thinking place."

The boat had an innovative twin hull, allowing a trap door opening from the inside of the boat to the water below. An armchair placed near the trap door made it convenient to do a little fishing and thinking at the same time!

Lagniappe

The road was dark under the overhanging trees. It curved upward toward the house, and we caught our breath. The house was huge. A Victorian summer home with different rooflines, including turrets, seemed to look down at us disdainfully from the height of its three storeys. Our previous elation at being admitted to the wooden fortress was suddenly diminished. Had we done the right thing to telephone for permission to come?

Our explanation for coming was quite simple and straightforward. "We are writing the libretto for a musical about early flight. Dr. Alexander Graham Bell has an important role in the musical, which is named *Seaplane*. We want to convey his personality correctly. May we come for an interview for perhaps, thirty minutes?"

We did not even know whom we would see. Someone had told us that Bell's granddaughters might be visiting Beinn Bhreagh. We wondered who had given us permission to come. When the front door opened, we received our answer. A member of the Bell staff met us, asked us to come in and explained that she had asked the granddaughters if we might come. As she led the way, we passed an enormous stuffed bear, standing upright in the hall. We walked into a comfortably furnished, hospitable room. Three older ladies were sitting across from each other in a triangle. We learned that they were Dr. Mabel Grosvenor, a retired pediatrician, living in Washington, D.C., Mrs. Carol Myers living in Miami and Washington and Mrs. Barbara Fairchild, also from Florida. We guessed that two were in their late seventies or eighties; one was close to ninety. All were as warm and gracious as we imagined that Dr. Bell would have been. We would remember their reassuring smiles as Charles Thomson had remembered the famous Bell handshake. (We had read *Alexander Graham Bell* by Edwin S. Grosvenor and Morgan Wesson who quoted Thomson, the Bell's butler and good friend, "Extending his hand with a genial smile, he shook my hand as if he had known me for years. During the entire eighteen years of my life, up to that time, I had never felt such a handshake. It electrified my whole being. I loved Mr. Bell from that moment, and if I had left that house that day never to see him again, I would never have forgotten that handshake."

Once they understood our mission, his granddaughters started reminiscing. They talked about musical evenings and their grandfather's playing the piano, his wonderful voice, the vibrancy and electricity in the air when he walked into the room. They said he was very kind and gentle and always interested in every person, no matter what their age or position. (These words were quite similar to words Helen Keller used when dedicating her autobiography to Dr. Bell.) They spoke of the strength of their grandmother, Mabel, and how as children, they were unaware that she was deaf because she was so adept at communicating. They mentioned how they knew not to be loud and wake their grandfather while he was sleeping in the morning. They remembered gatherings of people on the lawn. They said their grandfather's favorite dessert was floating island. They kept emphasizing the kindness of their grandfather and how he could concentrate his attention on one person. They identified pictures and mementos. Some of the travel souvenirs in the room, including a boomerang and fancy stirrups from South America or Spain had been collected by Gilbert and Elsie Bell Grosvenor. We assumed that Beinn Bhreagh had been kept much as it was when Dr. and Mrs. Bell had lived there.

When we told them that we would be staying at the Telegraph House Inn, Mrs. Myers excused herself to make a telephone call. When she returned, she said that she had called Telegraph House and asked them to put us in Room #1, where her grandparents had stayed on their first trip to Baddeck,. (We were more than pleased when the hotel complied with her request.)

When we rose to leave, the Bell granddaughters said good-bye to us as if we were long-time friends. And so we regard them in our memory of that day. Mrs. Myers offered to take us to the gravesite. She drove us to the highest point of Beinn Bhreagh to the spot where the Bells are buried. The view was magnificent. One could see for miles, and the setting was peaceful, even joyful to us, as we became mindful of two lives so wonderfully lived.

When we had said our thanks and good-byes to the ladies, little did we know that we would later come in contact with some of their family. Mrs. Myers' son, Dr. Gardiner Myers, professor of chemistry at the University of Florida and his wife, Jane, came twice to see the finished *Seaplane* in Pensacola. Could we have asked for any more lagniappe than our time at Beinn Bhreagh with three charming ladies? And what a great experience, culminating with a visit to the beautiful setting of the gravesites of Aleck and Mabel Bell, two people whom we had come to know better and to admire for their warm, human qualities.

We do not have the precise Bell family recipe for Dr. Bell's favorite dessert but here is our Alexander family recipe:

Floating Island

Beat until stiff 3 egg whites, slowly adding 3 T sugar and a pinch of salt. In a double boiler heat 1 pint of milk. Gradually drop egg white mixture by spoonful into heated milk. Poach these meringues on both sides, then carefully lift them onto a platter. Add any milk from meringues left in the platter to the remaining 1 pint of milk.

Beat 3 egg yolks with ½ c sugar and gradually add to heated milk. Cook this custard mixture over low heat until the mixture coats a spoon. Add ½ t each of vanilla and lemon flavoring. When all is chilled, place meringues in a glass bowl and pour the custard gently over them.

Photography credits:
Photographs of the houseboat on the first page of this chapter and the two pictures of Bell below are from the Gilbert H. Grosvenor Collection of Photographs of the Alexander Graham Bell Family (Library of Congress).
The photograph below of the gravesites is courtesy of Dr. Gardiner Myers, great-grandson of Alexander Graham Bell .

Bell Meadows: view from the Bells' gravesites at Beinn Breagh

Bell at age 29

Dr. Bell, Helen Keller and Annie Sullivan, 1894, at Chautauqua;
at a meeting to promote teaching speech to the deaf

Kate Chopin

1851 - 1904

The Melrose Plantation near Natchitoches, Louisiana
and The Kate Chopin House, Cloutiersville, Louisana

Kate Chopin

"She thought of Leonce and the children. They were a part of her life. But they need not have thought that they could possess her, body and soul. Mademoiselle Reisz would have laughed, perhaps sneered, if she knew. And you call yourself an artist! What pretensions, Madame! The artist must possess the courageous soul that dares and defies!"

The Awakening

".....an ecstasy of pain, the heavy odor of chloroform, a stupor which had deadened sensation, and an awakening to find a new little life to which she had been given being added to the great unnumbered multitude of souls that come and go."

The Awakening

Journey   Cane River Country

We started our Louisiana journey seeking the thinking place of Kate Chopin, a unique and outspoken novelist of the nineteenth century whose writings were sometimes at odds with most of her Victorian contemporaries. Her home has been preserved as a folk center museum in Cloutierville, near Natchitoches in the Cane River country.

Natchitoches, pronounced "Nack-a-tish" by locals, is the setting of *Steel Magnolias*, Robert Harling's poignant play made into a movie about five strong women in a small southern town.

After visiting nearby Melrose Plantation and learning the history of three very independent, creative women who lived at Melrose, we realized that our complete story must include, not only the strong-willed, unconventional Kate Chopin, but also three kindred "steel magnolias" of yesteryear.

Marie Theresa Coincoin, was a former African slave who was given her freedom and a small plantation by Claude Thomas Pierre Metoyer, the Frenchman father of her ten Franco-African children. With this beginning of Melrose, Marie Theresa and her sons, by dint of hard work and determination, added to the plantation until it became one of the largest, most successful in the area. Today, at Melrose, one may visit the original, colonial house, Yucca (c.1796), the African House (c.1800), the Big House (c.1833) and others (See section on Lagniappe).

The second strong woman, who became the chatelaine of Melrose in 1896, was Caucasian, Cammie Garrett Henry, who established an artists' colony, furnishing complete board, to such luminaries as William Faulkner, Roark Bradford, Rachel Field, Harnett Kane, Gwen Bristow, Lyle Saxon, Alexander Woolcott and many others. Cammie's only requirement was that the creative work be done "with sincerity." Francois Mignon, author of *Plantation Memories*, came for six weeks but stayed for thirty-two years, helping advance Cammie's desire to improve the gardens and the arts and crafts of the area. Many of the writers stayed at Yucca House, which was constructed of virgin cypress beams and walls of mud, moss and deer hair. It is said that Melrose's writers' huts have housed more of America's notable authors than any other single residence in the South.

The third strong woman was Clementine Hunter, the African-American painter, who became the most celebrated primitive artist in Louisiana. Clementine, a true original, once said, "I just do what my mind tells me to do." She worked as a cook for Cammie until a visiting artist discarded some tubes of paint. At the age of fifty, during the 1930's, Clementine began to paint on cardboard, then pieces of wood and finally, canvas. She recorded with humor and naiveté the African culture that she observed at Melrose. Asked why she had painted a rooster pulling a wagon, she replied, "I just got tired of seeing the mules and horses doing it all the time." Clementine continued to paint until nearly the time of her death at age one-hundred years.

Many of her murals are on the second-floor walls of African House at Melrose.

Melrose is just one of many plantation sites in the Cane River country. The narrow, meandering river, now technically a lake since it was dammed at two ends, once served as a waterway for the area. One may visit these plantation homes as well as many outstanding ante-bellum homes in Natchitoches at certain times, especially during the many festivals in the area. Natchitoches was an Indian name for "Place of the Paw-Paw" or "Chinquapins", a nut like an acorn. It was the earliest permanent European settlement in Louisiana. Today, history is re-enacted regularly in a simulated, early French fort with costumed actors and instructors.

The downtown section of Natchitoches is unique, with the main street bordered by wide lawns, sloping down on both sides of the narrow, picturesque Cane River, as featured in the movie, *Steel Magnolias*. Hospitable bed and breakfast homes, (such as the Jefferson House where we stayed and do recommend), overlook the river and make a visit to "Nackatish" and the Cane River country most memorable.

Vignette   Kate Chopin   1850 - 1904

Kate Chopin obviously didn't care whether she shocked people or not, thereby creating a wide swath of scandalized women and amused men. A few gentlemen may have been ostensibly outraged. Today, firmly established in the literary pantheon and in Women's Studies at most universities, Kate may be having the last laugh.

Kate was a feminist before that word had become popular. She wrote in the nineteenth and early twentieth century when "feminists" could be named and counted. She might have been dubious about inclusion in that group, probably preferring to be called simply, "independent or free spirited." Certainly, as a widow living in St. Louis with five sons and one daughter, she had to be careful. Before long, her daughter would make her debut. She definitely had to be more discreet and conventional. Living in St. Louis was quite different from living in the tiny hamlet of Cloutierville, in the northern Cane River country of Louisiana. That's where her liberated personality had emerged - on or soon after the death of her husband, Oscar.

Which came first – romance or her writing career? Did one spark the other? Or did monotony, boredom, the hot southern climate make her wish she were someone else, living in a different kind of world, anywhere but in Cloutierville in 1884?

Katherine O'Flaherty, Kate, was raised by her beloved mother and grandmother after her father died when she was five. Her mother had married Kate's father when he was thirty-nine and she was sixteen. Thomas O'Flaherty was a widower with one son. He needed to marry. Kate's mother, Eliza Farris, needed to marry for another reason. Eliza was the daughter of a widow with seven children. As was frequent in the society of that day, Eliza needed to rescue her family by marrying well, financially, that is. The matriarchy of strong women was established early in Kate's life with mother, grandmother and two aunts. Until the Civil War, Kate had a happy childhood, brightened also by her best friend and classmate, Kitty Garish. They became best friends for life, their contact becoming somewhat limited by Kitty's becoming a nun. Both went to the Sacred Heart Academy where they learned French and how to *be* French; they were taught the art of being a lady, with no bother for the essentials of managing a household. If the family could afford to send a daughter to school, it was commonly assumed in those days that she would never require knowledge of practical affairs. Kate was talented at music, took piano lessons every day and could also play by ear.

Then came the Civil War. Kitty moved away, her family ex--iled. Graduation from Sacred Heart was postponed. Kate's half-bother, George, released from military prison, died of typhoid fever. A band of German-American soldiers invaded the O'Flaherty household, commanded them to fly the Union flag, and according to a neighbor, committed an "outrage," the exact nature of which never became known. Strong women coped, but the impact of the War left its mark. The Sacred Heart Academy re-opened and Kate spent her time reading and copying chosen quotations in her notebook and writing poetry and essays. She was chosen a "Child of Mary," an election by both the nuns and the students. She won other honors at graduation, among them, the gold medal award for "excellence of conduct and proficiency in studies."

At eighteen she entered St. Louis "society," which she never cared for. She was considered beautiful and clever. Being clever was not always considered an asset in her day. Her first story, written when she was nineteen, was entitled, prophetically, "Emancipation: A Life Fable."

Now at a marriageable age, she met pleasant-looking Oscar Chopin, the gentle son of a wife-abusing physician. (To his credit, Oscar stood up for his mother who later died at the age of forty-two.) Oscar fell in love, and Kate fell into marriage, which was followed by a European honeymoon. Soon she was pregnant and, by this time, devoted to her husband. They moved from St. Louis to New Orleans where he was a cotton factor. In the hot, humid summer, wives and children would move from New Orleans to the beach at Grand Isle, joined by husbands on the weekend. If you have read *The Awakening*, Kate's most famous book, the one considered shocking more than a century ago, you can picture Grand Isle. Life in New Orleans offered books and music and stimulation of interesting people, although Kate and Oscar most enjoyed each other's company. They had five sons.

Then the blow fell. Depressed business conditions required Oscar to move his family to tiny Cloutierville where he opened a country store. Imagine the culture shock that faced Kate, again pregnant with her sixth and final child, a girl this time. If anything, Kate was an even bigger shock to the hamlet's residents than they were to her. She rode horseback astride, rarely side-saddle. With green eyes, the women noticed her fashionable riding habits, cut so daringly that her ankles showed. Her Parisian French was not their Arcadian French. To their disapproval, she sometimes helped her husband in his store. She was pretty and shapely. (They might have accepted her better in her later life when she became rather pleasingly plump.) At this youthful time in her life, she would stroll down Cloutierville's one street, holding her feminine parasol as she smiled at all the men she met. The women, whose friendship she needed, most likely shook their heads in disgust. "Can you believe it? That woman actually smokes! Cigarettes, which she rolls herself!"

A greater blow fell when Kate was widowed at thirty-two. Oscar died unexpectedly. Kate took over their affairs, as she had seen the strong women in her family do. She came in contact with the handsome, commanding, married, Albert Sampite. They had an affair. It ended when she left Cloutierville to live in St. Louis. Did it endure in her fiction?

In her St. Louis stories and novels, she changed the names of characters by switching letters – from "Albert" to "Alcee" or "Sylveste" to "Sylvere." The names of other people that she had known in real life, both men and women were disguised by slight manipulation of the alphabet. With common nouns, she was more specific, naming parts of the body that most writers refrained from mentioning.

In her new-old home in St. Louis, she looked forward to the companionship of her mother, Eliza, but her mother died within the year. If sorrow refines the talent of a writer, Kate Chopin had been through the furnace, and her writing gift was now burnished. She did start writing, regularly and with business-like organization of the stories that she sent out, seeking publication. She joined the prestigious, women's Wednesday Club, then resigned two years later. She did organize her own salon, which was attended by both men and women on Thursday evenings. In addition, strange to say, she continued to visit Cloutierville once a year. (Oscar's brother and family lived there, and she still owned her two-storied house until 1898.) She was also translating from the French, stories by Guy de Maupassant. She was teaching herself to write, and his style greatly influenced her own. By 1899 she had published two novels, a play, seventy-odd short stories, many essays, articles, poems, and reviews, as well as translations. In the next five years until her death of a cerebral hemorrhage in 1904, she published only a short story and *"Development of the Literary*

West: A Review." Next to *The Awakening, Bayou Folk,* a collection of short stories, is her best known work.

Kate Chopin may have been the main character of many of her stories, or she may have wished that the action she wrote about had indeed swirled around her.

Thinking Place

Not all journeys turn out just as we hope. Our trip to the Cane River country in search of Kate Chopin's thinking place is a case in point. Much of Kate's writing is about the people and places of this distinctive area of Louisiana, so we assumed that we would find her thinking place in her former home, which is now a folk museum. It was a faulty assumption. But, we found something equally or more interesting at nearby Melrose Plantation!

Although Kate continued to visit Cloutierville, she did most of her writing in St. Louis. One of her biographers said that she had her own writing room, which contained, besides a surface for writing, a daybed where she could nap or meditate. Kate herself mentioned a Morris chair, with a lapboard, beside the window where she could see a tree or two "a patch of sky, more or less blue."

We might have been tempted to put St. Louis on our list for future travels. Then sadly we discovered that of the three houses in which Kate lived, only one, the last one, is still standing.

The one we described earlier was from an article published in *The St. Louis Post Dispatch.* Accompanying the article was a watercolor sketch of the room by her son. This sketch was of the first house, which no longer exists. It did conform to the one requirement of all thinking places: "A dedicated place where the creative person goes on a regular basis."

Lagniappe   Cane River Country

Any trip to the Cane River Country is apt to give bountiful rewards of pleasure. Many memories of visitors would include the famous Natchitoches meat pies and hot tamales or the lighted Christmas scenes along the river or numerous pecan groves, promising many southern delicacies.

Natchitoches, "Nack-a-tish", is a gem of small town America and is like entering a movie set, as it once was for *Steel Magnolias*. The many plantations in the area helped us step back into the past, reminding us of the time when gracious living on one hand existed alongside backbreaking labor on the other hand. These were times of the melding of lives brought together by fate, but with the determination by many to endure and to make life better for the next generation.

No better example of the latter statement can be found than the impressive St. Joseph's Church, on a picturesque bend of the narrow Cane River, near Melrose Plantation.

Many members of the Church's congregation are descendents of a former slave, Theresa Coincoin. Her former French owner, was devoted to her and gave her many children, freedom and a tract of land which was gradually enlarged and became Melrose Plantation. Today many of her descendents are landowners and are successful in multiple businesses and professions.

We went to a worship service in the church, which in the past had been redecorated as a Protestant church for the film, *Steel Magnolias*. Afterwards, we visited the St. Joseph's Catholic Church Parish Hall, where they served gumbo. At the time, a spirited jazz combo was playing and singing. These warmhearted, friendly parishioners were comfortable with visitors and with themselves. We met some exceptional people.

Our lagniappe in Cane River Country was an even greater appreciation that people of diverse backgrounds had come together , established new and different pathways, then journeyed in good faith toward shared values and goals.

Kate Chopin

Cabin at Melrose Plantation

"Chicken Pullin' Flower Cart" inspired by Clementine Hunter collection; Ceramic by Lurline Didier Lemieux

Booker T. Washington

1856 – 1915

The "Oaks," Booker T. Washington's home in Tuskegee,
Alabama, and his desk in the study.

Booker T. Washington

"Let down your buckets where you are."

Address, Atlanta Exposition

"You can't hold a man down without staying down with
him."

Attributed

"No race can prosper until it learns that there is as much
dignity in tilling a field as in writing a poem."

Up from Slavery

Journey   Tuskegee

We had been to the town of Tuskegee and had briefly
viewed the Tuskegee Institute in past years, but we did not
know enough then to see adequately this very important and
historic part of the world. We returned twice on special journeys
to visit Tuskegee University, as it had become, and to learn more
about its two most famous personalities, Booker T. Washington
and George Washington Carver.

The town of Tuskegee is an old settlement that lies in the
rolling clay hills of southwestern Alabama between Mont-
gomery and Auburn. Nearby is the Tuskegee National Forest,
interesting for many reasons. (See "Lagniappe.")

On our initial return visit, we knew enough to inquire first
about visiting hours for the Booker T. Washington home and the
Carver Museum, but little else. We were in for some very pleasant surprises. Like signs of progress everywhere over the past
fifteen or twenty years, there have been many positive changes
in the campus, and we saw the striking Booker T. Washington
monument and his home for the first time.

When one visualizes the humble beginnings of the Institute
in 1881, with one small building and thirty students, one is

amazed at the magnitude of the campus development, now with over 160 buildings on 1500 acres. Today many of the early buildings, with traditional architecture, and the newer, more modern structures, blend together well. The site of the earlier buildings on campus is considered a part of the National Parks Service.

Near the gated entrance are the outstanding Booker T. Washington monument and the modern Visitors Center with restaurant and hotel accommodations. Adjacent to the latter is a pathway to the George Washington Carver Museum. (See next chapter about Dr. Carver.) In the near distance is the modern church tower, setting the tone for the campus.

When we walked up to the monument from the street, two busloads of students and their teachers were admiring the impressive structure. Each of them was very attentive and focused on the messages of the monument. They seemed very proud – and justly so.

The plaque near the monument reads as follows: *"The Booker T. Washington monument is a bronze statue designed by sculptor, Charles Keck. The Statue depicts Washington standing over a crouching black man, believed to have been a former slave, lifting the veil of ignorance from his face. The man is clasping an open book and sits on a plow and anvil. The open book represents Washington's opening the road to education and the plow and anvil correspond to the instruments of agriculture and industry, which were early educational principles of Washington's. The life course of Booker T. Washington was to shed the light of education on a race of people."*

The monument is considered the "center of campus" and was the site of the inauguration of military pilot training at Tuskegee Institute in 1941. On each side of the monument on the marble benches are the following inscriptions, both quotations from Dr. Washington:

"We shall prosper in proportion as we learn to
 dignify and glorify Labor."

And on the other side:
"and put brains and skill into the common occupations of life."

The inscription under the central figure of the monument states:

"Booker T. Washington 1856-1915.

He lifted the veil of ignorance from his people and pointed the way to progress through education and industry."

Across the street from the campus and just east of the main gate is the beautiful and substantial Victorian home of Booker T. Washington. The plaque near the home states:

"The Oaks, Booker T. Washington's Home, Tuskegee.

The residence of Booker T. Washington and his family was constructed eighteen years after he began his life's work, the establishing of Tuskegee Normal and Industrial Institute. The house was built on property owned by Dr. Washington, adjacent to the campus.

The house was later called The Oaks. Brick making and construction was completed entirely by Tuskegee students and faculty. Washington said, "The actual sight of a first class house that a Negro has built is ten times more potent than pages of discussion about a house that he ought to build or perhaps could build."

Robert R. Taylor, the first African-American graduate of the Massachusetts Institute of Technology, designed The Oaks."

———————

Vignette   Booker T. Washington 1856 - 1915

He was born into slavery in 1856, but by the age of twenty-six, Booker T. Washington was the first principal and had built from the ground up Tuskegee Institute, which became the most famous school for African-Americans in the world. A mere twenty-six years later, he was host to a U.S. president on Tuskegee's expanding campus in Alabama, soon becoming "Dr. Washington" and the guest of President Theodore Roosevelt in the White House. He became a sought-after speaker and a writer of note.

How did he accomplish so much in such a small amount of time? How could he have started at all when his resources were so meager?   The story of Dr. Booker T. Washington is a lesson in goal setting, persistence, ingenuity and faith—an example for people of all races everywhere.

It was illegal in Virginia for a slave to be taught how to read and write, so he received no training. The Emancipation Proclamation brought not only freedom when the War ended in 1865, but also the possibility of receiving an education. How could a young boy of nine pay for school? He worked in salt and coal mines in West Virginia for two years, and used his free time to go to school. When he was sixteen, he decided to go to Hampton Institute in Virginia. He didn't know whether he would be accepted. He didn't know anything about going to a fine school like Hampton. He didn't have a way to get there, but he set out with $1.50 in his pocket, hitching rides on a coach or walking, with 500 miles to go. He finally arrived, broke and hungry.

General Samuel Chapman Armstrong had founded Hampton Institute with the purpose of training teachers. In addition, he believed that each student should learn a trade. Washington was selected to be a janitor. Armstrong emphasized work and also "...study, hygiene, morality, self-discipline, and self-reliance." When Booker T. later founded Tuskegee Institute, he incorporated these standards into his goals for students. In 1875, he graduated with honors from Hampton Institute, actually at the head of his class. Three years later, still hungry for all the knowledge he could get, he enrolled at Wayland Baptist Seminary in Washington, D.C.

Remembering the exceptional student, General Armstrong called Washington back to teach at Hampton. Nine years later Harvard University asked him to give an address, awarding him an honorary degree, followed two years later by an honorary degree from Dartmouth College.

Somethings quite significant had happened in those nine years! General Armstrong was asked to nominate a white person to establish an educational institute for black people, the result of a political promise that had been made. Armstrong named as his choice, not the white person requested, but Booker T. Washington, who accepted the challenge. What subsequently happened was phenomenal!

When the school opened in 1881 the only resources were a shanty owned by a local church and funding of $2,000.00 a year, barely enough to pay the staff. Washington realized that the students themselves represented the Institute's most valuable capital. He chose to organize a curriculum similar to Hampton's. In addition to academic subjects, a practical education would be a requirement, along with emphasis on those personal characteristics he fostered. As the students learned brickmaking, carpentry, cabinetmaking, farming, shoemaking and other skills, they would also be learning to build their own school. He applied to Hampton Institute for a loan and was able to buy an abandoned plantation. The students lived up to what was expected of them. They started at five-thirty in the morning, frequently working until nine-thirty at night. They built their school. By 1888 the Institute had 400 students and owned 540 acres of land. Dr. Washington was able to attract good faculty, such as George Washington Carver, whose own story was as dynamic as Washington's.

In 1895, Dr. Washington addressed the opening of the Cotton States and International Exposition in Atlanta. His eloquence as an orator, a product of his early training at Hampton Institute, brought him recognition as a national figure. Another significant speech was "The Educational Outlook of the South," delivered to the National Educational Association meeting in Madison, Wisconsin. Others were the Peace Jubilee in Chicago, the Jamestown Exposition, and the Fourth Annual Peace Conference. Many considered him the major spokesman for African Americans.

His conservative views brought large sums of money to the Institute from such figures as Andrew Carnegie. In this period President William McKinley visited the campus, and later at the White House, President Theodore Roosevelt consulted with Washington about political appointments. Dr. Washington was conservative politically, due probably to his own gentle personality and his perceived need to co-exist peacefully with his white Alabama neighbors. He did not believe that African-Americans should campaign for the vote until they had proven themselves as citizens.

William Du Bois, African-American leader of the Niagara movement, provided respectful opposition to Washington's political views of accomodation in *The Souls of Black Folk*. Du Bois, one of the founders of the National Association for the Advancement of Colored People, argued that Washington's large financial responsibilities had made him beholden to the wealthy white public. He signed a statement (excerpted below) by twenty-two African-Americans: "Today in eight states where the bulk of the Negroes live, black men of property and university training can be, and usually are by law, denied the ballot, while the most ignorant white man votes. This attempt to put the personal and property rights of the best of the blacks at the absolute political mercy of the worst of the whites is spreading each day."

Dr. Washington spoke in rebuttal: "As a rule I believe in universal, free suffrage, but I believe in the South we are confronted with peculiar conditions that justify the protection of the ballot in many of the states, for a while at least, either by an educational test, a property test, or by both combined: but whatever tests are required, they should be made to apply with equal and exact justice to both races."

Thus the two leaders cogently expressed, in opposition, differences that could at least be expressed openly without fear.

Dr. Washington lived by a principle that he taught widely, "Put down your buckets where you are." (This was based on his story of finding fresh water where none was expected.) He had many problems, but he met them with equanimity. He received many awards and distinctions, and he founded several important organizations, among them the Negro Business League.

He traveled twice to Europe where he was asked to speak to many distinguished audiences and invited to study the conditions of peasants in Europe. In his time remaining, he managed to write forty books. Quite a record for a man whose first and only childhood book was Webster's blue back speller, which he proudly owned when he was eleven. His most famous book is his autobiography, *Up from Slavery*. Other titles include *My Larger Education, The Man Fartherest Down* and *Character Building*.

He was elected to the Alabama Hall of Fame and a Booker T. Washington Centennial three-cent stamp was issued.

His honors at Tuskegee included:

National Historic Monument by the U.S. Department of
  the Interior.

The Booker T. Washington Memorial Monument,
  sculptor, Charles Keck;

Dedication of the Booker T. Washington family home and

The Carver Museum as part of Tuskegee Institute and
  National Historic Site.

His life journey was short in duration but long in quality. The little boy who didn't have a name chose the surname of his country's first president, then learned later that his mother had called him Booker Taliaferro. Today the name, Booker T. Washington, graces the name of many schools and other institutions all over the United States.

Thinking Places

The impressive, large, two-storey Victorian house with gables stood on a corner shaded by huge trees. A National Park Service Guide opened for us Dr. Washington's home which had been temporarily closed for repairs.

Inside, we noticed the period furniture, Oriental rugs, now partially covered, and the unusual frieze in the handsome dining room. The hand-painted frieze pictured trees and lawns; it was a border just under the ceiling and encircled the room. Its different shades of green harmonized with the other furnishings. We noticed the dark woodwork and wondered if it were the "mission stain" developed by Dr. Carver from peanuts. All of the rooms were large and doubtless accommodated many students, faculty and visitors at Institute functions. We did not linger because we were anxious to see Dr. Washington's thinking place, which, as our guide explained, was on the second floor. At the top of the stairs, we entered Dr. Washington's study. It was a well-lighted, spacious room with windows on two sides. Almost immediately, we had that special, mystical feeling that we sometimes have when we visit someone's thinking place. Probably, we sense the person's presence. Dr. Washington's thinking place was unlike any we had visited before. It was the largest we had seen, and its furniture was the most unusual. Four pieces of furniture were heavy, ornately carved wooden pieces. One was a long table, which was centered in the room and rested on a turkey-red oriental rug. In the table's center was a three-handled silver tankard. A matching, richly carved, occasional chair was one of many chairs placed around the room. In one corner was his carved, wooden desk with matching chair. On the desk were two photographs, a marble inkstand, a china vase, a lamp and two stacks of small books. On top of one stack was *Present Forces and Negro Progress* by W.D. Weatherford. The other book's visible title was *Six Lectures on Architecture*. We learned that the rare and quite valuable furniture was the gift of Japanese parents in appreciation for both the education and the kindness that their daughter had received at Tuskegee.

Pictures on the walls were indicative of the life and career of Dr. Washington: large photographs of Presidents McKinley and Theodore Roosevelt, Martha and George Washington, diplomas or honorary degrees from Harvard, Dartmouth and from his Alma Mater, Hampton Normal and Agricultural Institute. A full-length portrait of Dr. Washington was placed over the mantle. On the floor was a large leather "medicine ball", which he used for exercising.

As we were leaving, we passed the mirrored hat stand where a derby, a straw hat and a walking cane must have remained since Dr. Washington was brought home, fatally ill, from New York where he collapsed while giving a speech.

The title of one of Dr. Washington's biographies, *Then Darkness Fled*, was used in a quotation by Martin Luther King, Jr., "So from an old clay cabin in Virginia's hills, Booker T. Washington rose up to be one of the nation's great leaders. He lit a torch in Alabama; then darkness fled."

Lagniappe

Our special gift from our visit to Tuskegee was an additional in-depth appreciation for Tuskegee alumnus, United States Air Force General Daniel "Chappie" James, the first African-American to be designated a four-star general in the U.S. Air Force. General James, a national hero, was well known in Pensacola, Florida, his birthplace and our hometown. He graduated from Booker T. Washington High School in Pensacola. His mother was recognized and celebrated in Pensacola for establishing and operating for years an outstanding private school for African-American children, many of whom were unable to pay the small tuition fee. It is little wonder that Chappie James, with his mother as a role model, would be successful. He stated that he always observed her "Eleventh Commandment, "Thou shalt not quit!"

As a four-star general, he was named Commander of the North American Defense Command. He served meritoriously in the Air Force in World War II, and in Korea and Vietnam. "I've fought in three wars," he said, "and three more wouldn't be too many to defend my country. I love America, and as she has weaknesses or ills, I'll hold her hand."

It all started at Tuskegee Institute. The military services were segregated, and Congress established an all-black, civilian Pilot Training Program at Tuskegee in 1941. Members became cadets and skilled flyers in the U. S. Army Air Corps in World War II. The segregated unit, eventually known as, the "Tuskegee Airmen," went on to serve in combat in Europe, achieving an impressive combat record, earning the respect of all, particularly the German pilots, who dreaded and avoided the "Schwartze

Vogelmenschen" or "Black Birdmen." Segregation ended in the Armed Forces in 1948, and the Tuskegee Airmen blended into the Air Force.

General Chappie James proved himself to be a distinguished flyer and leader in three wars. He attained the highest rank and position of influence and respect in the Air Force, but he retained his natural charm and sense of humor. He came back home to Pensacola, and at The University of West Florida at an informal gathering, he wowed the crowd when he sang "Hello Dolly." Everyone agreed that he could have had a successful career in music or the entertainment industry if he had so chosen. General Chappie James, aged 58 years, died in 1978, twenty-four days after his retirement. He is buried in Arlington Cemetery.

Tuskegee University honored the distinguished graduate with the massive building called the Daniel "Chappie" James Center for Aerospace Science and Health Education. President Ronald Reagan was there for the dedication in 1987. The 18.6 million dollar center includes: classrooms, and technical laboratories for the aerospace science engineering program; facilities for the Army and Air Force ROTC; library and Chappie James Museum; a 5,000 seat university arena/convocation center; other athletic facilities. The Tuskegee Airmen are honored in the courtyard, and the last plane that General James flew, an F-4C, is on display.

There are many other attractions for a visitor in the Tuskegee area: The George Washington Carver Museum; The Tuskegee's Airmen's Museum at the site of the old air field just outside of town; The Tuskegee National Forest with hiking and bicycle trails, horseback riding trails, rustic camp sites and a replica of Booker T. Washington's childhood home in Virginia. Our personal lagniappe was a better understanding of the many obstacles that had to be overcome by Washington, Carver and General Chappie James, with lessons learned from each of them: their positive attitudes, perseverance, willingness to work hard, adjusting to their times realistically and influencing change—and moving ahead for their own goals and those of their people.

Photographic credits:
Picture of Dr. Washington is from the George Washington Carver Museum collection, Tuskegee, AL.

Booker T. Washington   Dr. Washington's Study at The Oaks

Monument depicting Dr. Washington's lifting the
veil of ignorance; Tuskegee University campus

George Washington Carver

1861 or 1864 – 1943

George Washington Carver's Teaching
and Thinking Places in the Field and Laboratory.

George Washington Carver

"It is simply service that measures success."

"My soul's expression of its yearnings is its desire to understand the work of the Great Creator."

Speaking of his art and handicrafts

Journey   Tuskegee

On arriving at Tuskegee University, our priorities were seeing the campus, including the impressive Booker T. Washington monument, and then heading for the George Washington Carver Museum. Visiting Washington's home, The Oaks, had to wait until an appointed time the next afternoon.

We felt we were shaking hands with the past, an era that was beyond our comprehension, a time that was still reeling from the institution of slavery and the most devastating war in our history. We had come to visit the haunts of two great Americans, both born into slavery and both rising to amazing heights in education and national prominence.

Both men had chosen their names out of respect for America's first president. This reflected their attitude toward the country which provided them many opportunities, in spite of the social and educational handicaps that they faced.

The George Washington Carver Museum is an impressive structure and is near the center of activity on campus. It was developed with substantial support from a Carver admirer, industrialist Henry Ford. A fire in the Museum in the past, damaged part of Carver's collections and necessitated rebuilding, but there is still much to see today.

To more fully appreciate Carver before visiting the Museum, consider the eight cardinal virtues that he taught his students:

1) Be clean both inside and out.
2) Neither look up to the rich or down on the poor.
3) Lose, if need be, without squealing.
4) Win without bragging.
5) Always be considerate of women, children and older people.
6) Be too brave to lie.
7) Be too generous to cheat.
8) Take your share of the world and let others take theirs.

Perhaps the best place to start in the Museum is the small theatre downstairs, showing a video presentation. It starts with the touching story of Carver's early days on the Moses Carver farm, near Diamond Grove, Missouri. (Notice that Carver took the name of his owner, who later acted as his surrogate grandfather.) Roaming the surrounding woods and hills, Carver loved and revered Nature and started his interest in nurturing plants and collecting rocks. Some of his early collections were preserved and are now displayed in the Museum.

George Washington Carver (GWC) had to overcome racial barriers but he persisted, and at age thirty was admitted to Simpson College in Iowa as the first black student. He had interest in science, art and music. (Many of his subsequent paintings are on display in the Museum. Most, however, were destroyed in the fire.) Photographs of Carver's teaching farmers in the fields and students in the classrooms tell more of his story. A box-like truck, a "classroom on wheels", (called the "Jessup Wagon" for a benefactor) is on display in the Museum. GWC's interest and research in agriculture, especially peanuts and sweet potatoes, also are demonstrated in the Museum.

As an agricultural chemist or chemurgist, GWC was said to have extracted three to four hundred derivatives and uses for peanuts; and hundreds for soybeans, pecans and sweet potatoes. He made paint and stains from local clays. His final laboratory has been preserved in the Museum.

Vignette   George Washington Carver 1861 - 1943

What could a farmer do with an extra wagonload of peanuts? George Washington Carver set to work in his lab at Tuskegee Institute to find out. In the process, he developed 325 different uses for the simple nut—everything from cosmetics and food to dyes, paints and stains, medicines, even paper, soap and rubber.

Carver's goal in life was, as he stated, "to help my people." When he came to Alabama, "his people" were growing cotton on small, hard scrabble farms, where the soil had been depleted of nutrients. Cotton robbed the soil of nitrate, but buying nitrate took money the farmer didn't have. Without it in the soil, the cotton yield was low, perpetuating the cycle of poverty. Carver persuaded the farmer to adopt a crop rotation method of alternating cotton every other year with peanuts or legumes to supply the needed nitrogen. When a surplus of peanuts developed, Carver was determined to find a use for them. He did the same for an over supply of sweet potatoes.

If Carver had not been born with a tough strand of determination, he never would have become the practical, gifted dreamer, who started life as a small, sickly baby, born into slavery. Both he and Thomas Edison illustrated in their lives that hardships only strengthened their will. Edison was called the "Wizard of Menlo Park." Carver, too, was considered a wizard in his own field.

In his childhood the odds against Carver were increased when "bush-whackers" (the name for those who stole slaves for profit) kidnapped him, his mother and sister. By some miracle, Carver was rescued, but his mother and sister were never seen again. Moses and Susan Carver, his former owners, raised Carver and his brother, Jim, treating them with kindness.

Since Carver was too frail to work, he was allowed to roam the farmstead. As a very young boy, he developed his powers of observation, and Nature became his schoolhouse. He studied everything—insects, flowers, rocks, and weeds. He began growing plants, experimenting with different soils, the effect of sunlight and shade. Soon people were calling him the "Plant Doctor." The growing boy, still small, even made house calls on neighbors.

During these early years, he showed characteristics and developed beliefs that stayed with him for the rest of his life. He had a great desire to learn. No school was available to him, so he taught himself. He made his own playthings and was always full of ingenuity. Early on he came to believe that there is no waste in nature. He learned to love music by hearing Moses Carver play the violin at night. From Susan Carver he learned the alphabet and crocheting, which became a lifetime hobby.

When he was twelve, Carver left the only home he had ever known, but for a good reason. He wanted to go to school. The Carvers had been good to him, but their own education was limited, and Carver, a precocious child, had more questions than they had answers. He moved to the county seat in Neosho, boarding with the Watkins family in their three-room frame house. He returned to the Carvers on weekends. His teacher did not know much more than Carver, so he moved to Fort Scott, Kansas, supporting himself by doing a variety of odd jobs. He continued this pattern in several towns in Kansas, going to school, working and teaching Sunday school. Next he opened a laundry, and he made a small loan to buy land. Every action he took had one purpose—to obtain more education. With the help of several black families and one white family, he finally made it to Simpson College in Indianola, Iowa. It had not been a short journey. After he paid his fees at Simpson, he had ten cents left. With it, he bought cornmeal and suet for food. He found a small house to live in and set up another laundry with a boiler and wash tubs that he secured on credit.

He was popular with students; he had a gift for friendship, another lifetime trait. When fellow students discovered that he had no furniture, they took up a collection and left some in his room when he wasn't there. Sometimes they would slip concert tickets or a small sum of money under his door. He made high grades in spite of having to work constantly to support himself. Simpson College, a Methodist school, had an open door policy for all ethnic groups. Carver was the only black person. Three

Asian students were also enrolled. He still didn't have a high school diploma, but he took a full range of studies, including music and art. A teacher suggested that he take botany at Iowa State College of Agriculture and Mechanic Arts. Carver gave up his pursuit of art and said later that he felt he could do the most good for the greatest number of people in agriculture. He was ready for his next step, and when he later graduated from Iowa State, his former classmates at Simpson College sent him a bouquet of flowers. He received his Master's degree from Iowa State where he was the first black student and the first black faculty member.

He became a teacher, a gifted one, while pursuing his Master's degree at Iowa State. One of his students was a precocious six-year-old whom Carver allowed to go with him on his rambles in the woods. The child became in future years, Vice-President Henry Wallace, who later called Carver "the kindliest, most patient teacher I ever knew. He could cause a little boy to see the things which he saw in a grass flower."

In his Bachelor's thesis, Carver wrote,"...Man is simply nature's agent or employee to assist her in her work." Although he had many extra-curricular activities, the YMCA, music groups and playing the guitar and art, he settled down to specializing in hybridization and mycology, the study of fungi and plant diseases. He would always continue his interest in art, and he did receive a special honor in this field. One of his paintings was selected to represent Iowa in the World's Columbian Exposition in Chicago. This picture and other examples of his artistic bent are on display in the Carver Museum at Tuskegee. Two of his paintings were shown at the World's Fair of 1893. He was chosen a Fellow of the Royal Society of Arts, London.

In 1896 he received a fateful letter from Dr. Booker T. Washington, asking him to start and head an agricultural department and laboratory at Tuskegee. He debated the offer because he had also received one from Alcorn College, but he accepted Washington's offer. Assuming that his birth date was either 1861 or 1864, Carver was in his early thirties. He would stay at Tuskegee for forty-seven years, the remainder of his life.

Carver found no laboratory established at the Institute, so he set about making one out of discarded items that he salvaged, and he addressed whatever needs he found. He periodically examined the school's water and milk supplies for bacteria. "There is no study more important than foods," he said. He was concerned with poor nutrition and wanted to teach the farmers of the area to learn to dry foods for better preservation. He believed farmers could also vary their diets if they practiced crop rotation. On campus, he demonstrated how paints and stains could be made out of native clay, thus saving the Institute money. In the make-shift lab he and his students practiced what Carver called, "stove-top chemistry."

He reached out to farmers by inviting them to practical lectures and seminars. He issued bulletins on pertinent subjects. He made good use of the "Jessup wagon," named for a major benefactor. The wagon was fitted out with exhibits or equipment for whatever Carver was trying to teach, and it traveled to nearby farms and communities. He began to attract national attention. Henry Ford, among others, became a friend and supporter. Although Carver had a very high-pitched voice that was off-putting at first, he became popular on the lecture circuit. The Chancellor of the University of Georgia, Dr. Walter B. Hill said, "That was the best lecture on agriculture to which it has ever been my privilege to listen." An example of his content and style is the following excerpt: "There is not a single object in all the realm of animate nature that is not well organized. Indeed the work of creation was the work of organization. We would no doubt have made MAN first, without a place for him or food for his substance. I hold before you my hand with each finger standing erect and alone, and so long as they are held thus, not one of all the tasks that the hand may perform can be accomplished. I cannot lift. I cannot grasp. I cannot hold. I cannot even make an intelligible sign until my (fingers) organize and work together. In this we should also learn a lesson."

The "Principal," as Dr. Washington was called, and Carver did not always agree, largely due to differences in temperament. Carver was the artist-scientist and not an administrator.

Washington wanted Carver to attend national conferences and give seminars, but he was often frustrated by Carver's growing absences from campus. The two men had high regard for each other, and when Dr. Washington died in 1916, Carver felt bereft.

After his discovery of the many uses of peanuts, Carver was considered a "creative chemist" and became known as the "Peanut Man." A showman as well as an exceptional public speaker, he could be persuasive. "It takes a cow twenty-four hours to make milk. I can make from peanuts better, cleaner and more healthful milk in five minutes."

In his spare time, if there was any, Carver continued to develop his interest in art. He delighted in demonstrating how beauty can be created from humble materials. He was personally very thrifty also. On Sunday nights, he taught a Bible class to hundreds of students. He called his lab, "God's little workshop," and he said a prayer before entering it. His belief in the unity of all nature foreshadowed the ecology movement.

Although Dr. Carver validated many of his successful experiments, some were not pursued for practical reasons. According to Federer, Carver also demonstrated over one hundred eighteen uses for the sweet potato, over sixty for the pecan and dozens of uses for the soybean, okra, wild plum and cowpea. Most significant for today's needs was his suggestion that peanut products could be used for alternate fuels.

Honors poured in: a fellowship from The Thomas A. Edison Institute, a memorial cabin at Henry Ford's Greenfield Village and a nutritional laboratory in Carver's honor at Dearborn, honorary degrees, many radio programs about him and his work, schools named for him, membership in Kappa Delta Pi, honorary education society and Fellow of the Royal Society of Arts, London—and many, many more. His birthplace was made a national monument. He was inducted into the National Hall of Fame. Several postage stamps commemorated his work, the first to a non-president and the first to an African-American. In 1939 he received the Roosevelt Medal for outstanding contribution to Southern Agriculture. A half-dollar coin and a naval ship were named in his honor.

Most would agree, it was George Washington Carver the man, who was justly honored, even more than his work. The wonder is that against daunting circumstances, he not only survived but flourished—and helped others to flourish, also.

⌒∽∾∼⌒

Thinking Place

As a boy, George Washington Carver did much thinking in the woods and fields around Moses Carver's home. He fed his curiosity and taught himself a great deal about plants, rocks and creatures of the forest. With his strong religious faith, he felt a kinship to all of Nature. He was committed to trying to understand, to nurture and to preserve God's creation.

He remained an humble man in spite of his advanced education, his many accomplishments and national recognition. He wore old, shabby but clean clothing—always with a flower in the buttonhole of his coat. His wants were few. People who knew him said that he was always thoughtful and always thinking.

He lived in something of a dormitory setting, next to his laboratory. He also did a great deal of thinking in the fields of rural Alabama – about new ways he could improve the soil and the life of the farmers. He shared his information and thoughts with students in the classroom, and in the fields with continuing education classes facilitated by the Jessup Wagon.

Carver's regular thinking place at Tuskegee was in his laboratory, using chemistry methods for extracting products from the peanut and the sweet potato. His last laboratory has been preserved in the George Washington Carver Museum. A visitor may view his typical laboratory with bottles and jars, a Bunsen burner, a microscope, test tubes, a distilling set-up, multiple racks—and a large jar of peanuts.

One can visualize Carver working long hours in his laboratory, stopping to think and to figure in his notebook, frequently pausing "To talk it over with God," always convinced he was doing the Creator's work.

274

❨❨⌒◯⌒❩❩

Lagniappe   Alabama

George Washington Carver, scientist, educator, human-itarian and artist was a great American, inspiring teacher and, from all accounts, a wonderful human being. In spite of his humble beginnings as a slave, he overcame many obstacles. His thirst for knowledge and understanding, love of nature, faith, persistence and determination were admirable, and he still serves as a worthy role model.

Learning more in depth about the character and accomplishments of this good man was one of our special gifts, our lagniappe, from our visit to Tuskegee. But there was still more lagniappe on our trip home: seeing the monuments to the boll weevil and to the peanut in two southern towns!

Carver had long advocated and taught rotation of crops to restore the soil and, particularly, to plant peanuts and sweet potatoes as food and cash products. He said that dependency on one crop, cotton, would lead to more and more troubles for the farmer. The bollweevil invasion from Mexico in the 1890's reached southeastern Alabama in 1915. It had spread to South Carolina by 1921. This led to widespread economic devastation in the South. Planting and marketing peanuts helped to restore the economy in many areas. In 1919, the citizens of Enterprise, Alabama erected a monument to the boll weevil. In the center of the downtown main street is a large marble monument with a Grecian figure holding up in both hands a large boll weevil. The adjacent historical marker nearby reads as follows: "Boll Weevil Monument, December 11, 1919; In appreciation of the boll weevil and what it has done—as the Herald of Prosperity—this monument was erected by the citizens of Enterprise, Coffee County, Alabama." Farmers all over the South were forced to change to other crops, particularly peanuts and sweet potatoes, which proved to be much more profitable, eventually. The citizens of Early County, Georgia also demonstrated their appreciation for the peanut. In the courthouse square in Blakely, Georgia on a large monument adorned with a huge peanut is engraved: "The people of Early County, the largest peanut-producing center in the world, have erected this monument in tribute to the peanut which is largely responsible for our growth and prosperity. Not only has it contributed to higher living standards of the people engaged in its producing, manufacturing and marketing but has also become important to the better health of the people of the world as it is the source of some of our most nutritious and beneficial foods."

These two monuments represent two very important events in the history of the United States. The monuments also are symbolic landmarks attesting to the vision, intelligence and work of George Washington Carver who, with others, foresaw agricultural problems and proposed solutions through education, research and development of new products. Carver's efforts benefited all levels of society but uppermost always was his striving to improve the lives and conditions of the small farmer and rural people with limited resources and education.

Photographic credits:
All photographs of Dr. Carver are from the George Washington Carver Museum Collection, Tuskegee, Alabama.

George Washington Carver Museum
Tuskegee, Alabama.

George Washington Carver

Monument to the Boll Weevil
in Enterprise, Alabama

Monument to the Peanut
in Blakely, Georgia,

Carl Sandberg

1878 - 1967

Connemara, the Sandberg's home,
backyard and woods at Flatrock, North Carolina

Carl Sandburg

"I am the people - the mob - the crowd - the mass.
Do you know that all the great work of the world is
done through me?"

"I Am the People, the Mob"

"Hog butcher for the world, City of the big shoulders.
Tool maker, stacker of wheat,
Player of railroads and the nation's freight handler;
Stormier, husky, brawling,"

"Chicago"

"Sometime they will give a war and nobody will come."

The People, Yes

Journey   Flat Rock

Flat Rock, North Carolina, twenty miles from Asheville, sounds like it might be a long way from anywhere. Heading west on U.S. 25 toward Hendersonville, North Carolina, you know you are close to Connemara, Carl Sandburg's last home when you see the sign, "Flat Rock Playhouse." (This is an excellent regional theatre.) Turn left, and after a short distance, you're there. A short walk down a wooded path leads to a breath-taking view. At the foot of forested mountains, a glass-like lake reflects the distinctive Sandburg house. The scene gives a feeling of serenity and calm—and awe. In the house lived a happy and industrious family. Seeing their surroundings and how they lived makes one feel their vibrancy today.

Carl and Paula Sandburg, their daughters and a herd of prize-winning goats of distinctive breeds, moved to Connemara in 1945 to escape the harsh Michigan winters. They hoped to find a quiet place to work and to accommodate their expanding goat herd. Connemara, 245 acres of unspoiled beauty and 30 acres of pasture, was always a working farm. The Sandburgs lived here from 1945 until 1967 when Carl died at eighty-nine. The house is completely furnished as it was when Carl and Paula, with children and grandchildren, enlivened this simple but substantial home. His guitar in the living room looks as if it were placed there last night after he had sung for a family gathering. The upstairs room, one of Carl's thinking places, is described in a following section. The buildings on the grounds, including the barn, are well preserved by the National Park Service, which also cares for herds of goats of several different breeds. The Visitors' Center has educational materials and, at the time we were there, homemade fudge made from goats' milk.

We soon found out why the name "Flatrock." The backyard of the Sandburg house is one solid flat area of granite, quite flat and quite a rock! This topography must be common in the area. And, like the jingle advertising a hardy, high-performing truck, Carl Sandburg was "like a rock," rock-solid in his expressions of love of country and the common people.

Vignette   Carl Sandberg   1878 - 1967

By any reckoning, Carl Sandburg was an extraordinary man. His Swedish-born mother aptly described her young, exceptional son: "I only stand bewildered and would praise God for having molded his clay into so beautiful piece of ornament in His Kingdom."

The exceptional son also had an exceptional mother. She saved what little money she had to buy books for her small children. Her son Carl's dedication for his first and hand-lettered poems reads: "I dedicate them to one who has kept a serene soul in a life of stress, wrested beauty from the commonplace, and scattered her gladness without stint or measure: My Mother."

Some might say that these words also describe, in large measure, Carl Sandberg himself. He is probably best known for a poem of only six lines. The perfect metaphor, as familiar as a nursery rhyme, it is a tiny gem in the massive life work of Carl Sandburg. His mother might have said, "Ya! 'Tis goot!"

> "The fog comes
> on little cat feet.
> It sits looking
> over city and harbor
> on silent haunches
> and then moves on."

Who would guess that the same author would undertake a six-volume biography of Abraham Lincoln, which took thirty years to complete? In addition, he wrote a biography of Lincoln for children and one of Mrs. Lincoln, which was entitled, *Mary Lincoln, Wife and Widow*. President Franklin Delano Roosevelt personally guided Sandburg to the places in the White House associated with Lincoln. President Lyndon Johnson honored him also, as did Gustave, King of Sweden. Sandburg won a Pulitzer Prize for *Abraham Lincoln: The War Years*. It is most appropriate that Sandberg became a Lincoln scholar. Look at Sandberg's photograph. There is something in his face that is Lincolnesque.

Add to this monumental work many volumes of poetry. William Allen White, editor and critic, wrote to him, "Of all of today's modern poets, it seems to me that you have put more of America in your verses than any other..." *Complete Poems* won a second Pulitzer Prize for Sandburg in 1950. He also won a Grammy for his performance of Aaron Copland's "Lincoln Portrait." His poem, "Prairie," was featured in a prize-winning television documentary.

Next, consider his whimsical children's stories. When *Rutabaga Stories* came out, famed architect, Frank Lloyd Wright, wrote him: " Dear Carl, I read your fairy tales nearly every night—before I go to bed—they fill a long felt want—Poetry. I'll soon know them all by heart. ..."

The list continues. Ballads and folklore were issued in *The American Songbag* and *The New American Songbag*. Carl Sandberg was not only a poet. He was a musician. He sang and accompanied himself on the guitar and banjo on tours around the country. When he was at home, he entertained the family after dinner. Besides musical tours, he was also on the non-musical lecture circuit. His family regretted his absences from home, but the trips were frequently necessary for financial reasons. To the long list of volumes of both poetry and prose, add a novel and his autobiography. All of this came from someone who had had to quit school when he was thirteen, but who continued to read voraciously. When he was older, he put himself through Lombard College, withdrawing shortly before graduation. One of his greatest gifts from college was having a Professor Wright who insisted that Sandberg develop his talent. In their association, we see illustrated the importance of encouragement—or validation—in the development of creativity. Although Sandberg did not earn a degree from Lombard, he did receive in later years nine honorary degrees from prestigious universities.

Carl Sandberg was surely created from a very special clay. How was he molded? By hard work, from his earliest years, is one answer. The following is only a partial list of his jobs: "small odd jobs, 'a milk slinger' on a milk truck, learning the tinner's business, washing bottles, hobo, a soldier in Puerto Rico in the Spanish-American War, janitor, editor of the college yearbook (in return for tuition), vaudeville comedian, and general flunkey at the firehouse." He supported his eating habit by buying bananas and a loaf of stale bread with a total expenditure of fifteen cents a day. Probably his favorite job was selling stereographs. On a rented bicycle, he would ride into the countryside where he persuaded farmers that his marvelous stereograph would reproduce pictures of far-away places. On his off days he would walk long distances and spend time reading in some quiet place.

He bought a secondhand typewriter for $15.00 and began to write editorials on socialism. He was not interested so much in its theory as finding a practical process by which the common man, the people he knew, including his family, could find relief from their hard existence. His open mind could see both sides of the question and he wrote, "Against magnates, I haven't a word to say. For goodness of heart, for loftiness of purpose, and as regards mankind, they average as well as any class. The bourgeoisie and the proletariat both live in glass houses." What he wanted to do was to protect the workingman from unforeseen disasters. When more protective laws were passed, he gave up his active interest in the Social-Democratic Party, which he had once served as an organizer. It was through his interest in the party that he first met the love of his life.

Her real name was Lillian Steichen, a beautiful blonde, a Latin teacher, Phi Beta Kappa in college and a supporter also of the Social-Democratic Party. (Her brother was the world-famous photographer, Edward Steichen, who later became as close as a brother to Sandburg.) They met at party headquarters. With his first look at her, he knew they shared a destiny. She filled his heart with poetry.

"Paula" was his love-name for her. Hers for him was "Carl". (Previously everyone had called him Charles.) They were married the following June. Their ideas and their ideals were similar. She spoke for both of them when she wrote to Carl, "We shall do our best to do something—to leave some thing that we have produced here on earth as a bequest! But we'll remember that the life we live is more important than the works we leave."

Kept busy with a newspaper column and movie criticism for the paper, he was beginning to realize that what he wanted to do was to use his creative abilities. Even then, he was looking for his thinking place.

"There is a place for me somewhere, where I can write and speak as much as I can think, and make it pay for my living and some besides. Just where this place is I have small idea now, but I am going to find it."

Lecturing was one means of bringing in household income, and he was good at it. His rich voice, his whimsical, humorous manner captivated his audience. An extended tour satisfied his yen for travel—to see all he could of the country he loved next to his family– his own America.

Meanwhile, with a college background in genetics, and with the help of her daughters, Paula began to raise goats for extra income. Before long she was selling her three very special breeds to all parts of the globe. One of her nanny goats won the all-breed American championship in milk production and the world-wide Toggenburg championship.

As critical acclaim followed Carl's publication, the Sandbergs were able to buy property in Harbert, Michigan, where Paula designed their house. Michigan winters proved too cold for the goat herd that Paula was raising, so they moved to the idyllic spot in Flatrock, North Carolina, called "Connemara," taking all of Carl's 12,000 books and one complete herd of Paula's prize-winning goats.

All of the Sandbergs were hard workers who took pleasure in their work. Working on the *War Years*, Carl frequently spent sixteen to eighteen hours a day on research. The resulting eyestrain and headaches did not prevent his continuing. Meanwhile, life at Connemara settled to an agreeable routine for the remaining twenty-two years of his life. Carl had his own schedule. He worked in a third floor room, in his solitude, surrounded by his books and papers. Sometimes he would work outside, stripped to the waist, catching the sun on a porch or on the large, flat rock in the rear of the house. It was his nighttime habits that made him similar to other creative people like Charles Dickens. After the evening meal, followed by singing and playing the guitar for his family, Carl would then work on a current book. Sometimes he would take a stroll with Paula, but it was later in the evening when he would take his long rambles in the woods or the farm, recharging his creative battery.

A title of one of Carl Sandberg's own books sums up best this portion of his life, *The People Yes!* He truly loved people and the mystic union that bound them together.

He continued to receive honors. He received the National Institute of Arts and Letters gold medal for history and biography; the Albert Einstein College of Medicine's Humanities Award; Order of the North Star and later the Litteris et Artibus medal from the King of Sweden. One of his highest honors came on the anniversary of Lincoln's 150th birthday. It was an invitation to address the joint houses of Congress with the Cabinet, and the Supreme Court in attendance. Few private citizens were ever asked to speak before Congress, but of all Americans, Carl Sandberg was most connected with Abraham Lincoln. A standing ovation followed his speech.

When he died on July 22, 1967, at Connemara, Paula said, "I still have him through the pages of his books." That also applies to all who admire the man and his work.

Thinking Place

Carl Sandberg's study on the third floor was away from the activities of the rest of the house. Many books lined the walls in the room and in the hallway. Characteristic of Sandburg thriftiness, he used orange crates for small filing cabinets. (For younger readers: in the past, orange crates were oblong boxes made with thin strips of wood, about three feet long, divided down the middle, making two sections. They accommodated letter-sized papers, and the crates were free for the asking.) Sandberg did most of his writing in this room, and he wrote with his pencils whittled down to the stubs.

Some of Carl's thinking was done outside too. He sat on the front porch or on the large, flat rocks, which filled most of his back yard. He also liked to take long walks in the woods, usually late at night. Sometimes at dawn as he was going to bed, he would wave to the girls who were walking out to the barn to milk the goats. Carl Sandberg's thinking places also included the length and breadth of his beloved America, when he traveled widely on his lecture and concert tours and took trips to receive his many awards.

Lagniappe

What special, unexpected gift can come out of a place with such a plain name as "Flat Rock"? A visit to this scenic area is lagniappe enough: the forests, mountain vistas, the homes, the inns and bed and breakfast places and the town, Hendersonville, an All-American, Norman Rockwell kind of place. All are very much worth the trip as a final destination.

In addition, Carl and Paula Sandberg's home, reflecting the lives and work of two great Americans, leaves an indelible impression. Each made the most of the talent they had been given. Many people thought that Carl, a member of the American Academy of Arts and Letters, recipient of many honorary degrees, a two-time Pulitzer Prize winner, was also worthy of the Nobel Prize. Fewer may know that Paula herself was an international prize winner in breeding goats. The Sandbergs represent the best qualities of America, where this humble, hard-working, gifted couple could give back in full measure the blessings they had received from their beloved country.

Photographic credits:
Photograph of Carl Sandberg, balladeer, is courtesy of the Carl Sandberg Home and Museum, Flatrock, North Carolina. The photograph of Carl and Paula, by Edward Steichen is courtesy of the Steichen Foundation.

Carl Sandberg, balladeer   Connemara farm and goats today

Carl and Paula (Photo by her brother Edward Steichen)

"When we bought Connemara not only did we buy two hundred forty-five acres, we also bought a million acres of sky ..."

Paula Sandburg

Will Rogers

1879 – 1935

Will Rogers' Birthplace near Oolagah, Oklahoma, and a replica at the
Claremore Museum of his living room at Will Rogers Santa Monica
Ranch, near Pacific Palisades, California

Will Rogers

"I only know what I read in the newspapers."

-from a comic routine

"I joked about every prominent man in my lifetime,
but I never met one I didn't like."

-Epitaph

"Politics has got so expensive that it takes lots of money
to even get beat with."

- Syndicated newspaper article.

Journey   Oolagah and Claremore

As we traveled from Tulsa, Oklahoma toward Will Rogers'
birthplace near Oolagah and the Will Rogers Memorial at
Claremore, we joined the countless thousands who have made
this pilgrimage.

Why were we including Will Rogers, "the cowboy
humorist", actor and entertainer in this particular compilation?
The simple answer is that the talented Will had many
accomplishments, discussed further in the vignette that follows.
He was, indeed, a prolific writer and newspaper columnist, as
well as a radio commentator. He wrote six books, 4,000
syndicated columns, and scores of magazine articles. (He also
made 71 movies.) A CD-Rom has been produced, preserving
over 2 million words written by Will Rogers. Certainly, Will
Rogers was a creative person, a writer and much more. He
became a legend!

Many years before, we had visited the Will Rogers Santa
Monica Ranch, today a state park, in Pacific Palisades,
California. At the time we noticed that within view of his house,
he had a polo field where he would ask his friends to play. It
was not surprising that he was an expert horseman, but polo

seemed somewhat sophisticated for this homespun frontier man-turned movie star. Later, we learned that he never met a challenge he didn't like. Will's office and "living room" at the ranch was his thinking place where he did much of his writing.

In the Will Rogers Museum at Claremore, Oklahoma an exact replica of Will's Santa Monica Ranch living room has been constructed. On seeing this, we thought, as Yogi Berra might have said, "It was déjà vu all over again." Will would have appreciated Yogi's humor and maybe added a wisecrack something like this, "With me havin' two places like this, folks might accuse me of bein' two-faced—like some of them Washington politicians!"

Claremore , Oklahoma is not far from the bucolic little town of Oolagah, now a tourist attraction with a statue of Will, the cowboy, and his favorite horse, Comanche, at a fountain in the center of the town. Nearby is "Dog Iron Ranch", Will's birthplace. The substantial two-storey house, covered by clapboards, had been added to the original log construction part of the ranch house. This was a large ranch in its day, and Will's father was quite successful and prosperous. Today the house has been restored with attractive furnishings.

The more we observed and read about Will Rogers, the more we realized that learning about him is a journey in itself, with more discoveries down the road.

Vignette   Will Rogers   1879 - 1935

A Broadway musical restored to name recognition a man who was probably the best-known, most beloved figure of the 1920's and 1930's in America. He was an "Injun' Cowboy" who became a comedian, a humorist, a writer, a pundit and finally a news analyst. He was more popular than the then current U.S. president. *Life* magazine sent him this telegram on the night of the 1928 election, "All you know is what you read in the papers, and so you probably haven't heard that you were elected

President by the Great Silent Vote of this nation." For the rest of his life, Will Rogers was known as the "unofficial President of the United States."

The Broadway musical that "recreated" the charm, lovable nature and wit of this super-talented man was *"The Will Rogers Follies,"* and the most popular song of this mega-hit was one of Will's well-known sayings, "I Never Met A Man I Didn't Like." Not only did he like people, he helped them when he could. Once he hired seventy-five unemployed cowboys to do some work around his ranch. When reminded that the ranch tractor could do all that was needed, he replied, "Yes, I know but tractors don't eat." Later, when a movie filming finished ahead of schedule, Will himself paid the crew's salaries for the remaining time.

Will Rogers was part Cherokee on both sides, and proud of it. He was born in Oklahoma and proud of that, too. From both traditions he became a fine horseman, delighting in polo in later years, and in his expertise with the rope. He was once billed "the lariat champion of the world." He may not have actually won that title, but he later thrilled people all over the world with his amazing rope tricks.

In 1897 he enrolled in Kemper Military School, but though blessed with a photographic memory, school didn't interest him, and he quit after a year to become a cowboy, trail riding all the way to San Francisco. In 1900 he met Betty Blake, the love of his life, but it took eight years to rope her in. In the interim, great adventure lay ahead. Will was restless, and his father, Clem Rogers, who had moved to Claremore, gave him the "Dog Iron Ranch" near Oolagah, hoping to settle Will down. Will did work hard and increased his cattle holdings, but he had heard about wonderful ranches and cattle raising in Argentina and wanted to find out more about it. Like the prodigal son, Will told his father he wanted to sell his ranch and cattle and travel to Argentina. Clem Rogers wisely held on to the ranch for Will, but gave him three thousand dollars for the cattle.

When Will and a friend headed for Argentina, they were forced to go via England to find a ship sailing to Buenos Aires. After observing the gauchos and deciding Argentina was not a good place to make a living, Will returned to Buenos Aires. His money had nearly run out and there was only enough for one ticket, so Will paid for his friend to go back home. Needing to eat, Will took a job caring for a shipment of cows and mules to South Africa. Terribly seasick, as he had been also when crossing the Atlantic to England, he was miserable on this voyage for thirty-two days. "The veterinarian on board spent most of his time taking care of me." But, unknown to him, after a 600-mile cattle drive in South Africa, the beginning of his career in show business waited for him in Johannesburg. There he joined Texas Jack's Wild West Show, where he was a great success as "lariat champion of the world ."

Homesick for Oklahoma, he decided to head for home by way of Australia. Texas Jack put him in touch with a circus owner in Australia, and the "Cherokee Kid" sailed to "Down under" where he took a job with the circus before going on to New Zealand. Will expressed a great admiration for the land and people of New Zealand. Always seasick on the way, Will made it to San Francisco, and traveling by freight car, finally arrived home, where the prodigal son was welcomed with open arms.

Will had had a taste of and learned show business, using his lifelong, natural skills of riding and roping. Many shows followed with his performances pleasing the crowds at the St. Louis World's Fair, a burlesque show, Madison Square Garden, and a European tour where he passed the Kaiser on a bridle path in Berlin. At a club in London King Edward VII was in attendance. He had played most of the big cities in the United States when he finally persuaded Betty to marry him. They married in Rogers, Arkansas on November 25, 1908, "the star performance of my life," a happy Will said.

Real fame was on the way, and it arrived when Will started adding a humorous patter to his shows. "Will twirled his lariat, chewed on his gum, and scratched his head thoughtfully, 'Lemme see, folks'…and clever witticisms and comments about public figures flowed like an artesian well." He became a regular on the New York City stage shows, The Midnight Frolic and The Zeigfield Follies.

Will was hitting his stride, honing his own style of homespun, humorous comment about public figures, politics and daily events from the newspaper, simultaneously performing his incredible rope tricks. Richard Henry Little for the *Chicago Tribune* tried to describe it:

"The accomplished Mr. Rogers not only delights the audience with his amazing dexterity with the lasso, but even more with his running fire of small talk. The great beauty of Mr. Rogers' conversation is that he never is quite through. He makes a remark and apparently marks a period by doing some trick with the lasso, and the part of the audience that sympathized with his statement applauds madly. Then Mr. Rogers drops another remark that is diametrically opposed to his first statement and starts another section of the audience to great applause. But as this tumult dies down, he makes still another comment along the line of his original thought that is a trifle more pertinent than either of the first two and differs widely from them."

In 1911 two important events occurred. In August Will and Betty saw their first "airship," presaging Will's future love of flying. In October they saw the face of their first newborn whom they named William Vann. They would have three other children, losing Freddie to diphtheria, when he was two. All of the children would follow Will and Betty in their love of horses, riding, and the outdoor life.

Soon Will appeared in his first stage show, then in movies for a total of seventy-one films. Next, he went on the lecture circuit, averaging three to four speeches a week. Radio broadcasts followed. His radio contract netted him $350.00 a minute, an astronomical amount for those days, and he gave it all to charity. The American Red Cross and the Salvation Army and disaster victims were the recipients of his generosity. Then he started to tour the country, beginning in Elmira, N.Y and ending that tour in Boston. Meantime he began a newspaper column, writing a career total of 4,000 by-lines. He knew or performed for five U.S. presidents. Everywhere his performances brought tremendous ovations. After he had appeared at Carnegie Hall to loud applause, contractors allegedly had to shore up the rear wall to strengthen the building. Somehow he found time to write six books and to travel around the world three times.

Will Rogers had begun as a cowboy, then a roping whiz. He called himself the "Poet Lariat," and earned a place in the Guinness Book of Records for throwing three ropes at the same time, lassoing the rider and a horse, front and back. After success on the stage, Will became a screen star and was the highest paid actor in Hollywood.

In his full maturity, he became a pundit and a news analyst whose opinions were sought by world leaders. His wisdom was delivered with humor, but it contained a core of plain common sense and lack of pretense. He was concerned about the world situation, the conduct of nations and conditions in America, especially unemployment. He once said, "No country ever had more and no country ever had less. ... Ten men in our country could buy the world, and ten million can't buy enough to eat."

Will had flown many times for thousands of miles when he set out for Alaska with Wiley Post at the controls. Their plane failed to gain altitude and crashed at Barrow, Alaska at 8:15 PM, August 15, 1935. He was 55. The world went into mourning for the kind, shy, boyish man of great wit, wisdom and integrity - a man with a great heart. People asked themselves after the bulletin was broadcast," Where were you when you heard the news?" much as they later would when Pearl Harbor was bombed or when President John F. Kennedy was shot.

A memorial was built in Claremore, Oklahoma. Will, Betty and their infant son rest there today. At the dedication services, President Franklin Roosevelt's radio message was broadcast from Hyde Park:

"This afternoon we pay homage to the memory of a man who helped the nation to smile. ... And, after all, I doubt if there is among us a more useful citizen than the one who holds the secret of banishing gloom, of making tears give way to laughter, of supplanting desolation and despair with hope and courage, for hope and courage always go with a light heart. There was something infectious about his humor. His appeal went straight to the heart of the nation. Above all things, in a time grown too solemn and somber, he brought his countrymen back to a sense of proportion. ...When he wanted people to laugh out loud he used the methods of pure fun. ...And when he wanted to make a point for the good of all mankind, he used the kind of gentle irony that left no scars behind it. ...The American nation, to whose heart he brought gladness, will hold him in everlasting remembrance."

After President Roosevelt's remarks, Will's daughter, Mary, unveiled the bronze of Will Rogers. Later, at the U.S. Capitol a similar statue was unveiled at another ceremony when Will Rogers took his place in the Hall of Fame. (It has been reported that more than one U.S. President, since Will's time, have rubbed his statue's toe for luck.) An "Injun' Cowboy" with little schooling had completely stolen the nation's heart and mind and was now a significant part of history and warm, lasting memory.

Thinking Place

Will Rogers did a lot of thinking all over this world. He traveled widely, made a lot of observations, gave his opinions and wrote prolifically in his own style. He made fun of himself and sometimes signed his letters, "Yours Illiterately, Will Rogers."

On location, when filming a movie, frequently his big sedan was his dressing and living room. Often he sat on the car's running board, (only older readers will know much about running boards), and pecked out his communications on his typewriter. Will never wasted a lot of time studying scripts; his lines in movies and on stage were mostly ad lib.

Will probably did a lot of thinking while he was standing in front of an audience, punctuating his remarks with a different twist of his rope. More than likely, Will Rogers had more think-ing places than most folks.

One of Will's favorite places for creative activities and writing was his office and sitting room at his Santa Monica Ranch, in California, duplicated at the Claremore Museum. There is a large stone fireplace with a few items on the mantle; across the room is a small bed covered with a colorful Indian blanket. A coiled lariat hangs on the head of the bed. Will kept a rope handy for practicing lassoing a saddle mounted nearby.

A pull down map of North America and a globe on a stand attest to Will's interest in geography and travel. A small guitar on the wall reminds us that Will loved to sing and, in his own fashion, play the piano. On the floor is an attractive rug with an Indian design, possibly Cherokee. Central in the room is a chair and a small kneehole desk with an old typewriter sitting on it. Scattered on the small desk are newspapers and a few crumpled sheets of typing paper—as if Will might have just left his thinking place.

Lagniappe

Will Rogers, like Abraham Lincoln, was born in a log house, was "a man of the people", and had a folksy sense of humor. Today, years after their respective deaths, both are beloved and respected.

Of course, the magnitude of the life and contributions of "The Civil War-time President", "The Great Emancipator" are incomparable in the annals of history—but there are many similarities in the lives and qualities of Lincoln and Will Rogers, the cowboy-Indian entertainer, the prolific writer, columnist and movie star.

Some confusion over the birthplace of Will is easily explained. Will's father, part Cherokee, was a prosperous owner of a very large ranch in the Indian Territory. The ranch house, originally located between the towns of Claremore and Oolagah had to be moved to a nearby site when a lake was formed on the land in that area. A two-storey addition with painted, clapboard siding made the home quite comfortable.

When it was time for delivery of the new baby, Will's mother directed that they take her into the "log cabin" part of the house, so they could say that Will was born in a log cabin—just like Mr. Lincoln. Thus, his birthplace, formerly nearer tiny Oolagah, was said by Will's father to be in the larger town, Claremore, so people would know where it is. The ranch house and the Will Rogers Memorial may be visited today.

Similar stories are part and parcel of the Will Rogers story. Like Honest Abe's, his humor was straightforward and plain-spoken. He made fun of many subjects and groups, but his comments were never mean-spirited.

Our special gift from Will, our personal lagniappe, was his constant reminder to us of one of his kindred spirits, a beloved member of our family, JMF, who, like Will, "never met a man he didn't like."

Photographic credits:
Portraits of Will Rogers are courtesy of Will Rogers Memorial Museums, Claremore, Oklahoma.

Will in vaudeville days

Statue of Will and Comanche
at Oolagah, Oklahoma

Marjorie
Kinnan Rawlings

1896 - 1953

Marjorie Kinnan Rawlings' farmhouse at
Cross Creek, Florida, and her screen porch Thinking Place

Marjorie Kinnan Rawlings

"I am vibrating with material like a hive of bees in swarm.
I managed to get lost in the scrub the first day of the
hunting season— and encountered for the first time the
palpability of silence. So isolated a section gives a value
to the scattered inhabitants."

Letter to Maxwell Perkins

"Who owns Cross Creek? The red-birds, I think, more
than I, for they will have their nests even in the face of
delinquent mortgages. But what of the land? It seems to
me that the earth may be borrowed but not bought. It
may be used but not owned. It gives itself in response to
love and tending, offers its seasonal flowering and
fruiting. But we are tenants and not possessors, lovers
and not masters. Cross Creek belongs to the wind and
the rain, to the sun and the seasons, to the cosmic secrecy
of seed, and beyond all, to time."

Cross Creek

Journey   Cross Creek

We went to Cross Creek out of curiosity. The celebrated
books, *The Yearling* and *Cross Creek,* had been made into popular
movies. The author of both of these, Marjorie Kinnan Rawlings,
was well known and proudly claimed as a Florida writer.
(Actually, she had grown up in Washington, D.C. and graduated from the University of Wisconsin.) Another motivation for
going was one we had received from Thomas Jefferson, his
words embroidered on a pillow in our home. The much-traveled
Jefferson said, "If you are considering whether or not to go to a
place, go. You may not regret going, but you may always regret
not going."

A professional meeting in St. Augustine had adjourned, and obeying the Jefferson rule, which had become our mantra, we headed home by way of Cross Creek. Marjorie's farmhouse in the woods of central Florida was just as we expected it to be, very plain, functional and appropriate for the setting.

Unfortunately, it was getting late. Visiting hours were over, and the house would not open again until the next day. We elected to stay over. We were in the boondocks, the swampland, and the habitat of alligators, water moccasins, and coons, maybe even a panther or two. We found only one place to stay, a fish camp, offering very humble quarters in the midst of a marsh beside the river. It was not far from the Rawlings house. We told ourselves we were getting a flavor of Marjorie's life. Near total darkness surrounded the camp, and no one else was around. One of us probably had much more concern than Marjorie would have had about which of the local inhabitants might be crouching or slithering nearby.

We went to a local, rustic restaurant down the road. It was packed with people, many of whom had made the trip from Gainesville for the truly local cuisine—catfish, brim, eels or alligator, anything that could be fried. One of us ordered fried gator and pronounced it delicious until pangs of disloyalty made him remember that he was, after all, a University of Florida Gator.

Back at the fish camp, we settled down on the lumpy mattress, and were almost deafened by all the night sounds of the wilderness. We did enjoy our uncommon adventure–in retrospect. The next morning we were already waiting at the Rawlings' house when the Park guides arrived. The wooden, frame house, Marjorie's scrapbooks displayed on a table on the screened porch, the ancient typewriter—all conjured up what her life must have been like. We were glad we had come. Thank you again, Mr. Jefferson.

Our enjoyment of Marjorie Kinnan Rawlings was to continue soon when we journeyed to meet her husband, Norton Baskin, for a delightful experience.

Vignette   Marjorie Kinnan Rawlings 1896 – 1953

Both the life and work of Marjorie Kinnan Rawlings illustrate how much circumstance and place can affect creativity. Marjorie wrote so realistically about the swamps and palmetto scrub areas of central Florida that her readers thought she must be a native. (Florida does claim her as an esteemed writer since she lived most of her adult life in Florida. Her former home at Cross Creek is now a State park, as well as a National Historic Landmark.) Marjorie discovered Cross Creek quite by accident and — oh! the difference in her life!

It all started in 1928 when Marjorie and her husband, Charles, decided they needed a break from their newspaper work in cold and snowy Rochester, New York. They booked a cruise from New York City to Jacksonville, to be followed by a Florida vacation. As the ship was approaching Florida, did Marjorie stand at the ship's rail and wonder what lay ahead? In her wildest imagination, did Marjorie suppose that the beautiful country she was viewing, so different from Rochester, would become her home for the rest of her life? Did she even dream that she would meet Earnest Hemingway, Scott Fitzgerald, Margaret Mitchell, Thomas Wolfe, Robert Frost, Zora Neale Hurston, Mary McLeod Bethune as well as the legendary editor, Maxwell Perkins? Certainly she would not have believed that she would purchase an orange grove, which promised unremitting hard labor, with the results frequently trumped by bad weather. The one thing Marjorie knew was that she wanted to write — and not for a newspaper. Waiting at the dock to help facilitate the Rawlings move to a hotel was a woman they did not know. She was Zelma Cason. Remember the name.

Marjorie grew up in a suburb of Washington, D.C., but her father owned a farm in Maryland where they spent their summers, idyllic summers to Marjorie. When her father died, her mother moved to Madison, Wisconsin so that Marjorie and her brother could attend the University of Wisconsin. Marjorie made Phi Beta Kappa at the University and met her future husband. In May 1919, she married Charles Rawlings, and

307

changed her name. (Kinnan is always pronounced with an accent on the second syllable.) Two years later both Marjorie and Charles took jobs on the *Rochester Times Union* in New York. McClure's Syndicate, with a circulation of fifty newspapers, picked up "Songs of the Housewife," Marjorie's column. By dint of perseverance, Marjorie was successful, but she wished for literary success in another form. She had another concern. The foundation of her marriage was showing cracks.

After visiting in the state, Marjorie said, "Let's move to Florida!" Charles had two brothers in real estate in Florida who could help them do it. In July the brothers found some hammock property, partially planted in an orange grove, a pecan grove, extra land for truck farming, assorted farm equipment, two-hundred chickens, farm animals, a truck, an eight-room farmhouse and a four-room tenant house. It was hardly a prescription for a failing marriage, but in hopeful confidence, they moved in August, two months later.

The income from a prosperous farm would support their writing careers. They did not count on the huge expense involved in farming nor the threat of the Mediterranean fruit fly, not to mention extreme heat, devastating freezes, too much rain, not enough rain and windstorms. The two brothers quit after two years, and three years later, Charles decided he wasn't cut out for farming. Eventually, a divorce followed.

Except for loyal workers in the kitchen and in the orange grove, Marjorie was alone in an isolated, lonely part of Florida, thirty miles from Gainesville. The redeeming grace was her continued love of Cross Creek and a growing conviction that she had at last found what she should write about—this wilderness, teeming with wild life, but sparsely inhabited by a distinctive people who bonded with the land they lived on and were deeply affected by it. Later she would tell of a time when she was utterly lost in the scrub and overwhelmed by the silence. Instead of being afraid, she sat on a log and simply waited. A deep sense of peace came over her. It was the first day of the hunting season, and after an hour, she heard shots of the party searching for her. She never forgot this experience, and she resolved to know better the strong. enduring and stoic people called "Florida Crackers."

Soon afterwards, she made arrangements to live for two-and-a-half months with the Fiddia family. On another occasion, she lived for a week in the scrub with the family of an old hunter.

Marjorie now knew her writing sense of direction was true. She sat at her manual typewriter, placed on a table on her screened porch, and wrote for long hours. "Cracker Chitlings," written within a year after the move from Rochester was one of the first pieces that she sent out. *Scribners'* magazine bought it, and most significant for her future, chief editor, Maxwell Perkins, saw it—and liked it. From 1930 to his death in 1947, Marjorie became one of his stable of authors. Perkins also edited Hemingway, Fitzgerald and Thomas Wolfe, and it was through him that they all became acquainted with Marjorie.

After a number of short pieces of fiction, *South Moon Under* was her first major work. Besides garnering excellent reviews, it was chosen as a Book-of- the-Month Club selection. Her success or "arrival" was bittersweet because that time also marked the break-up of her marriage. How she dealt with the hurt of separation is a good illustration of her spunky character. She and her friend, Dessie Smith, courted danger when they took a one-hundred-mile trip on the upper St. John's River in a rowboat, powered by an outboard motor. For more of the details, read "Hyacinth Drift" chapter in *Cross Creek*.

Golden Apples, which took two years to write, was not the book she had wanted it to be. On the other hand, "Gal Young Un" won the O. Henry Memorial Prize. Recognition had come at last, but she had traveled a difficult road. This brief account has not described her own physical labor, and the problems and hardships involved in keeping the orange grove and farm activities going; nor has it mentioned the financial worries that beset her. For three years the farm was profitable; the next year it barely broke even and then it lost money. A check for a literary prize once arrived when she was down to her last can of soup!

Her finest moments still lay ahead. She continued to observe the backwoods, "Cracker" ways. She listened to stories of life in the primitive scrub, and she even went on bear hunts. She was now ready to write what would become a classic, translated into thirteen languages and made into a memorable movie, the touching story of a boy and his young deer, *The Yearling*. She won the Pulitzer Prize for it in 1939. *Cross Creek* followed with gratifying success; it was a major best seller. She was elected to the National Academy of Arts and Letters. *The Secret River*, a children's book, won The Newbery Prize.

Another measure of her fame was the number of famous people who came to Cross Creek to visit her. Once an indifferent cook, she now had become an expert—and an original. She wanted her guests to have a flavor of the region. Instead of serving asparagus, for example, she placed steamed okra on a plate, arranged like spokes in a wheel around a bowl of hollandaise sauce. Later she published the very popular cookbook, *Cross Creek Cookery*.

In 1941 she married Norton Baskin, a true gentleman she had known for many years. A very witty man, he must have kept her laughing. During World War II he served in the India-Burma Theater and came home very ill. She did little writing while she nursed him back to health.

In the summer for six years, she went to Van Hornesville, N.Y. and nearby Springfield Center where she worked on *The Sojourner*. It was a big book with a wide canvas, but it did not measure up to her Florida books.

Health problems began to consume her time as she tried to continue writing. Her greatest worry, however, was a legal case for invasion of privacy, brought by her previously good friend, Zelma Cason, who claimed Marjorie had maligned her in a book. You may remember that Zelma met the boat that brought the Rawlings to Florida. The jury ruled in favor of Marjorie, and it was a popular decision with those in the courtroom. Then Zelma appealed, and the case went to the Florida Supreme Court. With a 4-3 vote, the jury reversed the decision, fining Marjorie one dollar and costs of court. This needless action took five and a half years, $18,000 in legal fees for Marjorie, not to mention a few pounds of flesh. One good aspect was Marjorie's discovering how much her chosen community both loved and accepted her. Ironically, sometime afterward, the two women acknowledged their affection for each other. The end of the case came in 1948.

A heart attack in 1952 did not deter Marjorie from finishing *The Sojourner*, which was published in January, 1953. Then she began research on a biography of her good friend, the late Ellen Glasgow, in Richmond, Virginia.

She returned to Crescent Beach, Florida where she died of a cerebral hemorrhage on December 14, 1953. At the time of her death, perhaps she had the same peaceful, almost mystical experience that she had described when she was totally lost in the scrub, some twenty-two years earlier, and even before that, when she had called a similar experience "my glimpse of eternity."

At her funeral, Norton Baskin read from *Cross Creek* a passage that is eerily reminiscent of Isaak Dinesen (Karen Blixen) whose story was depicted in the movie, "Out of Africa." Her life paralleled Marjorie's in several major respects. Both writers are prime examples of how place and circumstance influence creativity.

"Who owns Cross Creek? The red birds, I think, more than I...Cross Creek belongs to the wind and the rain, to the sun and the seasons, to the cosmic secrecy of seed. And beyond all, to time."

Thinking Place

Marjorie Kinnan Rawlings did not always write about the Cross Creek country that made her famous. Maxwell Perkins, well known editor, advised her to "write about what you know." Marjorie knew his advice was sound and recognized that as far as literature was concerned, the wilderness country in central Florida was virgin territory. She set about making the people and the land of her new home in Florida come alive.

What better place to write than in her own rough-shingled cottage and farm that was literally carved out of the wilderness! In the hot, humid climate, only one choice for table and typewriter made sense—the screened porch. The over-hanging eaves protected from direct sun, and if there was a breeze, Marjorie would catch most of it. Her round table-top had a huge tree stump for a base. Typewriter, paper and a tall glass of spring water completed her needs. If she heard birdsong or the distant yell of a Florida panther, so much the better.

Sometimes, early in the mornings, she would prop up in bed and write first drafts in longhand—later, typing at her thinking place on the porch. Did she get lonely during the years when she lived alone? If she did, the independent woman that she was, would not have admitted it. Besides, she had many memorable friends—Jody and Ike, Idella and many more characters from her real-life experiences and imagination.

Lagniappe   St. Augustine

We learned that Norton Baskin, the widower of Marjorie Kinnan Rawlings, was living in St. Augustine, Florida. Carolyn, whose maternal grandmother was a Baskin, telephoned Norton, and the two of them discovered that they were, indeed, related. (Such a conversation between strangers is both acceptable and frequent in the Deep South.) At the time, we were investigating the court case when Marjorie was sued for slander by her former friend, Zelma Cason. Norton readily agreed to our coming to St. Augustine for an interview.

Norton Baskin had been the manager of a large hotel and restaurant in Atlanta, and then hotels in Ocala and St. August-ine, but he could have been famous as a stand-up comic and actor. In fact, he played a cameo role in the movie, *Cross Creek.*

We spent the afternoon with Norton, listening to his witty and frequently hilarious stories. He told us details of the Zelma Cason trial and the out-of-court story, and about Marjorie's friendships with many other writers, including Margaret Mitchell, Ernest Hemingway and others. He invited us to continue our conversation with dinner at his favorite restaurant and then to spend the night at his house! It was a delightful experience...continuous good humor and many belly laughs. We recorded some of our conversations, with his permission. For a complete transcript of much of our twelve-hour plus interview see *The Marjorie Kinnan Rawlings Journal of Florida Literature*, Vol XV, (2007).

Norton Baskin, raconteur, gentleman, and keen observer, became our friend. Our good fortune in knowing him was lagniappe indeed.

Additional lagniappe came when we joined The Marjorie Kinnan Rawlings Society, which promotes Marjorie's further acceptance as a major American writer. For minimal dues, one meets many fascinating people and hears exceptional programs. Rawlings was not only a fine writer but also an expert naturalist. She rambled through the woods, lived with families in primitive conditions, observed and recorded the flora and fauna of central Florida, as well as the life and times of its early inhabitants, called "Crackers." In deference to her talents, an MKR Society program may include identifying bird calls, plants or seashells, or discussing characters, relationships and plots in one of her many stories. In one of the meetings, the connection was made between Samuel Taylor Coleridge's "Kubla Khan" and Salt Springs (near Ocala), which Marjorie knew well. (See photo below of Marjorie spearing a crab at Salt Springs.) Naturalist William Bartram, in 1791, wrote of this bubbling spring and under-ground river spewing out sand and particles of shells. His vivid description may have been one of the inspirations for Coleridge in writing his now famous poem. This is another example of the wide range of topics that Marjorie and related subjects still bring to her readers and to the MKR Society.

Photographic credits: Pictures of Marjorie and Norton Baskin; and Marjorie at Salt Springs below are courtesy of the Department of Special and Area Studies Collections, George Smathers Libraries, University of Florida.

Marjorie Rawlings

Norton Baskin

Cross Creek

Marjorie spearing a crab at Salt Springs, the site which
may have inspired Coleridge's poem," Kubla Khan"

316

William Faulkner

1897 – 1962

Rowan Oaks, William Faulkner's
Home in Oxford, Mississippi and
his witting table and chair.

William Faulkner

"I decline to accept the end of man."

"The past is never dead. It isn't even past."

"Let the writer take up surgery or bricklaying if he is interested in technique. There is no mechanical way to get the writing done, no shortcut. The young writer would be a fool to follow a theory. Teach yourself by your own mistakes; people learn only by error. The good artist believes that nobody is good enough to give him advice. He has supreme vanity. No matter how much he admires the old writer, he wants to beat him."

Interview with the Paris Review,1956

Journey   Oxford, Mississippi

Oxford, Mississippi is a university town named for its famous counterpart, Oxford, England. To William Faulkner readers, a journey to Oxford, Mississippi is also a journey to the town of "Jefferson" and "Yoknapatawpha County," fictional locales of Faulkner's writings. Today the courthouse square in the center of town, the courthouse itself, has a commanding presence as it looms over "Yoknapatawpha County," whose real-life counterpart is Jefferson County with Oxford as its county seat. The courthouse was the model in *Sanctuary* where Temple Drake testified falsely against Lee Goodwin. Also, Faulkner used Hamilton Hill, an antebellum mansion on south Thirteenth Street, for the Compton family home in *The Sound and The Fury*. This "map-able" but fictitious locality in Faulkner's work is one of the most famous locales in literature. Faulkner referred to this land as " my very own postage stamp."

All roads in Oxford lead to William Faulkner's home, Rowan Oaks. Although quite southern in architecture, it is not a stately mansion, but its charm is the Faulknerian atmosphere it evokes.

An early settler built the original house in 1840. When the Faulkners acquired it in 1930, they chose the name Rowan Oaks from the legend related in James Frazier's, *The Golden Bough*. (Scottish peasants cut branches of rowan wood and placed them in the shape of a cross over the thresholds of their homes in order to ward off evil spirits and give those in the house peace and security.) Rowan Oaks is in a grove of oaks, and tall cedar trees line each side of the main walk. This setting gives a sense of privacy and protection. The house and its thirty-one acre grounds are now the property of the University of Mississippi; it is open only when the university is in session. Graduate students conduct tours through the Office of University Relations.

Faulkner sought refuge and privacy at Rowan Oaks for most of the last thirty years of his life except for interludes in Hollywood as a script writer and as writer-in-residence at the University of Virginia. Faulkner's yearning to relate to the British in their regard for privacy may have been reflected in his manner and his clothing, such as pictured in his English-style riding habit and tweedy coats. (As a young man he had volunteered for training in the Royal Canadian Air Force. World War I ended and he did not receive aviation training or his wings, but he returned home in an RCAF uniform complete with wings, and was properly photographed.) Willie Morris, admirer of Faulkner, had observed in his four years as a Rhodes Scholar at Oxford, England that the truest and most deeply appreciated impression an American can take from Oxford is "the almost universal deference paid there to privacy—privacy in the broad, human sense." While living in England we too learned to re-spect the privacy of strangers who were forced to share our table in a small restaurant. (When curiosity trumped the Brit's natural reserve, we were more than happy to share a conversation.)

Faulkner stated that the most important room in Rowan Oaks was the one he designed and added on to the house—his study or "office", as he called it, fashioned after the office of the masters of plantations of yesteryear—where they conducted all their business. This was his creative, thinking place at Rowan Oaks. Faulkner also built a brick wall, which extends from the corner of the house to the east porch to give him more privacy in the garden.

Today, a visitor sees little evidence of commercialism related to Faulkner's home. The sense of quiet dignity and refuge has been preserved at Rowan Oaks—in respect, perhaps, for the owner's long-term struggle for personal privacy.

Vignette   William Faulkner   1897 - 1962

Oh, the vagaries of Chance! Consider this about William Faulkner, Nobel Prize winner, and one of America's greatest writers. In 1944, all of Faulkner's seventeen novels, the then current number, were out-of-print except *Absalom, Absalom!* The New York Public Library listed only two of his books in its huge catalogue. It was difficult to find any of his books in a second-hand bookstore. Faulkner himself did not even own a copy of *The Sound and the Fury*, the personal favorite of all his novels. According to Malcolm Cowley, poet, critic, and literary historian, this state of affairs was Faulkner's "quoted value on the literary stock exchange." At this point, Cowley decided, with Faulkner's permission, to attempt *A Portable Faulkner*, as a sequel to his *Portable Hemingway*. Soon Faulkner was once more available in the market. (His lifetime literary output would grow to be: nineteen novels, five collections of stories, a collection of three short novels, two anthologies, several limited editions of his short fiction, two editions of his New Orleans sketches and two volumes of poetry.)

Who brought Faulkner back into prominence? Certainly not the critics, generally. They were not always in his camp. It was his fellow writers who respected his genius and promoted him. A partial list, besides Cowley, included: Robert Penn Warren, Conrad Aiken, Andre Malraux, Arnold Bennett, Caroline Gordon and Ernest Hemingway. Faulkner did "come back." The ultimate recognition of his lifetime achievement was his award of the Nobel Prize in Literature for 1949, given in 1950.

Faulkner did not like interviews or questions which delved into his private life. He felt that his literary work was the only proper subject for inquiry. Since he died forty-odd years ago, perhaps a few items may be mentioned. He was born in New Albany, Mississippi, but his family lived in Ripley, then moved to Oxford, Mississippi where he spent most of his life. He traveled for extended stays in New Orleans, Hollywood, New York, Europe, and Virginia. Later he went to Japan as a cultural ambassador for the State Department. Hard to believe, but Faulkner attended only two years of high school and one year at the University of Mississippi in Oxford.

To conservative townspeople of Oxford, Faulkner seemed eccentric in his old, tweedy jackets and various hats. Sometimes he went bare-footed in downtown Oxford. He was unemployed until he got a job at the post office. (He was later fired.) His nickname at that time was "Count No-count." He was an outstanding scoutmaster but was relieved because of his drinking. During this period, he was growing his creative wings. Later when he had to be away, he always missed his Mississippi home. The place he truly disliked was Hollywood, where he occasionally wrote movie scripts to support not only his wife, Estelle, daughter, Jill, and two stepchildren but also his extended family. Rowan Oaks, his pre-Civil War home, originally without electricity or indoor plumbing, was also a drain financially.

Money worries, family concerns preyed on his mind, but he was always fortunate in the loyalty and support of his friends, especially in New Orleans, New Haven and New York. He had friends in Oxford too, especially the men with whom he went hunting and fishing. Their testimony suggests that he was "a prince of a fellow" although they would have used different words to describe their hunting buddy. Alcohol abuse ran in his family; in fact, his father's problems were mirrored in his son. His father, Murry Faulkner, worked for the family owned railroad. It was his great pride and he had worked up in the organization, expecting to be its chief officer. Without informing him in advance, Murry's father sold the railroad, moved to Oxford, and Murry, with his wife's urgings, had to move the family to Oxford, also. Murry worked unhappily at a number of jobs and was frequently hospitalized with alcoholism. He and his son, William, were never close. Whatever his demons, eventually, William Faulkner also became an alcoholic with a tremendous capacity for whiskey.

Nothing deterred his writing. The wonder is that he was able to produce both the quality and the quantity of his work. He was always concerned for his creative life. He worried that the influence of Hollywood would kill his talent. It did not. The irony is that the movie moguls who did not always use the scripts that Faulkner had written while in bondage to the film industry, would later buy the movie rights to some of his books.

Faulkner's childhood sweetheart, Estelle, married someone else, but after her divorce, she and Faulkner married. It was not a happy union; abuse of alcohol by both partners was one reason. Faulkner had affairs with several other women, but he remained married to Estelle. He adored his daughter, Jill, and was fond of his two stepchildren.

Some first-time readers of Faulkner are intimidated by several elements of his style. He was a superb craftsman, but he was a modernist, thereby employing complex form; he attempted to explore and show the inner states of the mind, using interior monologue and his now well recognized, stream-of-consciousness technique. He would sometimes abandon chronological time and straight, linear narration. He used details tellingly for surface reality, and he aimed for strong characterization. Frequently his sentences were paragraph-long. Of his own involved and sometimes formless sentence, Faulkner said, "I'm trying to say it all in one sentence between one Cap and one period."

Another problem for the casual reader is the uncomfortable feeling that the text is full of symbolism, and the reader may be unsure of what it means. The following paragraphs may be helpful in understanding Faulkner.

Few authors have created an entire world as complete and as real as the imaginary Yoknapatawpha County. The sense of place was a significant part of Faulkner's creative vision. He liked to refer to his "own little postage stamp of native soil." It was enough because he believed that men everywhere, in whatever period, are essentially the same. The family is centrist in most of his books. Although his work is imbued with a sense of the South, Faulkner himself considered that he was writing, not about the South per se, but about the human situation. Faulkner spoke of this in 1962: 'The primary job that any writer faces is to tell you a story out of human experience—I mean by that, universal mutual experience, the anguishes and troubles and griefs of the human heart, which is universal, without regard to race or time or condition. He wants to tell you something which has seemed to him so true, so moving, either comic or tragic, that it's worth preserving."

Faulkner admired the following writers: Melville, Conrad, Balzac, Flaubert, Dickens, and Dostoyevsky. What he hoped most to accomplish, he expressed in the following phrase: "To create out of the material of the human spirit something which did not exist before."

He lived with a sense of history, not as a chronicle but as story. He said that he was still trying to put all of mankind's history into one sentence. His southern background was significant because the Civil War, the institution of slavery and the loss of the wilderness still seemed close to him, as it did to so many Southerners of his day. He owned the past upheavals as part of his own experience.

The concept of Time was an important concept to Faulkner. As he said, "There is no such thing as was— only is." We can only experience the past and anticipate the future in the present. There are two kinds of Time—clock or calendar Time and abstract Time, involving memory and thought. If these philosophical considerations are less important to you, the reader, take comfort in something else he believed: characters are more important than ideas. It is obvious that Faulkner can be read on more than one level. He was a writer of epics, but he was also a fine, comic writer. Before he wrote novels, he wrote poetry.

When he was awarded the Nobel Prize, he declined to attend the ceremony. He changed his mind when he considered what it would mean to his daughter, Jill, to be present and later to see Paris with him. He delivered his address in the famous hall in Stockholm. Few could hear him well because of his light, and high-pitched voice, but when the text was released, the public recognized that it was a masterpiece. Some have compared it to Lincoln's "Gettysburg Address." A brief excerpt follows:

> "… I believe that man will not merely endure: he will prevail. He is immortal, not because he alone among creatures has an inexhaustible voice, but because he has a soul, a spirit capable of compassion and sacrifice and endurance. The poet's, the writer's, duty is to write about these things. It is his privilege to help man endure by lifting his heart, by reminding him of the courage and honor and hope and pride and compassion and pity and sacrifice which have been the glory of his past. The poet's voice need not merely be the record of man, it can be one of the props, the pillars to help him endure and prevail."

Thinking Places

Faulkner probably had many thinking places during his early years, including a power plant described below, but his long-term favorite creative/thinking place was his "office" at Rowan Oaks which may be visited today. On a small wooden table an old, portable Underwood typewriter attests to the fact that Faulkner wrote many of his novels in this room. Also, on the table is an ashtray made from an old artillery casing. Nearby in the room is a daybed where he rested at times. On the wall, he wrote a detailed outline of *The Fable*. He needed a big space to write it all down. When you look at it, you may have an odd sensation that the author himself has just left the room. After all, Faulkner himself said that the past is not even past; the past and all we know of the future exist only in the present. This room is Faulkner's most famous thinking place.

Less well known, and certainly an unexpected thinking place, is the power plant in Oxford. Faulkner's father secured him the job as night foreman, assisted by a fireman. It required Faulkner's continually loading up a wheelbarrow with coal in the early evening. The fireman would then shovel each load into the boiler, assuring the regular and comforting hum of the generator. As the night wore on, the sleeping town needed less power, so from eleven until four, the fireman slept and Faulkner wrote. Assembling his onion-skin paper, Faulkner turned over the wheelbarrow and used its bottom surface as his desk. Unscrewing his fountain pen, he wrote quickly, steadily, confidently in long hand. His neat but diminutive script filled lines as straight as if drawn by a ruler. He did not waste paper. His own shorthand symbols could be hard to read once his copy got cold. As soon as possible, he typed out a second copy, making revisions as necessary. He sent a third perfect copy, still containing revisions, to the publisher. Once a book was printed, Faulkner did not read it again. He knew he would want to make changes.

Faulkner had other thinking places over the years, but the power plant must have had an advantage over all others. Solitude.

Lagniappe   Off the Square in Oxford, Mississippi

Our unexpected dividend in Oxford occurred in an old establishment just off the famous town square. It was the photographic studio of J.R. Cofield. We had no idea that this studio would itself have an interesting story.

One of us needed a photograph for a symposium to be held in Jackson, Mississippi soon thereafter. Someone recommended Mr. Cofield. When we entered the studio, we wondered if we should have just settled for a passport picture. The furnishings seemed—venerable. The lighting in the small room was subdued, but when J.R. Cofield walked in from the back room, we forgot our doubts. Mr. Cofield lit up that room. He made us feel like we were long-lost cousins, and we exchanged the usual statistics that southerners feel obligated to give on first meeting.

We adjourned to the back room and after fiddling with his camera, Mr. Cofield soon disappeared under the enveloping black cloth that added solemnity, even a touch of mysticism, to the procedure. That mood disappeared quickly when he started telling yarns, which fell into two categories—Bill Faulkner or the Ole Miss Football Team. Each story was better than the one before, and we hardly noticed when he squeezed the bulb and took the picture. By our laughter, he must have gauged which subject we preferred. Soon he was reminiscing exclusively about Faulkner. He said that every time Faulkner would get some new outfit or "costume," he would come in for a photographic session with J.R. The famous writer, or town character, whichever you prefer, was photogenic and quite handsome in his pictures, which made him look debonair and commanding. J.R. showed us his collection of Faulkner photographs, and we realized that Mr. Cofield was a talented artist. A movie star gazed at us from photographic paper. One of us wondered if Faulkner had an understandable vanity about being photographed or if he came to Cofield with some regularity because he was sending his picture to a female admirer.

J.R. Cofield had not finished with his yarns, each one hooked up to the next like railroad cars on a track. He finally concluded with what we judged to be his favorite, the engine of his memories of Faulkner. It did illustrate best the novelist's personality —from what we had read.

According to J.R., Faulkner was getting more and more irritated by the cars of rubber-necking tourists, mainly ladies, who would ride by Rowan Oak, always slowing down to get a glimpse of the resident monkey who wrote for a living. One day, as the cars were passing, Faulkner began to water the grass with a garden hose, "buck naked," J. R. said. "That kinda' stopped 'em," he chuckled. We had heard that story, but it was twice as funny when J.R. told us.

The photograph J.R. had taken of Jack, with its shadows and highlights, was quite flattering. A famous photographer, the friend of a Nobel Laureate, had taken what really was a distinctive portrait, even without the obligatory cigarette. Years later we realized that the picture had been lost, but we still had our lagniappe, our memory of an unforgettable character who made William Faulkner come alive for us.

Photographic credits:
Photograph of the cover of *William Faulkner: The Cofield Collection* which is now out of print. Courtesy of Larry Wells, Director, the Yoknapatawpha Press, Oxford, Mississippi

Book cover of J. R. Cofield's
collection of Faulkner pictures

The privacy of Rowan Oaks

Ernest Hemingway
1899 - 1960

Ernest Hemingway's home and
writing place at Key West, Florida.

Ernest Hemingway

"Grace under pressure."

His definition of guts

"Cowardice, as distinguished from panic, is almost
always simply a lack of ability to suspend the
functioning of the imagination."

"I know only that what is moral is what you feel good after
and what is immoral is what you feel bad after."

Death in the Afternoon

Journey   Key West

Like Robert Louis Stevenson, Ernest Hemingway was a true
citizen of the world. Both men sought adventure and were more
than willing to venture forth to distant lands and seas, writing
along the way.

As we followed Stevenson's pathways from Scotland to
France and California to Samoa, in like manner, many
Hemingway devotees may have traveled to Oak Park, Illinois to
Kansas City, Kansas; Paris; Spain; Italy; Africa; Key West;
Havana, Cuba and Ketchum, Idaho.

We have not yet visited Oak Park, ten miles outside of
Chicago, but judging from other reports, anyone interested in
Hemingway should go there. The Ernest Hemingway Foundation of Oak Park operates and makes available for visitors the
Hemingway birthplace and museum. Hemingway was born in
the Queen Anne style home in Oak Park. Frank Lloyd Wright
lived in Oak Park for over twenty years, and today it is said that
the village is a living museum of American architecture, containing "more buildings of national and international significance per capita than any other community in the United
States." Hemingway spent his first twenty years in Oak

Park, so this town and childhood summer vacations in the outdoors of the wilds of Michigan had considerable, influence on his life.

Our journey was to Key West—many miles and many events distant from Oak Park, in quite another world. Hemingway lived in Key West for over ten years, probably during his most prolific writing period. When Hemingway and wife, Pauline, arrived in Key West, their house was not ready, so they lived in an apartment above a Ford automobile showroom. There he established his habit of faithfully writing in the mornings when it was cooler, keeping the afternoons open for exploring. He worked hard on finishing *A Farewell to Arms*, and it was published in the fall of 1929. After two seasons in Key West, they moved into the house on Whitehead Street.

Hemingway's leisure time was often spent with friends at "Sloppy Joe's Bar," named for Joe Russell. Joe, Charles Thompson, and Captain Eddie "Bra" Sanders, along with some of Hemingway's friends from Paris, became known as "The Key West Mob." They frequently went on long trips to Cuba and other islands, pursuing tuna and game fish. The town was full of interesting characters and stories from which Hemingway probably modeled some of his writings.

After Ernest and Pauline divorced in 1939, Ernest moved to Cuba, and Pauline retained possession of the house until she died in 1951. Ernest then rented the house furnished. Upon his death, his estate sold it to a private party. In 1968, the house was designated a National Historic Landmark. Fortunately, the present owners give good care to the distinctive house along with a willingness to share this treasure of literary history with the public.

Vignette   Ernest Hemingway   1899 – 1960

The most significant story by Ernest Hemingway was never published. His own. Such a pity! His autobiography would have been a history of an era and some of its leading personalities.

Perhaps slanted, prejudiced, flippant, sometimes poetic, possibly obscene in places, it would have been colorful and eminently readable. Most likely, it would not have revealed the complex, conflicted, contradictory personality that was Ernest who later became "Papa," a role he delighted in playing— a man's man, a ladies' man, virile big game hunter, sports fisherman for marlin, Alpine skier, connoisseur of bull fighting and of good food and wine— and a handsome, famous writer!

It is amazing that a high school graduate, training himself by the style manual of *The Kansas City Star*, could produce a body of work that would win the Nobel Prize in Literature. Later in Paris, mentors who were at the top of the writing profession surrounded him and could have overshadowed him, but he had the fire in the belly to succeed and be a stand out. And he did. Hemingway understood the strength of the simple, declarative sentence as a building block in the creation of prose. The well known Hemingway style is his greatest legacy.

His childhood in a traditional American family, appears to have been a happy one in spite of tensions with his mother, Grace, who had kept him in lace-trimmed, long dresses until he was four, with a girlish haircut until he was six and in short pants until he was fifteen. His father was a successful, wealthy doctor who was an avid hunter, fisherman and taxidermist. He coached Ernest in these sports and taught him the manly art of boxing. Ernest and his father loved the outdoors. The family spent long summers in a rustic setting in the woods of Michigan. There, as a youngster, he played with members of the Ojibway Indian tribe. His mother said that when Ernest was a spunky child of two and asked what he was afraid of, his reply was, "fraid of nothing". In high school, he played football and also the cello in the school orchestra. He received from his mother, a talented musician, his love of the arts. Sixteen years later he would order a custom-made gun for big game hunting.

Even a reading of biographical information varies with the biographer. For instance, the boy with the "happy childhood" ran away from home when he was fourteen, but he did return to finish high school. He was seldom simpatico with his mother. On one occasion, after he was twenty-one, she ordered him to leave home until he learned to be respectful to her. His out-doorsman father backed her up.

All of this may give some insight as to how Ernest became the rough and tumble personality his public liked to read about but with varying reactions—envy, intrigue, fascination, dis-approval? Had he written an autobiography it might have had elements of mystery, bravery, betrayal, sensitivity, callousness, regret and probably great chunks of fiction because Hemingway had a habit of reinventing himself. He was content to write himself and his contemporaries into his novels and short stories, sometimes to their great and understandable displeasure.

Hemingway skipped college and worked for *The Kansas City Star* for six months until he joined an American ambulance unit in Italy in 1917. Within three weeks he was wounded with 227 bits of shrapnel, resulting in a long hospital stay where he fell in love with his nurse, later immortalized in *A Farewell to Arms*. (She rejected him then but later showed up in Key West. The romance was not resumed.) Although severely wounded, he had managed to carry an injured soldier to safety. The Italian government decorated him for bravery.

Working for a magazine in Chicago in 1921, he met the redheaded beauty, Hadley Richardson, also a talented musician, and announced on their first evening, "That's the girl I'm going to marry." And he did. Armed with introductions by Sherwood Anderson to Gertrude Stein and other literary figures, the couple moved to Paris. A job with The *Toronto Star Weekly* made it possible. In 1923, his first signed work appeared in *Poetry. Three Stories and Ten Poems* followed. Ernest and Hadley, now parents of a son, John, whom they called Brumby, were poor but happy. In his memoir, *Moveable Feast*, about this time in Paris he wrote, "If you are lucky enough to have lived in Paris as a young man, then wherever you go for the rest of your life, it stays with you, for Paris is a moveable feast."

Then another woman moved in with them—literally. She was Pauline Pfeiffer, who became his second wife. He lamented loving two women at once, and he did continue to write to Hadley through the years. He and Pauline had two sons. After his divorce from Pauline, in 1940 he married Martha Gellhorn, a respected journalist, who had followed Ernest to Europe. Mary Walsh was his fourth and final wife. Mary wrote of Ernest, he was…"heartless, thoughtless, selfish, spoiled, unappreciative, and egotistical and a publicity-seeking monster." Otherwise, we assume that she adored him. There were other dalliances, but Mary stayed with him to the end of his life, which came too soon.

Throughout his life he was open always to new experiences. He traveled, went big-game hunting, fished on his beloved boat, *The Pilar*, followed the bulls, entertained guests at his homes in Key West, Havana, and Ketchum, Idaho. After world-wide fame arrived, he also kept an apartment in Manhattan with one available at the Ritz in Paris and the Gritti in Venice. He had money enough to fulfill every desire.

Near the end, he and Mary were in Idaho where he was treated for deep depression, delusion and paranoia. He was suicidal. After receiving electric shock treatments, the hospital insisted that he was well enough for Mary to take home, and he did have good moments with her. However, the ironies pile up around this critical time. One is a statement written years before by his mother on the back of a photograph, "Ernest was taught to shoot by Pa when 2 1/2 and when 4 could handle a pistol."

In the early morning of July 2, 1961, while Mary was still sleeping, Ernest took the keys from the windowsill and un-locked the storage closet. He took out, not a pistol, but a shot gun. Mary said afterwards, "No one had a right to deny a man access to his possessions." We can only conclude that Ernest did not want to live when he judged that he was losing his creative power. He was sixty-one. One wonders what revealing book perished with him. An autobiography?

The mystery of Hemingway remains. How can we explain the destructive streak that destroyed his marriages or the dis-loyalty he showed to friends that had helped him and admired him, writers like Scott Fitzgerald, Robert Sherwood, Ford Maddox Ford and Gertrude Stein? (Admittedly, he did sustain some blows from the latter two.) On the other hand, how can we explain his inimical style, so spare, so distinctive, so frequently copied but seldom equalled? Martha Gellhorn, his third and least favorite wife, was a talented writer, who may have competed too much with her husband. Even so she said of Ernest, "He was a genius, that uneasy word, not so much in what he wrote as in how he wrote; he liberated our written language."

How could a man who so obviously reveled in everything around him and wanted to drain Life's cup, cause havoc in his own life? He stayed on uneasy terms with his parents, particularly his mother. Hemingway greatly admired his father and realized too late how much they had loved each other. (His father, depressed by bad health and financial problems, committed suicide.) Ernest loved and lost three wives before Mary, his fourth wife, who said that he married her to be his nursemaid. (That was said half in jest, but she did become a "nurse maid" for some of his work that was published post-humously.) Did Ernest Hemingway harbor a death wish? If so, was it the power that fueled his undeniable and rare creativity? Perhaps that could be put another way. Was fascination with Death a core element in his work? Certainly it appears in his two great war novels, *A Farewell to Arms* and *For Whom the Bell Tolls* and among other short stories, *The Snows of Kilimanjaro* and *Death in the Afternoon*, a story about bull-fighting, a ballet portraying chaos and civilization, a paean to valor.

Sensitive, generous, superstitious, primitive, contradictory, accident-prone, cool under fire, emotional, courageous, senti-mental. Each describes Hemingway in some situation. He did not exhibit interest in social concerns, labor disputes, for instance, nor was he overtly political except during the Spanish Civil War. He distrusted symbolism in writing although his readers supplied their own, especially interpretations of *The Old Man and the Sea*. He was not apparently a spiritual or religious person although he did mention attending mass when he wrote to his mother. It is only fair to acknowledge that the experts' differing views span the spectrum of opinion. Some extol the personal code of his heroes: honor, endurance, courage. Others insist that disillusion is not uppermost in his work. Instead, they point to his implied appeal to a higher set of ethical values than many men live by.

Edmund Wilson (according to James R. Mellow) tried to explain the paradox that was Hemingway by saying that Hemingway, Dickens, Joyce, Kipling had "developed a literature of trauma, working from...wounds that set these writers apart from society, producing a kind of alienation that was a strength and weakness of their genius." Hemingway was incensed by this assessment, particularly when Wilson called the public Hemingway, "certainly the worst-invented character to be found in the author's work." Hemingway expressed his anger by threatening to file an injunction forbidding Wilson's intent to publish.

With inadequately expressed appreciation for his crafting of many volumes of true sentences, it is only fair to let Hemingway himself have the last word: "A country, finally, erodes and the dust blows away, the people all die and none of them were of any importance permanently, except those who practiced the arts, and these now wish to cease their work because it is too lonely, too hard to do, and is not fashionable. A thousand years makes economics silly and a work of art endures forever."

Thinking Place

Hemingway believed in thinking places. He was never without one. When he and his first wife, Hadley, were newly married and existing on very little, he found the money to rent a writing-thinking place in a small hotel. He had to climb steep flights of steps to a small room on the top floor. The view across the rooftops of Paris must have been worth the climb. When it was too cold in his roof top aerie, he took his blue notebooks with him and wrote in the warmth of a café.

His most famous Thinking Place, one that may be visited today, is in Key West. Hemingway made his own place on the second storey of an old carriage house, connected by a catwalk to the main house. Very early in the morning he would slip out and write until noon, always careful not to "write out" but to leave sentences or thoughts to facilitate his beginning the next day. Some of his best work was written here while standing at a tall, shelf-like desk. He wrote in longhand but his Royal typewriter was nearby, as well as a Cuban cigar-maker's chair and mementos of past adventures. Hemingway was not lazy. He was disciplined and regular in his habits. He wrote every day whether or not company was visiting in the main house. He kept first drafts like graveyard wrecks, and scholars today may observe his method of composition.

In 1968 the house was made a National Historic Landmark. Visitors may see much of the unusual, original furniture, some of it Spanish antiques, accented by Venetian chandeliers. Hemingway had once given to Hadley, Miro's painting, *The Farm*. A copy is here. The original now hangs in the National Gallery in Washington, D.C. Picasso gave Papa a sculpture of a cat. A thief broke it, but a copy is part of the Hemingway house-museum.

Hemingway loved cats and dozens prowl through the gardens and porches. Some are direct descendents of those that Hemingway claimed. Probably one of the few fountains expressly built for cats is in the Hemingway gardens at Key West. Pauline fashioned a large clay jar that continuously overflows to an oblong container on the ground—the container was once a receptacle in the men's room at Sloppy Joe's.

When his marriage to Pauline, his second wife, was breaking up, he moved to Havana, Cuba. His first thinking place here was the Hotel Ambos Mundos, where he would write from eight-thirty a.m. to two or three in the afternoon.

Eventually he moved to Finca Vigia, Cuba, a house that his third wife, Martha Gellhorn, had renovated. Sometimes a circus atmosphere prevailed, exacerbated by servant problems. Possibly Martha, the skillful, professional journalist and novelist was not as interested in decorating as Pauline, who had added Spanish and Portuguese tiles, a modern kitchen and a swimming pool, the largest in Key West, to the home she shared with Ernest. The two houses had one thing in common. CATS! "Never laugh at a cat," Hemingway had once warned. "Dogs like it because they want to be pals with you. Cats don't want to be pals." "Friendless", one of Hemingway's favorite cats was allowed to drink milk and whiskey with him.

The thinking place did not work its magic during the 1940's.The decade following the publication of *For Whom the* Bell *Tolls* was a fallow time for Hemingway. He published nothing until 1950 with the appearance of *Across the River and into the Trees*, a disaster of a book, according to some. Perhaps Max Perkins could have helped salvage it, but Max had died in 1947. Hemingway redeemed his fading reputation with *The Old Man and the Sea*, published in 1952, winner of the Pulitzer Prize in 1953. Some believe that this slim volume clinched his winning the Nobel Prize in Literature. The Nobel Citation read, "... for forceful and style-making mastery of the art of modern narration."

Lagniappe

Key West is, no doubt, one of a dozen, unique, personality-cities of the United States. Our trips there were related to attending several of the Key West Literary Seminars, which convenes every January with famous writers as speakers and drawing cards. We had another motive for our first seminar, we must admit—to visit Ernest Hemingway's house. Now, strange to say, the first thing we think about when Key West is mentioned is cats—and not just the "Hemingway cats"!

Sunsets can be beautiful everywhere, but few places have capitalized—and commercialized—sunset-viewing as successfully as Key West. Almost every evening, a huge crowd gathers on the wharf, where ocean liners dock and often set sail just at sunset. The water's edge is like a county fair every evening with booths, vendors and entertainers. A modern-day Houdini steps out of his chains in record time, and various magicians, musicians, dancers, salesmen and artists vie for attention.

The major attraction that draws the most gasps for breath, oh's and ah's and hearty applause has been, for twenty-five years, Dominic the Frenchman and his cats. With a constant, heavily accented line of chatter, the Gaelic charmer addresses the crowd and his entourage of ordinary-looking house cats. But the cats are indeed quite extraordinary! Five to six of them sit on elevated perches like circus lions and tigers. They are totally disciplined and respond to their master's commands like animals in a Barnum and Bailey circus act. They jump long distances through the air from perch to perch, then through a small hoop, and finally they jump through a hoop which is in flames. They walk in tandem across a bar. The French master orchestrates all of this with an occasional, "set"! Evidently, the cats were unaware of Hemingway's conclusion that cats regard their owner not as their master but as their staff.

The only sight that competes with this spectacular performance is an even more spectacular sunset viewed from a ringside seat on the wharf.

At the Ernest Hemingway Home and Museum, one does not have to search for the famous cats. There are about sixty of them in the walled-in grounds of the house, and they are cared for and nurtured by the staff of the Museum. Each of the cats has a name listed. Some of them are pictured on the Hemingway Home and Museum web site. The number of cats is limited by careful planning. Many of the cats look like they are wearing "mittens" since they are "polydactyls", with extra toes, front or back, or both. Allegedly, a sea captain gave Hemingway a tom cat with extra toes, and it is presumed that these current polydactyls are descendents of Hemingway's original cats. Other cats on the Hemingway House grounds may have different origins.

We are not "cat people" normally since we have grown up with dogs and are currently subjects of a small, shaggy canine queen. But these Hemingway cats, each with a distinctive name, are very appealing and somewhat overwhelming as a group of "bobby-soxers" with their saddle-oxford-like paws.

The lagniappe of the lively cats of the Hemingway Home comes from a realization that these polydactyls may represent a living, direct link to a cat-lover of yesterday whose works still are quite alive.

Photographic credits: The two photographs of young Ernest Hemingway are courtesy of The Marcelline Hemingway Sanford Collection, The Ernest Hemingway Foundation of Oak Park.

Young Ernest Hemingway

LIÉUT. ERNEST M. HEMINGWAY—1918

Army Ambulance services

All of the sixty plus cats at the Hemingway House have recorded names. This is "Charlie Chaplin".

343

Eudora Welty

1909 - 2001

Eudora Welty House, Mississippi Department of Archives and History

Eudora Welty's Home in Jackson,
Mississippi and her Thinking Place

Eudora Welty

"I haven't a literary life at all, not much of a confession, maybe. But I do feel that the people and things I love are of a true and Human world, and there is no clutter about them. I would not understand a literary world."

Selected Stories of Eudora Welty

"The excursion is the same when you go looking for your sorrow as when you go looking for your joy."

The Wide Net

"The storm had rolled away to faintness like a wagon crossing a bridge."

A Curtain of Green

Journey   Jackson

Our arrival in Jackson at twilight was surreal. On the main highway, just a few blocks from Mississippi's domed Capitol, cowboys were riding their horses and bedding them down for the night at the Mississippi State Fairgrounds. Minutes later we passed the Washington D.C.-inspired "new" Capitol, then the old Capitol, now a museum. The fading sunset gave a special glow to the city.

On this, our return trip to Jackson after many years, searching for Eudora Welty's home, we felt as if we were visiting an old friend and tipping our hat to her! We had a special bond with Eudora Welty, as does any one who ever met her personally or through her writings. Years ago Eudora came to our city to receive an honorary degree from The University of West Florida, and we were asked by the University to be her hosts. Probably no one invited to our luncheon for her re-membered anything afterwards but Eudora's humor, her good spirits and her down-to-earth conversation. After she had received her honorary degree, she was asked to sit in a gazebo that had been especially constructed for her to sign books. When she looked at the long waiting line of people, including school children, she chuckled and said, "I feel just like Santa Claus!"

Eudora Welty worked for the WPA (a Depression-era Federal social service agency) in public relations, and traveled a great deal around her native state. On her own time she took many photographs, later published in *One Time, One Place.* (1978). She observed and documented the people, the places, the rural political rallies, the hog killings and the poverty of the era. She stated that in Mississippi, "the Depression was hardly a noticeable phenomenon in the poorest state in the union."

As we traveled through Mississippi, on our return trip in 2003, we were impressed with the general appearance of prosperity. Jackson is a beautiful, modern city with attractive, refurbished older buildings and many newer ones, including the Eudora Welty Library, relocated in 1986 in the heart of downtown. The library's Center for Mississippi Writers includes exhibits featuring Eudora, William Faulkner, Willie Morris, Tennessee Williams, and many others.

Books and the library had always been an important part of Eudora's life. As a little girl she often skated or rode her bicycle from her home to the library with a note from her mother stating that Eudora could check out any book she chose except for one author; however, Eudora was disappointed that she was allowed only two books at a time.

The old Capitol building is now an attractive museum; its excellent bookshop has a wide assortment of books by Mississippi writers. In the impressive rotunda of the Old Capitol building one can imagine the feelings expressed by friends and admirers on the death of Willie Morris, Eudora's close friend. Willie was the first writer to lie in state there, to be followed in turn by Eudora.

Down the street is the Mississippi Department of Archives and History, with bountiful resources. When we arrived in Jackson we went directly to the Welty House in Belhaven so we would lose no time looking for it the next day. Afterwards we looked for one of Eudora's favorite restaurants, the Mayflower

Café, still a busy and wonderful place to eat—indeed, a lagniappe experience and, by serendipity, meeting some one who could help us with the missions of our journey!

Vignette   Eudora Welty   1909 - 2001

Three-year-old Eudora plopped herself down on the back seat between her mother and their next-door neighbor. It was time for their usual Sunday afternoon drive. She looked up at both ladies, "Now talk," she commanded.

Thus from early childhood, Eudora Alice Welty began her lifelong habit of listening and observing and storing up impressions in her memory, which she called "my most precious possession." In *One Writer's Beginnings*, her too brief memoir, she said that she listened not to stories but for stories. She became famous for her rare power of observation and keen ear for dialogue. In one summary of her work, she wrote, "Writing fiction has developed in me an abiding respect for the unknown in a human lifetime, and a sense of where to look for the threads, how to follow, how to connect, to find in the thick of the tangle what clear line persists. The strands are all there."

Eudora could not have chosen a better time nor place to grow up in the south than Jackson, Mississippi. She could skate to the library where she tried to read every book. (Today the new library bears her name.) She frequently walked (or skated) through the Mississippi State Capitol on her small town errands, listening and observing. Millsaps and Belhaven were two prominent colleges in town. When the Weltys moved to a house across the street from Belhaven College, Eudora, from her upstairs bedroom, could hear the music students practicing.

Except for time spent away from home for education, travel, teaching and lectures, she spent most of her life in the same house on Pinehurst Street. She knew well her native state and loved it. At first, she was regarded as a local color writer. Then her readers became aware of the themes, the symbols, and the deeper meanings beneath the surface of her stories. She stated that she considered human relationships her real subject. In *One Writer's Beginnings*, she asks, "Can a sheltered life also be a daring life?" That she had a sheltered life may seem obvious, but she traveled frequently and had many friends famous in both literary and art circles. She had both a comic bent and an introspective side. As she once wrote,"I kept my ear to the ground and listened a lot."

The South, as Eudora knew it, had a talking culture. People talked on street corners, in drug stores, in the churchyard, after church. They had the time—more time than money. People gathered on front porches and verandahs in the early evenings and spoke of the past, of political candidates, of local gossip, suitably framed if children were present. There was radio, of course and a few favorite programs, but it was too hot to stay inside in the summertime. One story would always beget another, and if the talking continued into the late evening, one could always take a longer afternoon nap the next day. The oral tradition of story-telling was an important factor in her development. Eudora wrote that childhood learning was made up of moments. As she listened, she also listened for the unspoken. She was getting her perspective, "getting my distance," as she put it, her understanding of human events.

Accompanying her interest in writing was her early love of art. She liked to paint and later became a fine photographer. She was learning the principle of framing a subject, of finding its shape—knowledge she used in her writing. Akin to that, she was gaining a feeling for proportion and the importance of lights and shadows.

And so Eudora grew up as southern as her roots. Later she would write about the importance of place in fiction, so naturally the atmosphere of the South is evident in her work. No matter how much she enjoyed foreign travel or trips within the United States, she was content to be back home in Mississippi. She is revered and claimed by the South as a southern writer, and so she is, but she is more than southern. Her body of work has a universal cast.

Biographically, little seems to be made of the Ohio and West

Virginia influences on her and her family, but they were her roots also and are significant. Her father grew up in Ohio, her mother in West Virginia. Every summer the family would take the long automobile trip back to see their extended families. Eudora was close to her "northern family," her paternal grandparents and her maternal grandmother and their localities.   In *One Writer's Beginnings,* she wrote: "It seems likely to me now that the very element in my character that took possession of me there on top of the mountain, the fierce independence that was suddenly mine, to remain inside me no matter how it scared me when I tumbled, was an inheritance. Indeed, it was my chief inheritance from my mother, who was braver. It was what we shared; it made the strongest bond between us and the strongest tension." Continuing about West Virginia, she wrote that the high winds, which did not scare her, affected her awareness of the physical world, resulting in the importance of atmosphere in her stories.

The personalities of her parents also affected her sensibility, her developing strength, humor, warmth and sentiment that lacked sentimentality. Her caring and solicitous father rose to be president of his insurance company but died when he was only fifty-two. He was by nature cautious and taught Eudora and her two brothers how to be aware of outside dangers. In spite of this, he was the optimist. Her mother, a voracious reader, was the family pessimist but adventurous at the same time. She also had a highly developed sense of what was appropriate and what was not. With several striking clocks in the Tudor-style house, the family was always "time-minded." Eudora said that her parents had views of the world that were different from those of other parents.

From her adolescence onward, Eudora was quite tall for a girl, but she was very popular and voted "Best-All-Round-Girl" in high school. Throughout her life, she made many strong and lasting friendships with both men and women. She had a gift for friendship, both giving and receiving. And yes, she did know romance and returned the love of two men, although each love was tinged with sadness. Countless people have testified that in her presence one immediately forgot her lack of great beauty because her natural charm won the day. At a party, the guests would gravitate to wherever Eudora had settled herself. She was fun loving! Her genuine wit was spontaneous, an aspect of her quick mind. Add to that a soft voice and a southern accent that had a well-educated sound, and it is easy to understand why her lectures or readings were predictably, standing room only, whether at Cambridge or Oxford, England, New York or Wisconsin. She was gracious, kind, considerate of other people, honest to the penny, generous and anxious to help friends, family, beginning writers, and students. She undertook this on a personal level. She did not believe that her writing should be didactic, advance a cause or have political overtones. "Of all my strong emotions, anger is the one least responsible for any of my work."

Eudora attended Mississippi State College for Women in Columbus, Mississippi for two years and the University of Wisconsin, a very progressive school, where she graduated. She knew already that she wanted to be a writer. Her concerned father feared that she might not be able to support herself, but he bought her first typewriter, a red Royal. Later she would pin fragments of a manuscript together, thus re-arranging her work. (There were no computers then.) She never had a secretary until the very latter part of her life. After Wisconsin, she attended Columbia University's Business School on her father's advice. She liked New York but she returned home, a pattern that would be repeated many times, frequently because of needs of her family.

For a time she worked for the WPA throughout Mississippi and made 1200 photographs that had an important future. This job introduced her to the poverty and hardship endured by her fellow citizens. Suzanne Marrs has written a well-researched and most readable biography that sheds light on many of Eudora's associations. What of Eudora's relationship with her mother? Alike in interests, they had different temperaments and clashed on occasion. Certainly, Eudora seemed ambivalent about her mother's possessiveness, but later she would drive fifty miles nearly every day to Yazoo City to see her mother when it became necessary to put her in a nursing home.

When she wasn't writing, which would have been in the evening, Eudora revealed herself as the typical southern lady, who enjoyed cooking, entertaining out-of-town friends, giving and going to parties, and gardening. Visitors may now see her restored gardens and the interior of her house on appointment. When she was traveling, she was thrifty, usually seeking a cheaper room. She had to watch her finances when she was between stories or novels.

As the years have passed since the appearance of "Death of a Traveling Salesman," Eudora Welty's first published story, both readers and critics alike have come to regard her as one of the most important writers of the twentieth century. Numerous awards and honors underscore this. She won countless literary prizes, including the Pulitzer Prize, the O. Henry Prize twice in succession, and she received twice the Freedom Medal by two U.S. presidents and the French Legion d' Honneur. Perhaps it was by the vagaries of chance that the Nobel Prize eluded her. Surely it was the only one that did.

In her long life she wrote short stories, collected in four volumes; five novels; non-fiction, including criticism, memoir, essays and book reviews. Her greatest acclaim probably rests on her short stories which are even more illuminating if read more than once.

How may we describe the body of work that won such acclaim? Eudora said, "Everything I write teaches me as I go." She wrote of the family or of human relationships with a wide expanse of technique and elements: humor, satire, the grotesque, lyricism, impressionism, (sometimes bordering on the vague), realism, myth and fairy tales, and eccentricity. She was a master of dialogue, capturing the rhythm and the idioms of a region. Eudora believed that memory, unfathomable as it is, informs and shapes the present. The confluence or the convergence of the lives of different people in her own life fascinated and intrigued her. She may have explored the interior vision of women, but she was not a feminist. She acknowledged her debt to Jane Austen, E.M. Forster, William Faulkner and Anton Chekhov. She said that reading Virginia Woolf for the first time was a revelation to her.

If she had had no literary output, she probably would have achieved fame as a photographer. Before she had published anything, she had a show in 1936 in New York of photographs she had made for the W.P.A. Her pictures were also published by *Life* magazine in the 1930's. *Passionate Observer: Eudora Welty among Artists of the Thirties* was a companion book of her photographs for a show of the same name, organized by the Mississippi Museum of Art. Other exhibitions have been organized since her death at age ninety-two.

Eudora Welty revealed her essential compassion and her concern for human need in this statement: "My wish, indeed my continuing passion, would be not to point the finger in judgment, but to part a curtain, that invisible shadow that falls between people; the veil of indifference to each other's presence, each other's wonder, each other's human plight."

Thinking Place

The expression, "Bloom where you are planted," is most appropriate for Eudora Welty. She was planted and nurtured well in Jackson, Mississippi. With the exception of her school years at the Mississippi State College for Women, the University of Wisconsin, and Columbia University post graduate school in New York City, and a brief tenure (1944) on *The New York Times* staff, she bloomed and grew as a premier American writer, living essentially for most of her life in the same house her parents had built. She ventured forth periodically to teach writing classes in Jackson and beyond, to travel, and to receive myriad accolades and honors.

As they drove or walked along Pinehurst Street in the Belhaven area, often friends saw Eudora sitting at her desk near the front window, working away long hours on her old Royal typewriter. Since there was no air conditioning in the early years, the windows were frequently open.

Eudora's view from her upstairs room, her thinking place, was her front lawn, quiet Pinehurst Street and the Belhaven College campus. Willie Morris wrote, "Directly across the street from the Welty home was the music building of Belhaven College, and from the practice rooms the sounds of piano music would drift across Pinehurst Street, keeping her company through the long and solitary hours at the old Royal."

Eudora described it, "Though I was as constant in my work as the students were, subconsciously I must have been listening to them, following them. I realized that each practice session reached me as an outpouring. And those longings so expressed, so insistent, called up my longings unexpressed. I began to hear, in what kept coming across the street into the room where I typed, the recurring dreams of youth, inescapable, never to be renounced, naming themselves over and over again."

Lagniappe   Jackson

From all accounts Eudora Welty personally appreciated good food and served it to her guests. She also believed in the southern dictum that hospitality is an equal responsibility for guests as well as for the host. A friend once related that whatever the party, the guests, particularly the men, would gather around Eudora for her sparkling humor and unique insights. Her good friend, Willie Morris, once commented that Eudora was "quite simply the funniest person I have ever known." Once a young reporter came by appointment to interview her. The wonderful smell of southern cooking was coming from the kitchen, and he was delighted when she invited him to have lunch. For posterity he wrote that she had served the best snap beans that he had ever eaten.

But where were her prized recipes? On a hunch we made a discovery and found our lagniappe. At The Eudora Welty Library we found that Eudora had written "The Flavor of

Jackson" as a foreword for the thirtieth anniversary edition of *The Jackson Cookbook*. (Her style in describing food and social customs rivals that of culinary doyenne, M.F. K. Fisher.)

In the foreword, Eudora described the era of the 1920's when there were no prepared mixes, frozen foods or miracle appliances as "the era of the Madeira tea napkins." And, she continued, "Recipes, in the first place, had to be imparted—there was something oracular in the transaction—and, however often they were made after that by others, they kept their right names. I make Mrs. Mosal's White Fruitcake every Christmas, having got it from my mother, who got it from Mrs. Mosal, and I often think to make a friend's fine recipe is to celebrate her once more, and in that cheeriest, most aromatic of places to celebrate, in the home kitchen."

Mrs. Mosal's White Fruit Cake.

    1 ½ cups butter
    4 cups sifted flour
    2 cups sugar
    2 teaspoons baking powder
    6 whole eggs
    1 pound chopped pecans
    1 teaspoon fresh grated nutmeg
    1 pound crystallized pineapple
    1 pound crystallized cherries, half red, half green
    1 cup whiskey
    1 teaspoon vanilla

Cut fruit in small pieces and dust with one cup of flour. Cream butter and sugar well; add eggs 1 at a time. Sift dry ingredients with remaining 3 cups flour; add this to sugar mixture alternating with whiskey. When well blended, add fruit and pecans. Bake in tube pan at 225 degrees for about two hours. When done, pour ¼ to ½ cup whiskey over while still hot. Serves 20-24.

(Miss Welty wrote the foreword and contributed the recipe as an express gift to the Mississippi Symphony Orchestra via the

Symphony Guild's cookbook. We appreciate the permission from The Jackson Symphony League to share this valuable gift from the League's outstanding cookbook.)

This is now a cherished entry in our family cookbook. Too bad we couldn't get the formula for the broiled red fish and sauteed crab from one of Eudora's favorite restaurants, The Mayflower. Mr. Mike Kountouris (now deceased; his son, Jerry, is the present owner) did give us a hint. The hot sauce for the sautéed crab has generous portions of Worcestershire and butter. Pictures of Eudora Welty and of Willie Morris adorn the walls of the Mayflower Café. Mike Kountouris, a hero of World War II, knew Eudora. She came in often, and her favorite dish was any fresh seafood followed by hot apple pie with cheese. Mr. Kountouris said, "She was one of the nicest, most polite people I ever knew. Everybody liked her."

Another one of Eudora's favorite restaurants in Jackson can be visited today, Bill's Tavern. According to an account by Willie Morris, Eudora helped it to get started with her praise in the newspaper. Also, Willie had written that in 1994, at a birthday celebration at Bill's Tavern with Eudora's friends, a Greek belly dancer appeared with the following written above the dancer's navel, "Eudora Welty I love you!"

By serendipity, our conversation with Jerry Kountouris about Eudora and her friend, Willie Morris, was overheard by a young couple. They knew how we could get in touch with JoAnne Prichard Morris, the widow of Willie Morris. Talking with JoAnn by telephone laid the foundation for our later interview with her, and insights into our upcoming visit to Yazoo City and some of Willie's thinking places.

Photography credits:
The Welty home on the first page of this chapter and the picture below of Miss Welty typing are courtesy of the Eudora Welty House, Mississippi Department of Archives and History.

Windows of Eudora's thinking place overlooking Belhaven

Eudora at her thinking-writing place in her bedroom, by the window

View of the lawn and college from her window

Eudora Welty and Carolyn Fleming on the occasion of Eudora's
receiving an honorary degree at The University of West Florida

Willie Morris

1934 - 1999

The Morris' Home in Jackson Mississippi,
and a backyard Thinking Place

Willie Morris

"I came to the city and it changed my life. I was exalted by it, exulted in it. I was a young man at a great personal threshold in a place and a moment throbbing with possibility, observing America from here in its extravagant peaks and turmoils, giving myself to the town and it to me: a most American covenant."

-New York Days

"I knew the place better then than I knew my own heart -- every bend in the road -- and the cracks in every sidewalk. It was not in my soul then, only in my pores, yet as familiar to me as water or grass or sunlight. The town was poor one month and rich the next, and everything pertained to the land - labor and usury, mortgage and debt. We lived and died by nature, Anglos and Africans bound together in the whims of the timeless clouds. Our people played seven-card stud against God."

-Taps

Journey   Yazoo City

We were en route from Jackson, Mississippi to Yazoo City, some forty miles away, and thinking about Willie Morris. So much of his story brings a smile, a feeling of whimsy and a warm sense of shared humanity: his endearing name, "Willie"; his home county, Yazoo, which sounds like a Louis Armstrong jazz expression; his friendship with and love for his dogs, Pete and Skip, and other pets, about which he wrote with such humor and tenderness; his own remarkable story of a bright little boy, growing up in a small town in Mississippi and becoming the youngest editor of the oldest and most prestigious literary journal in America—in of all places—New York City. (Only Willie's "friend", William Faulkner, would consider the preceding sentence a short one.) He rubbed elbows with the most celebrated writers of his time, while maintaining his native

363

charm and identity with his small town, southern roots. One of Willie's books, *North Toward Home,* was highly acclaimed and called "The finest evocation of American boyhood since Mark Twain" by *The London Sunday Times.*

We had talked with JoAnne Prichard Morris, Willie's widow, earlier that day and inquired about Yazoo, the site of Willie's home and his thinking places. JoAnne answered immediately, "Willie did a lot of his thinking in cemeteries and, particularly, in the cemetery in Yazoo City." Fortunately for us, we had picked up a copy of the *Jackson Free Press* where JoAnne, in her column, answered questions from two readers asking where to go to escape Jackson—and cheap? Her answer to the readers was, "The back roads of Yazoo County." (Many of the roads seemed to be back roads.) JoAnn wrote: " In Yazoo County you can experience hills, Delta and prairie land. ...You'll find Indian mounds and rugged, cut-through roads that make the Natchez Trace seem like a faint imitation. There are creeks with petrified wood and prehistoric fossils. ...when you have the choice between a small road and a smaller one, take the smaller one first."

We took one of the back roads to Yazoo City and were impressed with the substantial houses along the way. There were none of the decaying cabins, which were so prominent over the landscape, throughout the South, a few decades ago. When we arrived in Yazoo City, we went directly to Willie's gravesite at the cemetery, and then rode by the house of his boyhood. A week later, we returned to Mississippi for a visit with JoAnne Prichard Morris to learn more about the incredible story of a boy, born in Jackson and raised in Yazoo, who made a giant circle, geographically, intellectually and emotionally; played a huge role in the literary world; then made his return journey, "South Toward Home," to a fulfilling life in Jackson.

Vignette   Willie Morris 1934-1999

Considering his prodigious talent, intellect, recognition and many prizes earned, it is difficult to summarize the life and work of the Mississippi-New York writer, Willie Morris, in a few paragraphs.(Willie liked to say, "I am an American writer who happened to be born in Mississippi.") To the incomplete list of Morris aspects stated above, Willie's intimate friends would add, "his great sweetness." For greater insight and understanding, we would refer the reader to his best-selling autobiography in two books, *North Toward Home* and *New York Days*. He was a prolific writer, and much of his other work is also revealing of his life and times.

Willie once said of himself, "I am and always will be a sports writer at heart." And he was one of the best, but he was so many other things as well: the valedictorian of his high school class; Phi Beta Kappa at The University of Texas; a Rhodes Scholar at Oxford for four years; the youngest editor in the history of *Harper's*. In just a few years he transformed it into an exciting periodical that reflected the significant issues and conditions of the times. He was first a journalist; in high school as a sports announcer, he read his own copy. At the University of Texas, as a freshman he served on the staff of *The Daily Texan*, becoming its fearless, crusading editor-in-chief when he was a senior. His years at Oxford interrupted his time on *The Texas Observer*, but when he returned he eventually became its editor-in-chief. These years reflect Willie's love of the land that had nurtured him and his angst over the racial divisions that were tearing it apart. As President Clinton said, years later, in a memoriam to Willie, "He showed us how we could love a place and want to change it at the same time."

After nearly a decade in New York City and another as a writer living in eastern Long Island, receiving honorary degrees and awards for his writing, he decided it was time to come southward to home. And he wrote, "I wanted to come home. It's no more complicated or simple than that. Besides, my nerve ends come alive when I cross the Mississippi line. I'm not exaggerating. It's got to have something to do with that whole business of the burden of memory—the memory that serves one's imagination as a writer."

He became writer-in-residence in Oxford at The University of Mississippi for ten years before moving to Jackson. Besides be-ing a journalist, he had become a novelist, essayist and writer of nonfiction. He was chosen Mississippi's favorite nonfiction author of the millennium by readers of *The Clarion-Ledger* of Jackson. The citizens of his final home knew him well and gave him honor.

He had grown up in Yazoo City, an only child who knew the freedom and the privileges that a small town frequently gives its young people. He knew love from his parents and his grandmother, Mamie. Usually accompanied by his dog, he explored the town, always looking for adventure. His growing-up time was richly captured in a movie, "My Dog Skip," and in a television feature, "Good Old Boy," filmed for the Disney Channel. He was all boy, playing baseball and basketball, becoming a star in each. He was full of mischief. He was full of kindness. There was no pretense in him.

Former Mississippi Governor William F. Winter was Willie's neighbor, across Purple Crane Creek, just up the hill. Knowing Willie well he said of him, "For those of us, who, like Willie, were, to use his word, ineffably affected by growing up in a Mississippi of myths and legends, of fantasy about what never was and hope for what might never be, of insufferable baseness and incredible goodness, he was the one who perhaps more than anyone else of our generation caused us to look within ourselves and discover there the joy and inspiration to sustain us through the good times and the bad."

Thinking Place   Yazoo City

Like most creative people who live in a variety of places, Willie Morris had many thinking places, but, as his wife JoAnne Prichard Morris had said, wherever he lived the constant place for Willie was the cemetery. According to Edwin Yoder, Jr., Willie"...had made friends with death. The friendship took the form of a passionate interest in cemeteries. He had prowled every notable burying ground from Oxford to Hollywood, from Boston to New Orleans—not in a spirit of morbidity but because their quiet precincts, the resting place of 'the great silent majority,' as Willie called the departed, offered a prism into the human comedy."

In *North Toward Home*, Willie wrote about the Yazoo City graveyard, "The cemetery itself held no horror for me. It was set in a beautiful hill, overlooking the whole town. I loved to walk among the graves and look at the dates and words on the tombstones. I learned more about the town's past here, the migrations, the epidemics, the old forgotten tragedies than I could ever have learned in the library. Sometimes we would bring our lunch." Willie said that in childhood they played games there because it was cooler.

"I remember we would watch funerals from afar in hushed awe, and I believe that was when I became obsessed not with death itself but with the singular community of death and life together—and life's secrets, life's fears, life's surprises." Willie also recalled that, in his high school years, when he stood on a distant hill ready to echo "Taps" on his bugle for the Korean War dead, he observed "the tableau below with its shining black hearse and the coffin enshrouded with the flag; and the gathering of mourners was like a folk drama with the earth as a stage." His novel, *Taps*, reflects this.

When Willie returned to Mississippi to serve as writer-in-residence and to teach at Ole Miss, he visited the Oxford cemetery and "Mr. Bill" Faulkner's grave frequently. "My dog Pete and I go out into the cemeteries not only to escape the telephone...but to feel the continuity with the flow of the generations. 'Living', William Faulkner wrote, 'is a process of getting ready to be dead for a long time.' "

When we visited Glenwood Cemetery in Yazoo City we found Willie's grave, thanks to JoAnne Morris' direction (near the sign Plot I-Odd Fellows on main entry road). There were signs of "life" around his gravesite, with which we imagined Willie would be pleased. Someone had decorated with colorful flowers and little windmills, along with Mardi Gras celebratory beads! Natives told us later that people come frequently "from everywhere," leaving flowers, notes and mementoes, including small bottles of spirits. Thirteen paces away is the grave of the

"Witch of Yazoo" surrounded by chains, one of which was broken. Willie had fun relating the legend in his book *Good Old Boy* and *Witch of Yazoo*. He had a book signing at the witch's gravesite at midnight!

In an essay, "A Love That Transcends Sadness" Willie wrote, "I have never been lonely in a cemetery. They are perfect places to observe the slow changing of the seasons and to absorb human history. ...In a preternatural quiet, one can almost hear the palpable, long- ago voices."

Home in Jackson

When JoAnne took us by their former home in Jackson, we were pleased that the current owner arrived shortly thereafter and cordially invited us into her very attractive and comfortable home. One of Willie's thinking places was the upstairs room where he could look out over the backyard lawn and Purple Crane Creek. JoAnne said also, that Willie enjoyed another thinking place, sitting in his lawn chair in the spacious backyard. Looking beyond the small creek, which occasionally overflows, one can see the home of Willie and JoAnne's friend and neighbor, William F. Winter, former governor of Mississippi.

At Willie's memorial service Governor Winter said, "... in the late 1960's when I first heard about Willie Morris and when I was looking desperately for some voices that would speak for what I thought the South was really about—of civility and courtesy and kindness and tolerance— not of rage and bitterness and bigotry, I found in his writings the special insight of one whose affection for his home state was not only undiminished but reinforced by his recognition of our weaknesses as well as our strengths and especially of our need to reach out more...and to erase barriers that separate us from one another..."

Governor Winter went on to say, "Willie found goodness and kindness in people wherever he met them. As an old Mississippi farmer said, 'He didn't cull nobody.' "

Lagniappe

We met Willie's wife, JoAnne Prichard Morris, in Jackson; weeks later, in New Orleans, we got together with Willie's son, David Rae Morris. What fine lagniappe! Although we met them separately for lunch as strangers, the two hours with each passed as quickly as a family gathering. We wanted to learn more about Willie from these two very special people in his life. When we parted, it was as new friends with a common interest.

We already knew something about Willie. He had written," I have a beautiful wife and three cats." Whoa! Everybody knows that Willie was a dog man. Who can forget the fox terrier that inspired the touching movie, "My Dog Skip" or Willie's essay, "The Day I Followed the Mayor around Town"? Pete, a black Labrador "with floppy ears and liquid brown eyes" was well known as The Mayor of Bridgehampton, New York. As Willie wrote, "When Pete, the Mayor, came to live with me, he reaffirmed the contours of my own existence." Pete also moved to Oxford with Willie. And then, in Jackson, three cats! Willie wrote about becoming their butler and servant. JoAnne's cats had won him over. He even wrote a cat story, *My Cat Spit McGee.*

As for his charming wife, in Willie's own words, "Jo Anne is not only one of the best human beings I have ever known, she is one of the smartest and just a highly talented editor... She's also one of the funniest people around when she is in the mood to be, and she's from the Mississippi Delta, as am I. We share the same kind of past and memories of people and things.... I am very fortunate." Paul Greenberg summed up JoAnne for himself and other literary colleagues, "If every idea begins as a great idea and becomes a great chore, JoAnne is the kind of editor who keeps a book, like a life, the way it should be: fun, moving, on track, a great cooperative enterprise, building up steam and shooting off cinders like the Dixie Express.... At his (Willie's) death, there is consolation in this: in JoAnne he was blessed."

JoAnne talked about Willie, reminiscing especially about his favorite thinking place, cemeteries, and how often he wrote about them with eloquence and feeling that must have inspired comfort and reassurance in his readers. She told us about the cemetery in Yazoo City where Willie is buried. "People come frequently from distant places and leave gifts at his gravesite," she said. Somehow we felt we were forging bonds with Willie, his honored ancestry and the land that is so unforgettable-- bonds we could not quite fathom. To use one of Willie's favorite words, "It was an ineffable moment." On this occasion, as we were leaving, we asked JoAnne to sign a book about Willie that we had just bought at the Lemuria Bookstore. "To my new friends," she began. We liked that.

David Rae Morris was born in Oxford, England while his father was a Rhodes scholar. Willie Morris became the youngest editor of *Harpers* when he moved back to the States and to New York City. David Rae's mother was also a talented writer on the national scene. Thus, David Rae grew up in New York and was educated there. Early in life he developed an interest and skill in photography. When his father moved to Oxford, Mississippi, he visited him often. Later David Rae moved to New Orleans to establish himself as one of its outstanding photographers. His photographs have appeared in *Time, Newsweek, USA Today, The New York Times,* and many other magazines and newspapers. David Rae and his father published a book together, *My Mississippi.* It was described as, "A father and son's eloquent portrait and personal evocations of modern Mississippi."

We wanted to talk with David Rae about his experiences with his father and to inquire if he had a picture of Willie in a cemetery. We chose the first one he showed us--Willie walking in the cemetery at Oxford, Mississippi with William Faulkner's gravesite in the distance! David Rae is a great combination of his Yankee, urban up-bringing and know-how--and his inborn, Southern gentlemanly manner. He is a jogger, obviously in good physical condition, who pays attention to his health. Also obvious was his pride and joy in his partner and their little girl.

We talked about Willie's interests in food and eating. David Rae said Willie was a "picky eater"; he was more interested in talking and socializing at the table than eating. He sometimes told the waiter "to bring four and a half French fries." He usually had a quart of milk at his bedside at night. He didn't cook often but, on special occasions he cooked what he called "The John Birch Society Beans" because "of immense internal reactions"..

No doubt, Willie Morris would be very proud of the continuing artistic contributions of the Morris family.

Meeting JoAnne and David Rae, two strong but gentle personalities, links to the past, confirmed our earliest impressions that we can receive lagniappe in so many relationships when we reach out and make our good luck happen. In Willie's words, "...to reach out more and to erase the barriers that separate us from one another."

Photographic credits:
The two pictures of Willie Morris are courtesy of his son, David Rae Morris, photojournalist/documentarian.

Willie Morris, portrait© by David Rae Morris

David Rae Morris©

JoAnne Prichard Morris

Willie Morris walking in the cemetery©, by David Rae Morris

Observations about Creativity and Creative People

"Medicine is a discipline pursued with passion.
Art is a passion pursued with discipline.
I have had pleasure pursuing both".
Arthur M. Sackler, M.D.

(Inscription at the Smithsonian Institution,
Arthur M. Sackler Gallery, Washington, D.C.)

After visiting the homes and thinking places, and studying the lives of the creative people reported in this book, we have observed some of their needs, habits and characteristics. Common to all of them were:

- Discipline in and passion for their work;
- Persistence and perseverance;
- A heightened imagination;
- A need for solitude and meditation;
- A desire for special thinking places.

Characteristics and habits shared by many of the individuals are as follows:

Many found long walks both helpful and necessary.
Charles Darwin walked daily around his thinking path, usually at the same hour;
Charles Dickens, a night walker, and *Thomas Carlyle* took long walks in the city;
Wordsworth, Kipling and Rawlings found inspiration tramping through the woods; *W.B.Yeats* and *Carl Sandburg* often walked

through the woods for most of the night. *Virginia Woolf* considered walking her "joy".

Willie Morris spent many hours walking in cemeteries around America.

<u>Some chose a talisman--or a common object for support, good luck or as their hallmark.</u>

Charles Dickens kept a green ceramic monkey on his desk.

Rudyard Kipling had a tiny, weighted seal and a small leather crocodile on his desk.

George Washington Carver always wore a fresh flower in his buttonhole.

Will Rogers made a cowboy hat and a lasso a part of his persona.

<u>Some paced back and forth in their thinking places, humming or barking out rhythmical utterances as they created new verses.</u>

William Wordsworth: "....later made this strolling, outdoor communication his own, 'booing and hawing' as he walked back and forth in his garden like a metrical shuttle, creating and memorizing his own verses for later dictation...."

Rudyard Kipling: "...pacing up and down in his study, humming to himself. Much of his best-known verse was written to a tune. He was utterly absorbed in it and oblivious to anything else."

<u>Some writers showed skill in reproducing the sounds, the manners, the daily life and customs of a vanishing era.</u>

Jane Austen is a prime example. She recognized this herself as she wrote in *Lady Susan*, "Here I have opportunity enough for the exercise of my talent, as the chief of my time is spent in conversation." She lived in a restricted environment but, as she chronicled the society of her times in the eighteenth century, she revealed her genius.

Rudyard Killing captured the flavor, the color and the mythic proportions of the British Empire.

Eudora Wetly was an exceptional listener and a keen observer with a gift for finding focus. The South of the twentieth century lives in her writings and her photographs.

374

<u>For many creative people, hardship and difficulty were considered a stimulus, not a deterrent, to their creative work.</u>
Robert Louis Stevenson, Dr. Booker T. Washington, George Washington Carver and Glenn Curtiss lived by this precept. Dr. Washington asked to be remembered not for the success he achieved but for the obstacles he overcame.

<u>Early recognition of one's strongest talents and gravitation to the field were beneficial to some.</u>
Wordsworth and *Yeats* found poetry early in their lives.
Thomas Carlyle appreciated the scholarly challenges of biography and history; he was totally dedicated and involved in his work from an early age.
Jane Welsh Carlyle found time on her hands in her marriage; she further developed her earlier skills in letter writing and became famous in her own right.
Thomas Edison followed his creative and entrepreneurial bent from an early age.
Alexander Graham Bell built on three generations of his family's study of speech and sound, later inventing the telephone.

<u>Using creativity to promote a viewpoint or a strong belief was important to some.</u>
Kate Chopin, in the vanguard of women's liberation in the mid-nineteenth century, wrote novels and stories advancing her conviction that women should have the right to independence.
Virginia Woolf's brilliance proved that the university education that she so desired, and full recognition of women, were not essential, after all, for becoming one of the foremost writers of the twentieth century.
Beatrix Potter's love of animals and nature, combined with her talent for drawing and story telling, vaulted her to fame and wealth, thus, allowing her to become a major financial contributor and conservator of the natural beauty of the Lake Country region.

The talent to create a world on paper as real as it is fictitious was common to all of these creative writers, with varying degrees, but some stand out in this respect.

William Faulkner made Yoknapatawpha so dynamic and realistic that his readers often are surprised to learn that it is imaginary and not truly a county in Mississippi.

Robert Louis Stevenson's stories about pirates, sailing ships, tropical islands and buried treasure are vivid memories and seem real to so many, especially since Long John Silver and other characters in the story have become a part of our culture and language.

The ability to see a need or problem, and the capability to create a solution through persistent experimentation and study were the hallmarks of the inventors' and scientists' lives described here.

Thomas Edison and *Alexander Graham Bell*, with divergent backgrounds, were indefatigable in pursuing solutions to theoretical problems and applying the results to widespread practical use, e.g., electric light, and the telephone.

Charles Darwin benefited from his early experiences and observations on his arduous voyage in his youth, then persisted with further experimentation and observations, finally making a major contribution to science and the understanding of the origin of life on our planet.

Glenn Curtiss, with meager formal education, had natural ability, inquisitiveness and a love of speed; his practicality, persistence and mechanical genius resulted in his playing one of the most important roles in the development of flight.

Some stand out as productive artists with the will and determination to live as their temperament and background dictated, resulting sometimes in an unconventional, personal lifestyle.

Vita Sackville-West, in spite of an unconventional life style, maintained a strong marriage until death. She had a remarkably prolific literary output and remained through the years, along with her husband, a leading authority on gardening in Britain.

376

Virginia Woolf's early exposure to intellectual pursuits and literary personages, as well as her membership in the Blooms- bury group, both stimulated and validated her independent spirit and lifestyle.

Ernest Hemingway, who lived a tempestuous life of adventure, did bring discipline to his writing habits and had a highly pro- ductive literary output for years.

Dylan Thomas crafted his remarkable poetry in spite of a tragic addiction.

<u>Some had a special capacity for using materials at hand or the unique elements of their own life to make something new.</u>
George Washington Carver worked in the laboratory to discover new ways to use common farm products, the peanut and sweet potato, to help the people around him and farmers everywhere.

Glenn Curtiss first worked on bicycles for which he built a motor; later, he used the motor in airships (dirigibles); and finally for aeroplanes–all in the same small shop close to his house and grounds in a small town. (Eventually, his company became the largest producer of airplanes in America at the time.)

Marjorie Kinnan Rawlings moved to an area strange to her, the swamplands and waters of central Florida, but she made the ex- otic wilderness the locale for most of her books, which have become classics.

<u>Some creative individuals were noteworthy for their originality and unique personal trademarks.</u>
William Butler Yeats and *Dylan Thomas* produced new sounds and symbols in poetry and in drama.

Edvard Grieg captured the spirit of his native land in music.

Will Rogers good-naturedly expressed the foibles of politicians and his fellow citizens.

George Bernard Shaw paraded idiosyncratic characteristics to reflect original viewpoints, irony and humor.

Charles Darwin possessed a highly calibrated sense of observation; he turned his scientific investigation into a theory that rocked both the world of science and the world of religion.

Beatrix Potter noted the tiniest details in her drawings of Nature.

Mark Twain and Will Rogers demonstrated in their lives and work the transforming power of humor.

Robert Louis Stevenson sublimated illness by creating gripping tales of adventure and poetry whose rhythm and images conjure up a world touched with wonder and imagination. In spite of his lifetime of illness he traveled widely over the globe. His life was even more adventurous than his many exciting stories.

Jane Austen, Charles Dickens, William Faulkner, Eudora Welty and *Willie Morris* exhibited through their style and their grasp of truth, the ability to deal with the commonplace, turning it into the universal.

Conclusions:

The Thinking Place and You

Do not be concerned if a garden hut with turntable or a thinkorium in the clouds is unavailable for you. You can create your own with no expense. Initially, your dedicated time of day for thinking may be more important than the place itself. Like J.K. Rowling, author of the *Harry Potter* series, you may find that a corner in a restaurant will suffice. A library, a spare bedroom, a secluded swing or chair in the garden, or perhaps a seat on a bus or commuter train may be the special place for you.

When you have found a congenial spot, which you use daily, the magic will begin. An ordinary hideaway will turn into a thinking place. There is something about the regularity and the accustomed place that frequently jumpstarts the creative process. It's like standing on "go," waiting for the race to begin. If inspiration doesn't come every time, the memory of those times when it has will bolster your confidence.

Finally, a thinking place may serve the role of matchmaker. It may introduce you to someone whose depths you hardly know —yourself!

Acknowledgements

To all the people and institutions who have helped us in writing this book, our gratitude is mixed with feelings of humility and inadequacy in recalling every person. If we have omitted anyone inadvertently, our apology—our disclaimer is a paraphrase of Tennyson in *Ulysses*—not, "I am a part of all that I have met," but rather," All that we have met is a part of us."

First, never last, our parents: Gilbert and Eloise Hammack Alexander and James and Ernestine Smith Fleming, who imbued in us the love of literature and the deep respect for people, like the thirty-one individuals we have featured, who chose to make a difference in their lives.

Our children: Deborah and Zan Fleming, Merry and Frank Thomasson, and Tina and Christopher Campbell for their great support, suggestions and encouragement; and our grand-children/ friends: Paige, Alexis and Claire Fleming; Frank, Drew and Jack Thomasson; and Barrett, Fleming and Caroline Campbell.

Special thanks to Frank Thomasson, III who suggested the title, "Thinking Places" and artfully designed and laid out the book in early form; and to Greg King who skillfully, helped bring it through in later stages. We are very grateful for the computer skills of Duncan McDavid (who rescued some of our pictures on slides to a digital form) and to The John Appleyard Agency and our artistic friends, Marybeth Pitman and Chitra Carroll for their expert help with producing the cover.

For reading parts or all of the manuscript and long-term encouragement, our thanks to our family, Babette Fleming, Mary Lou Fleming, Pat and Jack Butler, Phyllis and Bill Fleming, Rosemary Duncan, Pousinette and Bill Champlin; dear friends: Eleanor and John Appleyard, Ruth and Henry Cary, Dale and Art Doerr, Dorothy Dean Geiger, Marcia Jaquay, Betty and Ted

Nickinson, Julia and Bob Reid. Our gratitude also to Bette and Billy Wilson, our niece and nephew, who devoted a day to us as we followed the trail of Robert Frost, whom we hope to feature in a subsequent book.

We are grateful to the following institutions and their always helpful and capable staffs: The Learning Resources Center of Pensacola Junior College, West Florida Public Library, The University of West Florida Library, The British Museum, and the exhibits, resource centers and book collections connected with every thinking place that we visited. Our special thanks to The National Trust and English Heritage for sharing photographs with us and preserving the priceless legacy of gifted people who lived in England. We are indebted to those who individually and collectively in museums, societies and The National Park Service have safeguarded our American heritage. *We are particularly grateful to those individuals and institutions associated with each creative person described here as follows:*
Edvard Grieg: The Troldhaugen House and Museum in Bergen, Norway and especially for photographs of Troldhaugen by good friend, Ted Nickinson.
Mark Twain: Elmira College, New York, its reference library, and the Mark Twain Studies Center at Quarry Farm near Elmira; Patty Phillippon at the The Mark Twain House, Hartford, Connecticut.
George Bernard Shaw: The George Bernard Shaw House-Museum and a National Trust guide who made Shaw come alive. (The guide must be nameless to our shame.) Dorothy Bates and Laden and Minney for the Shaw cookbook; the book collection at the Shaw Festival, Ontario-on-the-Lake, Canada; the Festival itself for outstanding plays that we attended in three different years.
Glenn Curtiss: The Glenn Curtiss Museum, Hammondsport, N.Y. and the late Tony Doherty, curator and expert on Curtiss; Joseph Fleming for assistance in tracing the legacy of Glenn Curtiss in Miami; the *Seaplane* connection, (which led not only to Glenn Curtiss, but to Alexander Graham Bell and Mark Twain); Allen and Susan Pote for warm friendship and sharing exceptional musical adventures; Charles Champlin, native of

Hammondsport and emeritus columnist of *The Los Angeles Times* for encouragement; the late Admirals Maurice Weisner (who also led us to Stevenson in Samoa), Lloyd Mustin and Magruder Tuttle – and the late Anna Lamar Switzer – for information about the early days of naval aviation.

William Wordsworth: Hunter Davies, both personally and through his books on Wordsworth, Beatrix Potter and the Lake District.

Thomas and Jane Welsh Carlyle: Professor Brent Kinser, Professor Rodger Tarr, Peter Butler, John Kauch and the Carlyle House Museum, London.

Charles Darwin: Down House Museum, near London; Javis Gurr, English Heritage Photo Library, London.

Charles Dickens: The Honorable John Greaves, now deceased; Elliott Engel, professor, author and lecturer; Sophie Glade of The Charles Dickens Museum, London; The British Museum; The Charles Dickens Center, Rochester, England.

Wlliam Butler Yeats: Elderhostel for a course on Celtic culture and tours of Ireland.

Beatrix Potter: Hunter Davies and several fine Potter museums and exhibits in Cumbria, UK; Michelle Drasdol of the National Trust Photo Library, London.

Robert Louis Stevenson: The Robert Louis Stevenson Club, especially, the Honorary Secretary Alistair Ferguson, Edinburgh; The National Museum, Edinburgh; The Stevenson Museum, Monterrey, California; the RLS exhibit at the Trudeau Institute, New York; Vailima, the restored RLS House-Museum in Apia, Samoa and Rex Maughn, principal benefactor of Vailima, along with collaborator, Jim Winegar; the late Robert Van Dyke for gift of a book by Isobel Field, and for showing us his special collection of RLS memorabilia; special thanks for expert review of our manuscript by Jim Winegar and Hunter Davies; the late Ellen Schaffer, curator of The Silverado Museum in St. Helena, CA., for sharing her knowledge and love of RLS; and Elaine Grieg of the The Writers' Museum, Edinburgh for photographs and information..

Vita Sackville-West: Vita's son and author, the late Sir Nigel Nicolson for his warm welcome and loan of family photographs.

Acknowledgements

Dylan Thomas: Laugharne, Wales, which became Dylan's inspiration and hometown; Ann and Paul Jaycock, proprietors of Golden Arms Inn, Llanarthne, Carmarthen, Wales, for the recipe for the incomparable Sticky Toffee Pudding; the school nearby that presented a music program in Welsh, "the language of Heaven"; the Dylan Thomas Gift Shop for providing tapes and Welsh sweets; the Jeff Towns collection in Sansea ,Wales for the picture of young Dylan.

Thomas Edison: Michelle Ortwei and Edward Wirth at the Edison National Historic Site, West Orange, New Jersey; Edison's summer retreat, Chautauqua Institute, NY and its library; Cathy Thompson, for material on Edison's home and laboratory in Fort Myers, Florida.

Alexander Graham Bell: his three granddaughters, Dr. Mabel Grosvenor, Mrs. Carol Myer and Mrs. Barbara Fairchild for a visit and pleasant interview at Bienn Breaugh; Bell's great-grandson, Dr. Gardiner Myers, for kindly reviewing our manuscript, and for providing an important photograph, and a unit of the fabled tetrahedron; The Bell Museum, Baddeck, Nova Scotia, and The Bell House-Museum, Brantford, Ontario; Gilbert M.Grosvenor and the Gilbert H. Grosvenor Collection of Photographs of the Alexander Graham Bell Family (Library of Congress).

Kate Chopin: The Folk Museum, Cloutierville, LA.; Laurie Tate of Melrose Plantation, near Natchitoches, LA.

Booker T. Washington: the National Park Service for opening his home, The Oaks, for a private tour; The Daniel "Chappie" James Center, Tuskegee, AL.

George Washington Carver: The Carver Museum at Tuskegee, AL, an introductory tape and several photographs from the exhibits of the Museum.

Carl Sandberg: Lynn Savage of the Carl Sandberg Home National Historic Site, at Flat Rock, NC; Laura Platt Winfrey of Carousel Research, New York City of the Carl Steichen Estate, for permission to use photographs.

Will Rogers: Will Rogers Museum at his Santa Monica, CA ranch; Steve Gragert of the Will Rogers Memorial Museum at Claremore, Oklahoma for photographs.

Marjorie Kinnan Rawlings: her House-Museum at Cross Creek, Florida; Norton Baskin, her husband, now deceased, who gave us a twelve-plus hour interview and stay in his home; The Marjorie Kinnan Rawlings Society; including Dr. Brent Kinser, Anna Lillios and Dr. Roger T. Tarr; Carolyn Winebarger, for her excellent transcription of our interview with Norton Baskin; Flo Turcott of the Department of Special and Area Studies Collections, George Smathers Libraries, University of Florida.

William Faulkner: Rowan Oaks, his House-Museum with University of Mississippi student guides; J.R. Cofield, photographer, Oxford, MI, now deceased, for his memories of his frequent photographic subject, William Faulkner. Larry Wells, director, Yoknapatawpha Press, Oxford, MI, for permission to show the cover of J.R.Coffield's book.

Ernest Hemingway: Gwenda Conner of the Ernest Hemingway Foundation of Oak Park; the Ernest Hemingway House-Museum at Key West, Florida; Dr.Allen Josephs, acknowledged Hemingway authority, professor and writer; Miles Frieden, executive director of the Key West Literary Seminar, which has featured Hemingway family members and experts in the past.

Eudora Welty: The Eudora Welty Library of Jackson, Mississippi; Miss Welty's neice and literary executor, Mary Alice White; Rick Fountain, friend and community leader, Jackson; Amy Steadman of the Eudora Welty House-museum; The University of West Florida, which gave Miss Welty her 28th Honorary degree (out of the total of 39) and asked us to be her hosts during her stay in Pensacola. The Jackson Symphony League for allowing us to quote from the foreword of their exceptional cookbook and a recipe by Eudora Welty.

Willie Morris: Jo Ann Prichard Morris, his wife, for an informative interview in Jackson, Mississippi and her subsequent valued review of the section on Willie Morris; David Rae Morris, Willie's photograper-son, for an interview in New Orleans and the use of David Rae's photographs of his father; the late Mike Kountouris, Jackson restauranteur, for his memories of both Willie Morris and Eudora Welty.

Bibliography

We have quoted many of the authors listed below freely and indicated these with quotation marks. Any echo of a word, phrase or quotation without proper acknowledgement is an unintentional mistake which we sincerely regret.

Jane Austen
Bloom, Harold, *Jane Austen* , Chelsea House, New Haven, 1986.
Cecil, David, *A Portrait of Jane Austen,* Hill and Wang, New York, 1978.
Engel, Elliot, *A Dab of Dickens and A Touch of Twain,* Pocket Books, New York, 2002
Honan, Park, *Jane Austen, Her Life,* St. Martin's Press, New York, 1987.
Lane, Maggie, *Jane Austen's World, The Life and Times of England's Favorite,* Adam's Media Corporation, Avon, MA,1997.
Nobles, David, *Jane Austen, a Life,* Farrar, Straus and Giroux, New York, 1997.
Southam, B.C. *Jane Austen, The Critical Heritage,* Rutledge & Kegan Paul, London 1968.

Alexander Graham Bell
Eben, Dorothy, *Genius at Work,* (Alexander Graham Bell), Viking Press, New York, 1982.
Grosvenor, Edwin S. and Wesson, Morgan, *Alexander Graham Bell, The Life and Times of the Man Who Invented the Telephone,* Abrams, New York, 1997.
Langille, Jacqueline, *Alexander Graham Bell,* Four East Publications, Ltd., Tantallon, Nova Scotia, 1989, 2001.
Lewis, Cynthia Copeland, *Alexander Graham Bell,* Dillon Press, Bloomington, 1991.
Linder, Greg, *Alexander Graham Bell, a photo-illustrated biography,* Bridgestone Books, imprint of Baker Books, Grand Rapids,

Michigan, 1999.

Thomas and Jane Carlyle
Bloom, Harold, *Thomas Carlyle*, Chelsea House Publishers, New Haven, NewYork, 1986.
Collis, John Stewart, *The Carlyles*, Dodd, Mead and Co., New York, 1971.
Froude, James Anthony, *Froude's Life of Carlyle*, abridged and edited by John Clubbs, University Press, Columbus Ohio, 1979.
Holme, Thea, *The Carlyles at Home*, Oxford University Press, New York, Toronto, 1965.
Kaplan, Fred, *Thomas Carlyle, a Biography*, Cornell University Press, Ithaca, New York, 1983.

George Washington Carver
Mansfield, Stephen, *Then Darkness Fled, George Washington Carver*, Cumberland House Publishing, Inc., Nashville, 1999.
McMurry, Linda O., *George Washington Carver, Scientist and Symbol*, Oxford University Press, New York, 1981.
Neyland, James, *George W. Carver*, Melrose Square Publishing Co., Los Angeles, 1991.
Federer, William J., *George Washington Carver---His Life and Faith in His Own Words*, Amerisearch, Inc., St. Louis, 2003.

Kate Chopin
Chopin, Kate, *The Awakening*, Dover Publications, Inc., Mineola, New York 1993, (c.1899).
Toth, Emily, *Unveiling Kate Chopin*, University Press of Mississippi, Jackson 1999.
Toth, Emily, *Kate Chopin*, Morrow, New York, 1990.

Glenn Curtiss
Curtiss, Glenn H., *The Curtiss Aviation Book*, Frederick A. Stokes Company, New York, 1912.
Reynolds, Clark G., *Admiral John H. Towers, The Struggle for Naval Air Supremacy*, Naval Institute Press, Annapolis, 1991.
Roseberry, C.R., *Glenn Curtiss, Pioneer of Flight*, Syracuse University Press, Syracuse, 1972 and 1991.

Charles Darwin

Darwin, Charles, *The Voyage of the Beagle*, (Darwin's Preface, 22nd edition, 1845) P.F. Collier, New York, 1937.

Bowlby, John, *Charles Darwin, A New Life*, W.W. Norton & Co., New York and London, 1991.

Brown, E.J., *Charles Darwin, a biography*, Princeton University Press, 1996 and Knopf, Random House, 1995-2002.

Brunt, Peter Ludwig, *Darwin, A Man of Enlarged Curiosity*, Harper and Row, New York, 1981.

Eiseley, Loren, *Darwin's Century*, Anchor Books, Doubleday, New York, 1958 and 1990.

Moore, John, *The Darwin Legend*, Baker Books, Grand Rapids, Michigan, 1994.

Keynes, Randal, *Annie's Box: Darwin, His Daughter and Human Evolution*, Riverbend Books, New York, N.Y. 2002.

Charles Dickens

Ackroyd, Peter, *Charles Dickens*, Harper Collins, New York, 1990.

Brown, Ivor, *Dickens and his Time*, Thomas Nelson and Sons, Ltd. London, 1963.

Engel, Elliot, *A Dab of Dickens and A Touch of Twain*, Pocket Books, New York, 2002

Huxley, John and Kettlewell, H.B.D., *Charles Dickens and His World*, Viking Press, New York, 1965.

MacKenzie, Norman and Jeanne, *Charles Dickens*, Oxford University Press, New York and Oxford, 1979.

Mankowitz, Wolf, *Dickens of London*, Macmillan & Co., Inc., New York, 1976.

Murray, Brian, *Charles Dickens*, A Frederick Ungar Book Continuum, New York, 1994.

Thomas A. Edison

Adair, Gene, *Thomas Alva Edison, Inventing the Electric Age*, Oxford University Press, New York, 1996.

Baldwin, Neil, *Edison , Inventing the Century*, Hyperion, New York, 1995.

Bryan, George S., *Edison, The Man and His Work*, Garden City

Publishing, New York, 1926.

Cramer, Carol, *Thomas Edison,* Greenhaven Press, San Diego, 2001.

Frost, Lawrence, *The Thomas A. Edison Album,* Superior Publishing Co., North Hill, CA and Winchester, MA, 1969.

Simons, William Adams, *Edison, His Life, His Work, His Genius,* Bobbs-Merrill, 1934.

Thulesius, Olav, *Edison in Florida,* University Press of Florida, Gainesville, 1997.

Simpson, Jeffrey, and Solomon, Paul, *Chautauqua, An American Utopia,* Harry N. Abrams, Inc. 100 Fifth Avenue, N.Y. N.Y. 1999.

William Faulkner

Blotner, Joseph, *William Faulkner,* Random House, New York, 1974 and 1984.

Blotner, Joseph, *Selected Letters of William Faulkner,* Random House, New York, 1977.

Brooks, Cleanth, *William, Faulkner, Toward Yoknapatawpha and Beyond,* Yale University Press, New Haven, 1978.

Cates, Stephen B., *Stephen B. Faulkner, The Man and the Artist,* Harper and Row, New York, 1987.

Cowley, Malcolm, *The Faulkner-Cowley File,* The Viking Press, New York, 1966.

Cowley, Malcolm, *The Faulkner Reader,* Random House, New York, 1929 to 1954.

Howe, Irving, *William Faulkner, A Critical Study,* Elephant Paperback, Ivan R. Dee, Chicago, 1952.

Oates, Stephen B, *Faulkner, The Man and the Artist,* Harper & Roe, New York, 1987.

Cullen, John B., *Old Times in the Faulkner Country,* University of North Carolina Press, Chapel Hill, 1961.

Minter, David, *William Faulkner, His Life and Work,* Johns Hopkins University Press, Baltimore, 1980.

Edvard Grieg

Abraham, Gerald, *Grieg: A Symposium,* edited by Abraham Gerald, Greenwood Press, Wichita, 1971.

Gilman, Lawrence, *Nature in Music and Other Studies in the Tone-*

Poetry of Today, Books for Libraries Press, Freeport, New York, 1966.

Horton, John, *Grieg,* Dent, London, 1974.

Ernest Hemingway

Baker, Carlos, Ernest *Hemingway, Critiques of Four Major Novels,* Charles Scribner's and Sons, New York, 1962.

Baker, Sheridan, *Ernest Hemingway, An Introduction and Interpretation,* Holt, Rinehart and Winston, Inc., New York, 1967.

Hemingway, Ernest, *A Moveable Feast,* Charles Scribner's Sons, New York, 1964.

Hemingway, Gregory, *A Personal Memoir,* Houghton Mifflin, Boston, 1976.

Hotchner, A.E., *Papa Hemingway,* Random House, New York, 1966.

Mellow, James R., *Hemingway, a Life Without Consequences,* Houghton Mifflin Co., Boston, New York and London, 1992.

Meyers, Jeffrey, *Hemingway,* Harper and Row, Publishers, New York, 1985.

Reynolds, Michael, *Hemingway in the 1930's,* W.W. Norton, London and New York, 1997.

Sandison, David, *Ernest Hemingway, An Illustrated Biography,* Octopus Publishing, 1998 and Group Ltd. & Chicago Review Press, Inc., Chicago, 1999.

White, William, editor, By-*Line: Ernest Hemingway,* A Bantam Book and Charles Scribner's Sons, New York, 1967 and 1968.

Rudyard Kipling

Birkenhead, Lord, *Rudyard Kipling,* Random House, New York, 1978.

Manley, Seon, *Rudyard Kipling, Creative Adventurer,* The Vanguard Press, Inc., New York, 1965.

Mason, Phillip, *The Glass, The Shadow and the Fire,* Harper and Row, New York 1975.

Kipling, Rudyard, *Something of Myself,* edited by Thomas Pinney, Cambridge University Press, Cambridge, 1990.

Kipling, Rudyard, *Selected Prose and Poetry of Rudyard Kipling,* authorized edition, Garden City, New York, 1937.

Shakane, Vasant A., *Rudyard Kipling, Activist and Artist,* Southern

Illinois University Press, Carbondale and Edwardsville, 1973.

Stewart, J.I.M., *Rudyard Kipling*, Dodd, Mead & Co., New York, 1966.

Willie Morris

Bales, Jack, editor, *Conversations with Willie Morris*, University Press of Mississippi, Jackson, 2000.

Eulogies and Published Tributes, *Remembering Willie*, University Press of Mississippi, Jackson, 2000.

Glusker, Irwin, *A Southern Album, Recollections of Some People and Places and Times Gone By*, Oxmoor House, Birmingham. Alabama, 1975.

Morris, Willie, *The South Today, One Hundred Years after Appomattox*, Harper and Row, New York, 1965.

Morris, Willie, *North Toward Home*, Houghton Mifflin, New York, 1967.

Morris, Willie, *Good Old Boy, a Delta Boyhood*, Harper and Row, New York, 1971.

Morris, Willie, *Shifting Interludes*, edited by Jack Bales, University Press of Mississippi, Jackson, 2002.

Morris, Willie, *Taps*, Houghton Mifflin Company, Boston and New York, 2001.

Morris, Willie, *Terrains of the Heart and Other Essays on Home*, Yoknapatawpha Press, Oxford, 1981.

Morris, Willie and David Rae, *My Mississippi*, Yoknapatawpha Press, Oxford, 1981.

Beatrix Potter

Aldis, Dorothy Keeley, *Beatrix Potter, Atheneum, 1969*.

Buchan, B.D., *The Story of the Creator of Peter Rabbit*, Frederick Warne, London, 1998.

Davies, Hunter, *Beatrix Potter's Lakeland*, photography by Cressida Pemberton-Pigott, Frederick Warne, London, 1988 and 1999.

Mayer, Ann Margaret, *The Two Worlds of Beatrix Potter*, Creative Education Children; Chicago Press, Chicago, 1974.

Potter, Beatrix, *The Journal of Beatrix Potter from 1881 - 1896*, Frederick Warne, London, 1966.

Taylor, *So I Shall Tell you a Story, Encounters with Beatrix Potter*,

Frederick Warne, London, 1993.

Marjorie Kinnan Rawlings

Bigelow, Gordon E., *The Literary Career of Marjorie Kinnan Rawlings*, University Press of Florida, Gainesville, 1966.

Fleming, Carolyn and Jack, "Gentlemen Story-Teller: A Conversation with Norton S. Baskin," *The Marjorie Kinnan Rawlings Journal of Florida Literature*, Vol XV, Gainesville, Fl, 2007.

Nassif, Patricia, *Invasion of Privacy, The Cross Creek Trial of Marjorie Kinnan Rawlings*, University Press of Florida, Gainesville, 1989.

Parker, Idella, with Bud and Liz Crussell, *From Reddick to Cross Creek*, University Press of Florida, Gainesville, 1999.

Rawlings, Marjorie, *Blood of My Blood*, edited by Anne Blythe Meriwether, University Press of Florida, Gainesville, 2002.

Rawlings, Marjorie, *Cross Creek*, Grosset and Dunlap, by arrangement with Charles Scribner's and Sons, New York, 1942.

Rawlings, Marjorie, *The Yearling*, Scribners', New York, 1938.

Tarr, Roger L., editor, *The Private Marjorie, The Love Letters of Marjorie Kinnan Rawlings to Norton S. Baskin*, University Press of Florida, Gainesville, 2004.

Tarr, Roger L. and Kinser, Brent E., editors, *The Uncollected Writings of Marjorie Kinnan Rawlings*, University Press of Florida, Gainesville, 2007.

Will Rogers

Carter, Joseph H., *Never Met A Man I Didn't Like, the Life and Writings of Will Rogers*, Avon Books, (Morrow), New York, 1991.

Day, Donald, *Will Rogers, a Biography*, D. McKay Co., 1962.

Rogers, Will, *Reflections and Observations*, Thorndike Press, Waterville, 1993.

Sonneborn, Elizabeth, *Cherokee Entertainer*, Chelsea House Publishers, New Haven, 1993.

Yogoda, Ben, *Will Rogers, a Biography*, Alfred A. Knopf, New York, 1993.

Vita Sackville-West
Caws, Mary Ann, *Vita Sackville-West, Selected Writings, Macmillan,* London, 2003
Glendinning, Victoria, *Vita: Life of V. Sackwell-West,* Knopf, 1983.
Nicholson, Nigel, *Portrait of a Marriage: Vita Sackville-West and Harold Nicolson,* Simon and Schuster, University of Chicago Press, 1998.
Sackville-West, Vita, *The Edwardians,* Avon (Morrow), New York, 1976.
Sackville-West, Vita, *English Country Houses,* Collins, 1941
Sackville-West, Vita, *Pepita,* Doubleday, Doran and Co., Garden City, N.Y.
Varlow, Sally, *A Reader's Guide to Writers' Britain,* England, Scotland, Wales, Tourist Boards, Prion Books, Ltd., London, 1996.
Woolf, Virginia, *Orlando,* (a biography of Vita Sackville-West), Random House, New York, 1993.
DeSalvo, Louise and Leaska, Mitchell, *The Letters of Vita Sackville-West and Virginia Woolf,* Cleis Press, Inc., San Francisco.

Carl Sandburg
Crowder, Richard, *Carl Sandburg,* Twayne Publishers, New York, 1965.
Niven, Penelope, *Carl Sandburg,* Charles Scribners & Sons, New York, 1991.
Sandburg, Carl, *Always the Young Strangers, an Autobiography,* Harcourt, Brace and World, New York, 1952, 1953.
Sandburg, Carl, *The American Songbag,* A Harvest Book, Harcourt, Brace & Company, New York, 1927 and 1990.
Sandburg, Carl, *Chicago Poems,* Dover Publications, New York, 1994.
Sandburg, Carl, *Rootabaga Stories,* An Odyssey Classic, Harcourt, Brace and Company, New York, 1922 and 1990.
Sandburg, Margaret, editor, *The Poet and the Dream Girl, The Love Letters of Lilllian Steichen and Carl Sandburg,* University of Illinois Press, Urbana and Chicago, 1999.
Steichen, Edward, editor, *Sandburg, Photographer'sView: Carl Sandburg,* Harcourt, Brace and World, Inc., New York, 1966.

George Bernard Shaw

Coolidge, Olivia, *G.B. Shaw*, Houghton Mifflin, Boston, 1968.

Ohmann, Richard M., *Shaw, The Style and The Man*, Wesleyan University Press, Middlebury, Vermont, 1962.

Holdroyd Michael, *The Search for Love*, Vol. I, Random House, New York, 1988; Dodd, Mead and Company, New York, 1965.

Holdroyd, Michael, *The Pursuit of Power*, Vol. II, Random House, New York, 1989.

Laurence, Dan C. *Letters*, Dodd, Mead and Company, New York, *1965*.

Peters, Sally, *Bernard Shaw, The Ascent of the Superman*, Yale University Press, New Haven, London, *1996*.

Weintraub, Stanley, *Shaw, An Autobiography, 1856-1898*, Weybright, & Talley, New York, 1969.

Robert Louis Stevenson

Alailima, Faye, *Aggie Grey, A Samoan Saga*, Mutual, Honolulu, 1991.

Alailima, Faye, *My Samoan Chief*, University of Hawaii Press, Honolulu, 1986.

Bell, Gavin, *In Search for Tusitala, Travels in the Pacific after Robert Louis Stevenson*, Picador, McMillan General Books, London, 1994.

Bell, Ian, *Robert Louis Stevenson*, Mainstream, Edinburgh, 1992.

Davies, Hunter, *Teller of Tales, In Search of Robert Louis Stevenson*, Sinclair-Stevenson, London, 1994.

Field, Isobel, *This Life I've Loved*, Longmans, Green, New York, 1937.

Furnas, J.C., *Voyage to the Windward, The Life of Robert Louis Stevenson*, Faber & Faber, New York, 1951.

Lapierre, Alexandra, *Fanny Stevenson, A Romance of Destiny*, Carroll and Graf, New York, 1995.

McKay, Margaret, *My Violent Friend, The Story of Mrs. Robert Louis Stevenson*, Dent, 1969.

Michener, James, *The World Is My Home, A Memoir*, Random House, New York, 1992.

Rankin, Nicholas, *Deadman's Chest, Travels after Robert Louis Stevenson*, Faber & Faber, New York, 1987.

Stevenson, Robert Louis, *Travels with a Donkey*, Heritage, New York, 1957.

Dylan Thomas

Ferris, Paul, *Dylan Thomas,* Dial Press, New York, 1977.

Hall, Guy B., *Remembering Poets, Reminiscences and Opinions,* Harper& Row, New York, 1978.

Kershner, R.B., *Dylan Thomas,* American Library Association, New York, 1976.

Michaels, Sidney, *Dylan,* Random House, New York, 1964.

Thomas, Caitlin, *Life with Dylan,* Thomas Holt, 1987.

Swyddogol, Llawlyfr, *Dylan Thomas Boat House,* official guide-book, Carmarthen District Council.

Mark Twain

Blair, Walter, editor, *Selected Shorter Writings of Mark Twain,* Houghton Mifflin Company, Boston and The Riverside Press, Cambridge, 1962.

Hoffman, Andrew Jay, *Inventing Mark Twain, the Lives of Samuel Langhorne Clemens,* William Morrow, New York, 1977.

Lasky, Kathryn, *A Brilliant Streak: The Making of Mark Twain,* Harcourt, Brace & Co, San Diego.

Lyttle, Richard B., *Mark Twain, The Man and His Adventure,* Atheneum, New York 1994.

Twain, Mark, *Adventures of Huckleberry Finn,* edited by Henry Nash Smith, Houghton Mifflin, Riverside Editions, Cambridge, MA, 1884, Cambridge, England, 1958.

Twain, Mark, *Tales, Speeches, Essays and Sketches,* Penguin Books, 1994.

Booker T. Washington

Washington, Booker T., *Up from Slavery,* A Signet Classic, Penguin Putnam, New York, 2000.

Washington, Booker T., *Great Lives Observed,* Prentice-Hall. Inc. Englewoods Cliffs, New Jersey, 1969.

Washington, Booker T., *My Larger Education,* Doubleday, Page & Co., Garden City, N.Y., 1969.

Eudora Welty

Black, Pattie Carr, Editor, *Eudora Welty, Early Escapades,* University Press of Mississippi, Jackson, 2005.

Bloom, Harold, editor, *Eudora,* Broomall, PA: Chelsea House

Publishers, London, 1999.

Marrs, Suzanne, *Eudora Welty, A Biography*, Harcourt Inc., Orlando, 2005.

Russell, George, *The Candle of Vision*, D. Appleton-Century Co, New York, 1943.

Waldron, Ann, *Eudora, a Writer's Life*, Doubleday, New York, 1998, 1969.

Welty, Eudora, *A Curtain of Green and Other Stories*, A Harvest Book, Harcourt Brace Jovanovich, New York and London, 1936 and 1979.

Welty, Eudora, *Delta Wedding*, A Harvest Book, Harcourt Brace Jovanovich, New York and London, 1945 and 1979.

Welty, Eudora *One Writer's Beginnings*, Harvard University Press, Cambridge, 1948.

Welty, Eudora, *Photographs*, University Press of Mississippi, Jackson, 1989, 1997.

Westling, Louise, *Eudora Welty, (Women Writers)*, Barnes and Noble Books, Totowa, New Jersey, 1989.

Virginia Woolf

Bell, Quentin, *Virginia Woolf, a Biography*, Harcourt Brace Jovanovich, 1972.

Johnson, Manly, *Virginia Woolf*, F. Ungar, 1973.

Noble, Joan Russell, *Recollections of Virginia Woolf*, William Morrow, 1972.

Rose, Phyllis, *Woman of Letters, a Life of Virginia Woolf*, Oxford University Press, London, 1978.

Spater, George, *A Marriage of True Minds, an Intimate Portrait of Leonard and Virginia Woolf*, Harcourt Brace Johanovitch, New York, 1977.

Sprague, Claire, *Virginia Woolf, a Collection of Critical Essays*, Prentice Hall, 1971.

Woolf, Virginia, *To the Lighthouse*, A Harvest Book, Harcourt, Brace and World, Inc., New York, 1927 and 1952.

Woolf, Virginia, *A Room of One's Own*, Bloomsbury Classics, Bloomsbury Publishing, Ltd., London, 1928 and 1993.

Todd, Pamela, *Bloomsbury at Home*, Henry Abrams, New York, 2000.

DeSalvo and Leaska, *The Letters of Vita Sackville-West and Virginia Woolf,* Morrow, New York, 1985.

William Wordsworth

Beatty, Fredericka, *William Wordsworth of Dove Cottage,* Bookman Associates, New York, 1964

Davies, Hunter, *William Wordsworth, A Biography,* Atheneum, New York, 1980.

Hebron, Stephen, *William Wordsworth,* Oxford University Press, New York, 2000.

Manley, Seon, *Dorothy and William Wordsworth, The Heart of a Circle of Friends,* The Vanguard Press, New York, 1974.

William Butler Yeats.

Foster, R.F., *W.B. Yeats, A Life,* Oxford University Press, London, New York, 1997.

Foster, R.F., *Apprentice Mage, The Arch Poet,* Oxford University Press, London, 2003.

Hebron, Stephen, *William Wordsworth,* Oxford University Press, London, 2000..

Mac Liammoir, Michael and Boland, Evan, W.B. *Yeats and His World,* The Viking Press, New York, 1971.

Touhy, Frank, *Yeats,* Macmillan Publishing Co., Inc., New York, 1976.

Yeats. W.B., *The Autobiography of Yeats,* The Macmillan Company, New York, 1969.

Yeats, William Butler, *Memoirs,* edited by Denis Doneghue, Macmillan Publishing Co., Inc., New York, 1973.

Printed in the United States
By Bookmasters